Towards a Theology of Relationship

Towards a Theology of Relationship

Emil Brunner's Truth as Encounter in Light of Relationship Science

Michael Berra

PICKWICK Publications · Eugene, Oregon

TOWARDS A THEOLOGY OF RELATIONSHIP
Emil Brunner's Truth as Encounter in Light of Relationship Science

Copyright © 2022 Michael Berra. All rights reserved. Except for brief quotations in critical publications or reviews, no part of this book may be reproduced in any manner without prior written permission from the publisher. Write: Permissions, Wipf and Stock Publishers, 199 W. 8th Ave., Suite 3, Eugene, OR 97401.

Pickwick Publications
An Imprint of Wipf and Stock Publishers
199 W. 8th Ave., Suite 3
Eugene, OR 97401

www.wipfandstock.com

PAPERBACK ISBN: 978-1-6667-3765-3
HARDCOVER ISBN: 978-1-6667-9734-3
EBOOK ISBN: 978-1-6667-9735-0

Cataloguing-in-Publication data:

Names: Berra, Michael [author]

Title: Towards a theology of relationship : Emil Brunner's truth as encounter in light of relationship science / Michael Berra.

Description: Eugene, OR: Pickwick Publications, 2022 | Includes bibliographical references.

Identifiers: ISBN 978-1-6667-3765-3 (paperback) | ISBN 978-1-6667-9734-3 (hardcover) | ISBN 978-1-6667-9735-0 (ebook)

Subjects: LCSH: Brunner, Emil, 1889–1966 | Interpersonal relations—Religious aspects—Christianity | Theology—Doctrinal | Theology

Classification: BX4827.B67 B47 2022 (print) | BX4827.B67 (ebook)

08/01/22

Scripture quoted by permission. Quotations designated (NET) are from the NET Bible® copyright ©1996, 2019 by Biblical Studies Press, L.L.C. http://netbible.com All rights reserved.

Scripture quotations marked (NKJV) are taken from the Holy Bible, New King James Version®. Copyright © 1982 by Thomas Nelson. Used by permission. All rights reserved.

To my sons Yannick and Gian.
May my ceiling become your floor.

Contents

List of Figures and Tables | xi
Acknowledgements and Encounters along the Way | xiii
Abbreviations | xvii

Introduction | 1
  a) Relationships Are Booming | 1
  b) Evangelical Shibboleth: A Personal Relationship with God | 3
  c) Emil Brunner: Unique among Relational Theologians | 5
  d) Motivation, Methodology and Structure: Building on
      Brunner in Light of Relationship Science | 9

I: Truth as Encounter: Emil Brunner, the Relationship Theologian | 13

1. Relationship: Emil Brunner's Leitmotif | 18
  a) Existential: Relationship as Praxis | 21
  b) Epistemological: Relationship as Theological Leitmotif | 26

2. Why Building on Emil Brunner? | 36
  a) Why Not Brunner? | 36
  b) Why Brunner? | 47

II: Personal Correspondence: Emil Brunner's Leitmotif | 65

3. Personal Correspondence: Preliminary Considerations | 67
   a) Brunner's Evolving Terminology | 67
   b) The Problem of Systematizing Personal Correspondence | 71
   c) The Question of Structuring Personal Correspondence | 73

4. Personal Correspondence as Ontic Basis | 79
   a) Personal Correspondence as Primordial Relationship | 80
   b) Responsory Actuality as Actual Relation | 84
   c) Conclusions and Outlook | 90

5. God-Towards-Human: The Call to Restoration of Personal Correspondence | 94
   a) The Mediator: Jesus Christ, the Incarnated Word | 98
   b) Immediated by the Holy Spirit, Mediated through the Church | 105

6. Human-Towards-God: The Answer to Restoration of Personal Correspondence | 115
   a) The Turning from Faith as Believing Something | 116
   b) Happy Asymmetry: God First, Humans Second | 119
   c) The Importance of Reciprocity in Freedom | 120
   d) Faith as Self-Disclosure in Loving Responsiveness | 122

III: The Analogy of Relationship: Personal Correspondence in Light of Relationship Science | 127

7. Analogy of Relationship: Preliminary Considerations | 129
   a) What Is a Relationship? | 129
   b) Relationship Science as Point of Reference | 131
   c) A Working Theory of Analogy | 137

8. Comparing Human and God-Human Relationships | 143
   a) A Personal Relationship with God? | 143
   b) A Close Relationship with God? | 146
   c) An Intimate Relationship with God? | 158
   d) Conclusion: The Analogy of Relationship | 169

IV: Towards a Theology of Relationship | 175

9. The Analogical Argument | 178
   a) The Categorical Argument | 178
   b) The Existential Argument | 178
   c) The Epistemological (Theological) Argument | 179

    d) The Argument towards a Theology of Relationship | 179
    e) Objections | 180
10. Outlook: Ten Propositions Expanding Emil
    Brunner's Leitmotif of Relationship | 189
    a) Material: Towards a Systemic Theology of Relationship | 192
    b) Existential: Towards an Intimate Relationship with God | 197
    c) Formal: Towards a Communication of Relationship | 204

Epilogue | 213
Appendix: A Brief Introduction to the Major
    Frameworks of Relationship Science | 217
Bibliography | 227

List of Figures and Tables

Figure 1: A pyramidal typology of relationships | 136

Figure 2: Including other in the self (IOS) scale | 148

Figure 3: The questions and interconnection of the five major conceptual models of relationship science | 218

Figure 4: Dimensions and styles of attachment | 224

Table 1: Overview of Brunner's "theathropology" | 91

Table 2: Overview and comparison of human relationships (relationship science) and God-human interaction (Emil Brunner) | 170

Acknowledgements and Encounters along the Way

MY PERSONAL STORY TOWARDS a theology of relationship revolves—unsurprisingly—around relationships. I have been brought up in the context of a traditional Swiss evangelical free church. While the talk about *a personal relationship with Jesus* was omnipresent, its effects were by and large non-existent in my own life and in my perception of others. While my mother's faith was simple, childlike, and real—and I want to thank her for this example—my view and experience of *the faith* was nonetheless a rule- and fear-based mixture of dos and don'ts. In my teenage years, I was on the brink of giving up Christianity and I owe it to my existential religious fear and to the love and persistence of some of my youth group's leaders (thank you Lukas Weiss and Peter Hefti) that I did not follow through. During that time, a book played—for the first but not the last time—a major role in my life: Keith Green and his biography *No Compromise*. His example and later also his music set me on a path towards a real relationship with God. One of this journey's milestones was an actual journey to the US; I was almost nineteen and thought of it as a half-year time-out with God. During that time, it was not primarily other people who had the most impact—although I had many challenging encounters (thanks to Jesus People USA and the many strangers I met on the road)—it was their absence and God the Holy Spirit's sometimes tangible presence in my extensive times of solitude.

Later I started my theological education at the Theologisches Seminar St. Chrischona near Basel and reflected my experience theologically. Near the end of seminary, I began to realize that I was as dissatisfied with the abstract-philosophical tendencies within academic theology as I was with the pietistic-evangelical interpretations of the Bible. At that time, a newly acquainted professor, Dr. Andreas Loos, added fuel to those flames and I made my first steps within a relational understanding of theology with a bold (and immature) thesis about original sin. Ever since, *relationship* was the golden thread in my theological thinking. However, I was not drawn to academia and started my Christian "career" as the national director of youth ministry within the Evangelical Free Churches in Switzerland. This position allowed me to launch a widespread material called *R3—radical relationship* that reached youth groups across the German-speaking countries of Europe and even Latvia. Later, I was called to an innovative church to help build its young adults ministry and this relational focus remained central to my theological work that was mainly built around praxis (sermons, courses, etc.). I have to thank my congregation for bearing my many attempts to reformulate every topic from a relational viewpoint.

While I was independently developing "new" relational reformulations, I later learned that others had already developed very similar takes on dogmatic issues and I want to thank them, people like Dr. Gregory Boyd, for unknowingly encouraging me to proceed in this direction. However, this relational take on central biblical truths like sin, faith, love, justice, heaven, and hell, to only name a few, had its greatest impact on the people I served—including myself. To perceive, how analogies taken from human relationships not only opened a new and deeper understanding of the nature of God but also broke through walls of hardened sceptics, was not only fascinating but, in the truest sense, mind-blowing! That said, it dawned on me that this relational view was nothing new, but actually very old, and that the "original" had been buried and simply needed rediscovering. I also realized that far too often church ministry and academic theology diverged; for the loss of the people both were intended to serve. I only knew a few pastors or theologians bringing both together, one important example being my friend Prof. Dr. Stefan Schweyer, yet I realized that this was my calling: being a pastor-theologian and theologian-pastor. Consequently, I started to think about doing a doctorate as a side project from my work as a pastor. Thanks to the church board of the Kirche im Prisma in Rapperswil, Switzerland—the church I am currently serving—I had the liberty to pursue a part-time PhD. Admittedly, the path to my research proposal was a rocky one since my vision was too large for a PhD thesis and since at this stage of my life, I wanted to make an investment that would not only contribute something "interesting" but make an impact. During this process, I realized that the expression *relational theology* was already occupied and with its breadth not very helpful. A friend of mine, who had already played a role in encouraging me to do a PhD, Daniel Vassen, set me up for the right direction by casually mentioning Emil Brunner's *Truth as Encounter*. At first, I did not pursue this track but then, in my desperation, I looked into this unlikely "midwife" for my thesis and was taken aback: Emil Brunner appeared to be the perfect conversation partner.

Since then, many have contributed to the success of this project. First and foremost, my first supervisor Dr. Graham McFarlane who helped me focus my proposal, taught me to write well in English (at least much better) and most of all was an incredible encourager. Also, my second supervisor, Dr. William Atkinson who pointed out some crucial flaws in my proposal and work. Furthermore, I want to thank Prof. Dr. Alister McGrath whose book *A Reappraisal* contributed to bringing Emil Brunner back to the theological landscape and introduced me to his work; it was also very kind of him to meet me in person and discuss some of my questions concerning Brunner. Many others have made small contributions that made this work possible or at least improved it: Célina Brändle, who left her social psychology textbook on our terrace, which introduced me to relationship science; Bill Johnson, by stimulating and enlarging my understanding of God as a good father; and casual discussion partners like Dr. Stefan Leuthold, Adriano Montefusco, Dr. Manuel Schmid, Prof. Dr. Ralph Kunz, Prof. Dr. Volker Rabens, Prof. Dr. Tobias Künkler, Prof. Dr. John Barclay, Prof. Dr. Ingolf Dalferth, Dr. Raphaela Meyer zu Hörste-Bührer, Dr. Kenneth Kovacs, Paul Schneider, Stefania Cimino, Mike Scheuzger, Michael Candrian and many more I cannot remember anymore.

Last but not least, I want to thank my wife Barbara who supports me like no one else and who is, to me, an embodiment of a theology of relationship; and my sons, Yannick and Gian, who bore my sitting in the armchair reading and who are the ultimate test for the relevance of my theology of relationship: may my ceiling become your floor.

Abbreviations

The standard abbreviations are according to the *SBL Handbook of Style*.

TM	Translation mine
ETR	English translation reference page
GR	German reference page
IOS	Including other in the self

Introduction

THIS BOOK WORKS—AS THE title suggests—towards a theology of relationship. While this scope is rather broad, the focus lies on the vertical dimension, the God-human relationship. The driving question is the following: What does the Swiss theologian Emil Brunner contribute to a theology of relationship for the twenty-first century? Consequently, Brunner's central analogy of relationship is analyzed in light of current relationship science in order to build a solid foundation for further research aiming in the same direction. However, before we start it makes sense to consider the broader context.

a) Relationships Are Booming

We live in an era of relationality and relationships. While the actuality and the content of these terms[1] are debatable, the present, nevertheless, might be considered a unique point in history as relations are considered of utmost importance in almost every field of science and society which is often referred to as a "relational turn."[2] Clearly, pop culture is permeated by the topic of relationships, reflected in songs, movies, books, and self-help workshops. Social networks like Instagram, Twitter, Facebook

---

1. See section 7a for a detailed definition of these terms.
2. See, e.g., Shults, *Theological Anthropology*, 11–33; Fretheim, *God Enters*, 4; Dépelteau, "Relational Turn"; Quick, "Taking a Relational Turn"; Fernández, "Taking the Relational Turn," 163; Selg, "Two Faces," 27.

and YouTube appear to be dominant means of personal and relational "transportation."[3] However, this relational focus is not only the status quo of everyday life but also increasingly pervades academia in a variety of disciplines and forms.[4] For example, on the one hand, even in non-social fields like physics the relationships are now emphasized over the substantials.[5] On the other hand, the rise of neuroscience has shown that the human brain "is designed for social relationships,"[6] which brings us to the social sciences. Since relationships are the epicenter of human existence,[7] a turn from individuals to relationships is perceivable in the field of psychology, especially represented by the so-called *relationship science*, which will be investigated and instrumentalized in Part III. Furthermore, pedagogy experiences a movement to relationships taking center stage[8] and even in business literature, an understanding of human relationality and relationships is considered key.[9] With that said, all of the above is reflected and summarized in particular grand theories within sociology focusing on relations and relationality. One of the foremost and most influential examples is Hartmut Rosa's *Resonanz* (resonance), a sociology of world relationship. Rosa's opus magnum reflects on (late) modernity's loss of and quest for meaningful connection—resonance—to each other, the world, and also the "vertical," the transcendent.[10] However, Rosa is not simply interested in a description or diagnosis of humanity's relationality and being in the world. He rather proposes resonance as a radical,

---

3. For a brief critical evaluation of these virtual relations, see Lynch, *Ecclesial Leadership*, 141, 144–45.

4. A good example for the intersection between pop culture and the sciences is the bestselling book Brooks, *Social Animal*.

5. Shults, *Theological Anthropology*, 18–19. Shults mentions particle physics, quantum theory, and chaos theory as examples. However, his view is questioned as too lopsided by Wisse, "Truly Relational Theology," 151–52.

6. Kenrick et al., "Evolutionary Life History Perspective," 13. See also Beckes and Coan, "Integrative Neuroscience of Relationships," 703.

7. Regan, *Close Relationships*, 18–19; Reis et al., "Emergence of Relationship Science," 559; Gergen, *Relational Being*, xv.

8. See, e.g., Krautz, *Beziehungsweisen und Bezogenheiten*; Künkler, "Relationalität und relationale Subjektivität"; Künkler, *Lernen in Beziehung*; Brozio, *Vom pädagogischen Bezug*. Brozio also draws from relationship science.

9. See, e.g., Hochman, *Relationship Revolution*; Covey, *Seven Habits*, 7–11. Covey implicitly draws on relationship science's *interdependence theory* (see the appendix for its basics) for his framework.

10. Rosa, *Resonanz*, 522, 596, 599–600, 621, 623–24, 677, 688, 706–7, 722, 739.

normative conception, a leitmotif for human flourishing and the good life.¹¹ As such, Rosa's study transcends sociology and brinks on a philosophy that characterizes, encapsulates, and echoes the current turn to relationality very well.¹² Hence, the context is set for the main field and question of this book: what about relationality and relationships in Christian faith and theology or, even more specifically, the relation between God and humans?

b) Evangelical Shibboleth: A Personal Relationship with God

Unquestionably, relationships have always been central within Christianity, be it human relationships or the relation to the divine. Within all the different strands of the Christian Faith, "the thinking of God in relationship and as reason of all relationship represents a persistent 'identity marker.'"¹³ This is reflected in a rich history of Christian spirituality, in hymns and modern worship songs and also in the general behavior and faith-praxis of common Christians around the globe: God and faith are personal and relational.¹⁴ That said, there is one Christian strand that has especially emphasized a personal relationship with God: Evangelicalism.¹⁵ As such, the expression "a personal relationship with God or Jesus Christ" is one of the central markers of this movement¹⁶ and can encompass the whole of the Christian life; accordingly, it is widely preached¹⁷

---

11. Rosa, *Resonanz*, 19, 53, 59, 62, 747–48, 756. We will further evaluate Rosa's proposal in section 10b.

12. For a similar, less encompassing, Anglo-American conception, see Gergen, *Relational Being*. He writes as a psychologist (influenced by John Thibaut and *interdependence theory*), yet sketches a sociology and philosophy.

13. Hartenstein, "Relationalität als Schlüssel," 165 (TM).

14. For a recognition of this fact from the field of psychology see, e.g., Ickes et al., "Closeness as Intersubjectivity," 357.

15. It is not unproblematic to define *evangelical* and to clearly distinguish it from *charismatic* or *fundamental*. Furthermore, the history of Evangelicalism in England or the US, although connected, is different from its history in, e.g., Germany or Switzerland. For an in-depth discussion of these issues, see Bebbington, *Evangelicalism*; Stanley, *Global Diffusion of Evangelicalism*. For works considering the future of evangelicalism in light of current issues, see Gushee, *After Evangelicalism*; Noll et al., eds, *Evangelicals*.

16. See, e.g., Schulz and Plüss, "Evangelikalismus," 114–16.

17. For a study on the content of American Protestant churches, see Witten, *All Is Forgiven*.

and used as a distinction from and even dissociation against other forms of religiosity and spirituality. However common this expression and focus on a personal relationship, it is recently and increasingly challenged even outside of academia and from within the evangelical movement.[18] While accrediting some value, common points of discontent prevail, namely, that this phrase and concept is not found in the Bible, is only a metaphor, and appears too individualistic.[19] Further critique concerns the confusion it produces about the nature of the relationship one can have with God, that it is the language of secularity,[20] and that it has a therapeutic inclination.[21] Consequently, it is proposed that instead of "the language of relationship" one should use "the language of faith" like *being in Christ*[22] or speaking of a *covenant* with God.[23] Others are more differentiated and perceive that the validity of the phrase and concept depends on its meaning, on the definition of *relationship* and *personal*. Preston Sprinkle, for example, points out that *personal relationship* can wrongly mean private or individual[24] but also, justly, that it is a real relationship with real persons involved.[25] Thus, it certainly is probable that the historical and societal context has altered the meaning of the expression[26] and that it has become an empty phrase that could be called an evangelical "shibboleth." Personally, I can understand and confirm this somewhat disrespectful label and the corresponding critique. Having grown up in a traditional Swiss evangelical free church, talk about a personal relationship with Jesus was ubiquitous but so were the above-mentioned problematic side effects that accompany this expression. Later I started my theological education at the *Theologisches Seminar St. Chrischona* near Basel and reflected my experience theologically. As a consequence, I began to realize that I was

18. For an alternatively Catholic critique see, e.g., Boyd, "Problem."

19. Spalink, "Personal Relationship with God"; Suk, "Personal Relationship with Jesus."

20. Suk, "Personal Relationship with Jesus."

21. Witten, *All Is Forgiven*, 35, 53, 130–32.

22. Suk, "Personal Relationship with Jesus." See also his deeply personal book: *Not Sure*. Interestingly, the content of his conclusion, while rejecting the terminology, is very similar to what will be proposed as *personal correspondence* in this work.

23. Spalink, "Personal Relationship with God." This is one of the objections that will be discussed in more detail in section 9e.

24. Hinting at Johnny Cash's song "Personal Jesus."

25. Sprinkle, "Having a Personal Relationship with Jesus."

26. For some insights into the history of the phrase *personal Savior*, see Viola, "Origin of Personal Savior."

as dissatisfied with the abstract-philosophical tendencies within academic theology as I was with the pietistic-evangelical interpretations of the Bible, which lead to a quest for a third way.

Thus, while we acknowledge and underscore many of the critical points being made, the central thesis of this book holds that the human's interaction with the divine actually is very personal and is very much an actual relationship. Furthermore, it will be proposed that, therefore, the analogy and language of relationship is the most adequate mode to speak about the Christian faith and consequently should be the leitmotif in theology. This undertaking and its motivation are implicit in the work's title *Towards a Theology of Relationship*. Having said that, besides the observation that in theology over centuries "Western thought has suffered from a systematic blind spot for relations"[27] while focusing on abstractions, the widespread lack of reflection concerning the God-human relationship might be considered an almost equal shortcoming.[28] Thus Thomas Oord comments, "the nature of this 'relationship' is rarely examined, but a necessity" since "the answers we give to fundamental questions have an impact upon every area of life."[29] However, there are some more or less contemporary exceptions to both of these shortcomings that should be mentioned, theologians who have given relationality or relationship a focal position within their thought. Some of them (it is by no means a complete list) will be adumbrated in the next section and consulted throughout this work as discussion partners.

c) Emil Brunner: Unique among Relational Theologians

Famous Swiss theologian Karl Barth is considered by some as one of the prime examples of a relational theology[30] but has only been examined exclusively from a relational perspective in the last two or three decades.[31] Within the same timeframe, many so-called open and rela-

---

27. Brümmer, *Model of Love*, 33–34, 156. See also Gunton, *The One*, 6; Balswick et al., *Reciprocating Self*, 21; Sanders, *God Who Risks*, 39.

28. Boschki, *Religionspädagogik*, 17–18, 405. Boschki refers to theology as well as to pedagogy. See also Sattler, *Beziehungsdenken*, 332–34, who perceives the theological reflection primarily within the category of *covenant*.

29. Oord, *Uncontrolling Love*, 27.

30. See, e.g., Balswick et al., *Reciprocating Self*, 32; Cavey, *End of Religion*, 37.

31. See, e.g., Meyer zu Hörste-Bührer, *Gott und Menschen*; Deddo, *Theology of Relations*.

tional theological conceptions have emerged, associated with names like Gregory Boyd,[32] Thomas Oord,[33] John Sanders,[34] Clark Pinnock,[35] John Polkinghorne,[36] William Curtis Holtzen,[37] and others.[38] A third major stream of a relational understanding of God, in particular, and the Christian faith, in general, is the trinitarian theology represented by a variety of theologians like the Greek Orthodox John Zizioulas,[39] the Catholic Gisbert Greshake,[40] the Protestants T. F. Torrance[41] and Colin Gunton,[42] the Lutheran Robert Jenson,[43] the Baptists Stanley Grenz[44] and Stephen Holmes,[45] the Charismatic Thomas Smail,[46] and Karl Barth being considered among them as a forerunner. Whilst these three major theological strands come closest to a comprehensive theology of relationship, however, in chapter 2 they are briefly evaluated, and explanation is given for why this book will not be based on any of them.

That said, there have been other relational theological endeavors.[47] From the Catholic tradition there is most famously Karl Rahner,[48] but also lesser-known theologians like the German Reinhold Boschki with his work on religious education *"Beziehung" als Leitbegriff der Religionspädagogik*, or Dorothea Sattler's soteriology *Beziehungsdenken in der*

---

32. See, e.g., Boyd, *God of the Possible*.
33. See, e.g., Oord, *Uncontrolling Love*.
34. See, e.g., Sanders, *God Who Risks*; Sanders, *Theology in the Flesh*.
35. See, e.g., Pinnock, *Openness of God*.
36. See, e.g., Polkinghorne, *Love*; Polkinghorne, *Entangled World*.
37. See, e.g., Holtzen, *God Who Trusts*.
38. For a brief introduction, see Oord et al., *Relational Theology*. For an in depth overview and a history of open theism, see Schmid, *Gott ist ein Abenteurer*.
39. See, e.g., Zizioulas, *Being as Communion*.
40. See, e.g., Greshake, *Der dreieine Gott*.
41. See, e.g., Torrance, *Trinitarian Faith*.
42. See, e.g., Gunton, *Promise of Trinitarian Theology*; Gunton, *The One*.
43. See, e.g., Jenson, *Systematic Theology*.
44. See, e.g., Grenz, *The Social God*; Grenz and Ford, *Created for Community*.
45. See, e.g., Holmes, *Quest for the Trinity*.
46. See, e.g., Smail, *Like Father, Like Son*.
47. For an alternative list, see Holtzen, "Dei Fide," 62–63.
48. See, e.g., Rahner, *Grundkurs des Glaubens*. For a summary of his relational focus, see Boschki, *Religionspädagogik*, 283–88. Rahner appears in many respects (e.g., God's self-disclosure) very similar to Emil Brunner (see chapter 5).

Erlösungslehre, and the works of Stefan Oster;[49] to name a few. There is also a growing number of biblical scholars and exegetes discovering *relationship* as a central hermeneutical leitmotif. Some German examples are Hans-Joachim Eckstein's studies on faith,[50] Walter and Raphaela Bührer's collective volume *Relationale Erkenntnishorizonte in Exegese und Systematischer Theologie,* Emmanuel Rehfeld's study *Relationale Ontologie bei Paulus,* or Volker Rabens's Pauline and Johannine studies.[51] John Barclay could be mentioned as a well-respected British scholar, his relational lens being exemplified by his book *Paul and the Gift,* and Paul Anderson, as an American proponent, with his relational focus on the Gospel of John.[52] Examples of some more encompassing biblical theologies with relationship as center are presented by Terence Fretheim concerning the Old Testament,[53] and by Scott Duvall and Daniel Hays for the whole of Scripture.[54] Furthermore, theologians like Peter Knauer,[55] Wilfried Härle,[56] and in a sense also LeRon Shults,[57] offer *relational ontologies.* Some theologians contribute to a relational understanding of God-human interaction with love as focal point, such as Vincent Brümmer and his important philosophical-theological works,[58] Edward Vacek,[59] John Peckham,[60] Gerald Bray's relational systematic theology,[61] or Anders Nygren's classical work.[62] There are also some relational theological anthropologies or ethics revolving around divine-human encounter like

---

49. See, e.g., Oster, *Person-Sein.*
50. See, e.g., Eckstein, *Glaube als Beziehung*; Eckstein, *Gerechte.*
51. Rabens, *Holy Spirit and Ethics*; Rabens, "Sein und Werden."
52. See, e.g., Anderson, *Living Waters.*
53. Fretheim, *God and World*; Fretheim, *God Enters.*
54. Duvall and Hays, *Relational Presence.*
55. See, e.g., Knauer, "Ontología Relacional"; Knauer, *Glaube kommt vom Hören*; Knauer, *Verantwortung des Glaubens.* Knauer was influenced by Gerhard Ebeling who was one of Emil Brunner's students.
56. See, e.g., Härle, "Relationale Erkenntnistheorie."
57. See, e.g., Shults, *Doctrine of God*; Shults, *Anthropology.*
58. See, e.g., Brümmer, *Personal God*; Brümmer, *Love.*
59. Vacek, *Love.*
60. Peckham, *Love of God.*
61. Bray, *God Is Love.* Sadly, Bray confirms some of our critique of the evangelical use of *personal relationship with God* since he does not or only poorly define the terms and takes them as a given.
62. Nygren, *Agape and Eros.*

James Loder's contribution to a relational framework and understanding of the Christian life,[63] Vern Poythress's *Redeeming Sociology*, or important studies at the intersection with psychology.[64] Others focus on the task of theology itself like Miroslav Volf's relational manifesto for a renewal of theology *For the Life of the World*, and Bernd Hilberath et al.'s proposal of a *communicative theology*.[65] Last but not least there are attempts towards a relational missiology.[66] Besides these academic works, there are many pop-theological and even apologetical books for a wider audience that refocus and redefine a personal relationship with God; Bruxey Cavey's *The End of Religion* being a fine example.

Overall, all of these efforts make valuable contributions towards a theology of relationship, yet many of them lack definitional clarity concerning the terminology of relationship and none of them attempts or achieves an encompassing theological conception.[67] However, we believe that such a conception is needed since "an approach that argues within the framework of relationship-reality [*Beziehungswirklichkeit*] comes—not in all but some areas—to certain conclusions that a differently oriented approach could not achieve."[68] Thus, this cannot be accomplished by looking merely at the ontological grounds, or the biblical foundations, or the anthropological and the ethical consequences for the Christian life and praxis, or the language and communication, or the missional implications, or the theological task itself; one has to look at the whole and all of those subfields combined.[69] As a result, as will be argued in Part One, there is only one theologian who explicitly has attempted such an extensive endeavor with *relationship* or *encounter* as his leitmotif,[70] or

---

63. See, e.g., Loder, *The Logic of the Spirit*. For a reappraisal of Loder's work, see Kovacs, *James E. Loder*. Interestingly, Loder was strongly influenced by Emil Brunner and by one of Brunner's students.

64. See, e.g., Balswick et al., *Reciprocating Self*; Sandage and Brown, "Relational Integration (Part I)"; Majerus and Sandage, "Differentiation of Self"; Sandage et al., "Relational Spirituality"; Shults and Sandage, *Transforming Spirituality*.

65. See, e.g., Hilberath et al., *Communicative Theology*.

66. See, e.g., Wan, "Relational Missiology."

67. Today, these encompassing conceptions are increasingly considered unwanted. "Postmodernity" is generally considered putting *meta-narratives* on death row (see, e.g., Lyotard, *La condition postmoderne*; Vanhoozer, *The Cambridge Companion to Postmodern Theology*, xiii).

68. Meyer zu Hörste-Bührer, *Gott und Menschen*, 321 (TM).

69. See, e.g., Volf and Croasmun, *Life of the World*, 1, 6–7, 11, 33, 64, 81.

70. See, e.g., Brunner, "Intellectual Autobiography," 12; Brunner, *Dogmatics II*, v–vi; McGrath, *Emil Brunner*, 171.

at least is considered the first one to have tried,[71] and who has not been mentioned thus far: Emil Brunner. The Swiss theologian was and is on a par with Karl Barth in almost every respect,[72] and yet for a long time he was hardly mentioned in theological discussions.[73] Notwithstanding, we hold that Brunner has much to contribute towards a theology of relationship and that his voice might even be more relevant for our "postmodern" times than for his own era.[74] Hence, this book builds on Emil Brunner's legacy and works towards a theology of relationship by critically assessing his approach and contribution, thus laying the groundwork for future projects with Emil Brunner as their signpost.

d) Motivation, Methodology and Structure: Building on Brunner in Light of Relationship Science

Admittedly, this book is a claim, a call, for a specific way of "doing" theology.[75] To express it with the words of Miroslav Volf: "It is a manifesto. In writing it, we implicitly request not simply that you 'take and read.' Instead, we ask you to 'do something': change the way you do theology and help change the way others do it as well."[76] While this might not be the intended purpose of a doctoral thesis, it most certainly is the motivation for this book: towards a theology of relationship. As such, we agree with Bruxy Cavey who "preaches":

> For too long, people have assumed that religion is how we connect with God, whereas relationship is how we connect with people. The original lesson of the Bible is that our connection with God should be a lot more like our relationships with other persons—intimate, unscripted, authentic.[77]

---

71. Jewett, *Concept of Revelation*, 68.

72. For example, with about nine thousand pages, his life's work has about the same volume as Karl Barth's *Church Dogmatics* (see Rössler, *Person und Glaube*, 19). More will be discussed in Part One.

73. See section 2a.

74. See, e.g., Leiner, *Gottes Gegenwart*, 276.

75. Meaning the whole task of theology and not merely the theological method by referring to the much more encompassing German *Theologie treiben*.

76. Volf and Croasmun, *Life of the World*, 7.

77. Cavey, *End of Religion*, 196.

Furthermore, we ask the same questions as Terence Fretheim:

> What if we took the word relationship seriously? What if we spoke of the Godhuman [sic] relationship as real and genuine? What if we understood the relationship with God to be a relationship of integrity . . . ? If we did this, what are the implications of such an understanding?[78]

Therefore, our admitted bias is put to the test by the considered study of the grounds and foundation of this call for a theology of relationship, which will be the bulk of this book.

Structural overview: Part I is the opening "bracket" of the broad and encompassing vision towards a theology of relationship, whereof Part IV is its closing bracket, arguing for a theology of relationship based on Brunner and outlining some of its ramifications in the form of hypotheses for future research. As Parts One and Four contribute to the vision towards a theology of relationship based on Emil Brunner, Parts Two and Three investigate its basis and qualification by "drilling deep" into the hard ground of its theological implications. Since Brunner's encounter motif is analogically taken from human relationships, this analogy is under scrutiny.

Part I introduces and establishes Emil Brunner as "relationship theologian" and sketches his grand vision of *encounter* as theological leitmotif based on his central monograph *Wahrheit als Begegnung*. Chapter 1 gives an overview of Brunner's existential and theological focal point of *Truth as Encounter* and also traces his biographical journey towards this leitmotif. This is the precondition for chapter 2 that argues for building on Emil Brunner, by converging on the question of the decline of his theological reception and proposing his unique position over and against other major relational theological conceptions and proponents.

Part II portrays Brunner's leitmotif of *personal correspondence*, hereby accomplishing a twofold goal: first, its detailed exposition and second, its justification. Chapter 3 deals with some important preliminary issues concerning Brunner's way of thinking, which conduces to a better overall understanding of his dogmatic considerations throughout chapters 4, 5, and 6. These chapters explore the nature of the God-human relationship, first its ontic basis, secondly God's role in it, and finally the human's role. As a result, five characteristics of the intended relationship

---

78. Fretheim, *God and World*, 16.

between God and humans are extracted: *freedom, asymmetry, reciprocity, self-disclosure*, and *responsiveness*.

In **Part III** the proposed taxonomy is used as a basis for our analogical reasoning, as the God-human interaction is compared to human relationships depicted by relationship science. The introductory chapter 7 considers the difficulty of the relationship terminology, followed by the justification of relationship science and the proposal of a working theory of analogy as a basis for the comprehensive comparison in chapter 8. A positive analogy of relationship is summarized, differentiated, and established.

In **Part IV**, the positive results from Part III will be sharpened by the proposal of an analogical argument in chapter 9 that leads to relationship as a theological leitmotif. After defending this reasoning against potential objections, the circle will be closed by returning to Brunner's implementation of this leitmotif in chapter 10. Based on a brief evaluation of Brunner's contribution, a way forward towards a theology of relationship will be sketched by introducing ten propositions for future research.

Throughout this work, the necessary methodological justifications will be presented alongside the argumentation. However, some methodological considerations already require attention. Firstly, at the heart of this book lies analogical reasoning and an analogical argument. While the thorough treatment of the methods on which our reasoning is based on will be explicated in the respective chapter,[79] an extract sheds light on our argument's structure. Based on Mary Hesse and Paul Bartha our working theory of analogy holds that good analogical reasoning must treat first and foremost each domain's specifics and relations separately (called *vertical relations*) before comparing them with each other (called *horizontal relations*). In other words, one must have a detailed understanding of each, God-human and human interactions, prior to examining the analogy itself. Consequently, in Part II and III each domain receives extensive consideration to accomplish good analogical reasoning and a sturdy analogical argument. Secondly, within this work usually the generic term *God* is used to refer to the divine and the reason for this is twofold: On the one hand, *the divine* appears to be abstract and impersonal, which is the very thing Brunner and also this book argues against. On the other hand, *God* is a collective term for the specific trinitarian hypostases and as such encompasses all of them. However, where due, God will be treated

---

79. See section 7c.

specifically as Father, Son (Jesus Christ), and Holy Spirit.[80] Thirdly, discussions with a variety of theologians will be in the main text only when relevant for the main argument or the point being made[81] and other valuable cross-references, be it confirmations or critiques, will be treated in the footnotes—thus increasing the flow of reading and the focus of the reader. Lastly, an appendix is added, an introduction to relationship science, for the convenience of readers who are not as familiar with the whole area, whose basic knowledge is presupposed.

---

80. See, e.g., sections 2b; 5a; 5b; 8b; 8c.
81. See especially sections 2a; 2b; 9e; and chapter 10.

I

Truth as Encounter
Emil Brunner, the Relationship Theologian

ALMOST ALL THE SCHOLARS agree that *Truth as Encounter*[1] is the centerpiece of Emil Brunner's theology. Indeed, it could be described as the hinge that connects his earlier thought with his later. Alister McGrath calls this relational conception "a Leitmotif of Brunner's later thought, tending to be amplified rather than modified."[2] That said, whilst the relationship-focus was already present before his Uppsala-Lectures, it was only after *Wahrheit als Begegnung* that he chose the language of personal

---

1. In 1938, *Wahrheit als Begegnung* was released as a printed version of the Olaus Petri Lectures delivered 1937 in Uppsala, Sweden. In 1943, the English translation was published under the title *The Divine-Human Encounter*. Although this title rendered the relational dimension of Brunner's content well, Brunner himself repeatedly mentioned that he was unhappy with it because the central aspect of truth was lacking (see, e.g., Brunner, "Intellectual Autobiography," 12). In 1963, a second, enlarged edition of *Wahrheit als Begegnung* was released because Brunner wanted to clarify that he had only tackled the theological questions in the first edition and not some philosophical or epistemological viewpoints in general. The first part of this second edition was titled *The Christian understanding of truth in relation to the philosophico-scientific understanding*, adding another fifty pages to the original text. One year later, 1964, the English translation of this second edition came with a new title: *Truth as Encounter*. It can be assumed that this was due to Brunner's intervention, and he then jokingly granted his absolution to the publisher for his earlier shortcomings (Brunner, *Truth as Encounter*, 1).

For the sake of simplicity this book will only refer to this second edition *Truth as Encounter* save instances where a specific reference to the first edition is meant and necessary.

2. McGrath, *Emil Brunner*, 171.

encounter.³ Thus, McGrath notes that Brunner's "main phase of . . . theological development was essentially complete with [its] publication."⁴ However, McGrath is not alone in this assessment. Frank Jehle concludes that with Brunner's Uppsala-Lectures his theological process came to a certain goal. From then on (1938–66) some prefer to call it Brunner's phase of personalism when he came to a settlement with himself and was able to define his own position apart from Karl Barth's. What followed was an unfolding of this theme.⁵ Jehle also notes that this development was nothing new, but rather a topical continuum in Brunner's thought.⁶ He quotes Arthur Rich who praises Brunner's *Truth as Encounter* as his "most weighty piece of writing" and considers its importance not yet appreciated enough by far.⁷ Rich also points to the genius of the "simpleness" of Brunner's work:

> Only those who have worked through, grasped, and understood a thing in its essence will be touched by the truth and be able to bring it to simple, comprehensible, and understandable words. It is about simpleness [*Einfachheit*] that has nothing to do with simplicity [*Simplizität*], but is a sign of maturity, truth, and validity. Emil Brunner is and will undoubtedly remain a role model in this respect, which one can only emulate.⁸

It is of interest to note various commentators' opinions regarding Brunner's work. For instance, Brunner's eldest son perceives in his father's theological personalism the center around which everything in his ethics revolves.⁹ Matthias Zeindler calls Brunner's "thinking in terms of relationship" (*Beziehungsdenken*), as outlined in *Truth as Encounter*, the "key to Emil Brunner's complete works."¹⁰ David Cairns sees it as "perhaps the most brilliant of Brunner's books, . . . the most original thing that he has written."¹¹ Paul Tillich, on the other hand, counts Brunner's *The Divine-Human Encounter* as his "possibly most suggestive book,"

---

3. McGrath, *Emil Brunner*, 126.
4. McGrath, *Emil Brunner*, 181.
5. Jehle, *Emil Brunner*, 353.
6. Jehle, *Emil Brunner*, 348–49.
7. Jehle, *Emil Brunner*, 580 (TM).
8. Rich, "Denken," 81–82 (TM). Cited also in Jehle, *Emil Brunner*, 580.
9. Brunner, *Mein Vater*, 208.
10. Zeindler, "Emil Brunner," 94–95 (TM).
11. Cairns, "Theology of Emil Brunner," 303.

calling his epistemology, explicated in that work, "both Biblical and existentialist and, most important [sic], adequate to the subject matter with which theology has to deal." For Tillich, Brunner's "concept of encounter" is "highly useful in a situation where the word 'experience' has lost any definite meaning."[12] John Hesselink quotes Heinz Zahrnt for whom Brunner's relationship-concept of personal correspondence "is a most pregnant representation of his fundamental theological concern."[13] Gerhard Gloege, in turn, considers this personalism as the main feature of Brunner's theology.[14] Bernard Meland even postulates that Brunner's relationship-focus is the determining factor to "understand Brunner's total theological endeavor" and that "any attempt to refute Brunner's theology must come to terms with the issues which this intention raises."[15] Thus, we have seen so far that there is not much discussion concerning whether or not Brunner's relationship motif proposed in *Truth as Encounter* is the centerpiece of his theology and consequently earns him the title of a relational or relationship theologian.[16]

Brunner himself makes it very clear that a close relationship between humans and God is the basic leitmotif of life, his theology, and theology in general. In his popular booklet *Our Faith* he writes about the meaning of human life: "God created us for fellowship with Himself. Fellowship with God is, so to speak, the substance of human life."[17] Later he widens the scope and adds a definition of eternal life: "It is life *with* God, *in* God, *from* God; life in perfect fellowship."[18] In essence, this simple and practical focus—fellowship with God—is the goal of Brunner's academic, professional, and personal lifework.[19] Whereas this layperson's expression of God-human interaction could and should be enough, Brunner

---

12. Tillich, "Brunner's Epistemology," 99. After his praise Tillich then critically questions whether "person-to-person encounter is the only valid analogy" of God-human interaction and whether it is possible to "establish the divinity of the divine in merely personalistic terms."

13. Hesselink, "Reappraisal," 41.

14. Gloege, "Gläubiges Denken," 59.

15. Meland, "Thought of Emil Brunner," 165. See also Hauge, "Truth as Encounter," 133. A similar statement has been made about Barth's theology in Deddo, *Theology of Relations*, 153.

16. See, e.g., Thompson, "Emil Brunner," 65–77.

17. Brunner, *Our Faith*, 108.

18. Brunner, *Our Faith*, 151.

19. See Maurer, "Keine neue Orthodoxie," 98.

explains, it is not so simple since for centuries much speculation and abstract thought has found its way into the church. Indeed, it is through the lens of such misunderstandings that the original biblical message and its corresponding terminology are now interpreted. Some of these misconceptions have poisoned the whole of Christian teaching and are therefore especially dangerous. Consequently, new terms and a new conception are needed to correct those detours and lead back to the simplicity of the message, promise, and practice of fellowship between God and humans. To precisely this task, which Brunner deems sadly necessary, he has devoted his theological enterprise with its central conception explicated in *Truth as Encounter*.[20] This is not an easy task:

> To track down such a presupposition—foreign, even contrary, to the Bible itself—is therefore as difficult as it is necessary: difficult because it cannot be discovered in a single article of doctrine but extends through the whole of it; necessary because it has alienated from its peculiar meaning the entirety of Christian doctrine. The "sickness," figuratively speaking, lies not in a localized abscess or in a deformed organ but, rather, in the corruption of the blood, which thus secretly spreads the corruption into all organs.[21]

This metaphor of body and blood illustrates well how Brunner has taken on this task. In *Truth as Encounter*, as a true Doctor of Theology, he makes the diagnosis and proposes the cure for the corrupt blood: relationship as theological leitmotif. In the rest of his works, he then explicates how this blood affects the whole of the theological "body."

In summary, Brunner's concern is essentially twofold, like two sides of the same coin: First, he is concerned with the existential, the actual relationship between God and humans, which is the core, the epicenter around which everything else revolves. Second, he consequently proposes this relationship as epistemological "glasses" leading to his theological leitmotif. This Part, therefore, will first address Brunner's understanding of and development towards relationship as existential core and, secondly, its epistemological consequences for theology. Chapter 3, based on this depiction of Brunner's thought, makes a case for building this book on Brunner; first, by dealing with the question as to why Brunner is

---

20. Brunner, *Wahrheit als Begegnung*, 69–70; ETR 67–68.

21. Brunner, *Truth as Encounter*, 68; GR 69. Interestingly, a very similar metaphor is used by Brooks, *Social Animal*, 235, to depict the difference between *change* and *reform*.

almost forgotten today and by exploring the possibility that misreadings or ignorance of his theology may have contributed to the demise of his theological influence; secondly, by evaluating other relational theologies and comparing them with Brunner's approach.

1

Relationship
Emil Brunner's Leitmotif

ENCOUNTER, RELATIONSHIP, PERSONAL CORRESPONDENCE or even *faith*—for Brunner all these different terms describe different aspects of the same existential reality:[1] God-human interaction, which, according to Brunner, lies at the center of everything. While Part II will examine how Brunner interprets the biblical testimony of this interaction in detail, for now, a brief overview must suffice by quoting Brunner at length.

> The biblical revelation of the Old and New Testaments is about the relationship of God to mankind and mankind to God. It contains no doctrine of God per se and none of the human[2]

---

1. The question of Brunner's terminology will be further investigated in section 3a. In this work, referring to Brunner, we treat *encounter* and *relationship* interchangeably since he generally does that too. However, for some differentiations of the terms, see sections 7a and 8a.

2. In the English translations of Brunner's works, and normally also in secondary literature, inclusive language is absent due to the time they were published. This fact becomes painfully obvious with the term *man*, which is a lot more gender-specific in English than the German original *der Mensch*. Albeit, etymologically the word *man* has neutral roots it appears to be more masculine than the neutral German *Mensch*. However, in this book the usual synonyms for *man* are not sufficiently synonymous due to the anthropological focus especially in chapter 6. For example, the term *humanity* can also be understood as a trait of a human that is humane (see, e.g., Ensminger, *Christian Theology of Religions*, 83–84). Humankind, like *humanity*, depicts the whole human race, while *der Mensch* depicts the individual human as being part of the whole (a corporate person), which is important for Brunner. *Human being* refers to the being of the human and *human person* makes a statement of "its"

per se. . . . This relationship is not timeless, arising from the world of ideas, dormant or static, . . . but this relationship is an event. . . . God "enters" into a relationship with the world, with humanity, he deals with them, for them, and in a certain sense also against them; but he acts always in relation *to them*, and he always *acts*.[3]

Brunner calls this relationship an event and an act; it clearly is more than a theological principle. This act of God's entering is precisely and primarily his act of self-revelation in Jesus Christ. Yet, since it is a true relationship—this is important for Brunner—it is not only God who is acting:

> Similarly, humans are also seen as those who are not per se something, but rather as those who are placed in a certain relationship with God from the outset and now relate themselves to him, positively or negatively, obediently or disobediently, faithfully or unfaithfully, in accordance with God or God forsaking.

---

being a person; both cases are already unwanted, philosophical statements, especially undesirable in the treatment of Brunner's theological anthropology. This last sentence leads us to another difficulty: to depict a *human* as an "it" goes against the core of Brunner's I-You and I-it differentiation and therefore cannot be used neutrally. To use the inclusive pronoun "they" instead would be elegant, yet problematic in erasing the corporate nature of *der Mensch* and replace it with something foreign to Brunner, namely, humanity as a collection of individuals rather than a corporate entity (see the translation note in Barth, *Religion*, x). Surprisingly, the most recent works on Brunner from Brown and McGrath do not treat these obvious and important difficulties and questions; McGrath, for example, usually translates *humanity*. Since some of the same problems occur with Barth's works, many solutions have been attempted; most of them not satisfying overall (see, e.g., Deddo, *Karl Barth's Theology of Relations*, 11). As it has been put concerning Barth's work: "not only the clarity but also the content . . . would be altered by eliminating gendered language" (Barth, *Religion*, x); the same is true of Brunner's. Consequently, we propose that for this book the least offensive, most accurate, yet a little wooden compromise is to use *the human* with the pronoun *he* (understood generic, not masculine) whenever other synonyms for *der Mensch* fall short of the intended meaning (for the same "solution" see the translation note in Barth and Marga, *Word of God*, xi). This precisely reflects the German original *der Mensch*, usually combined with *er*. In addition, when citing the original English translation of Brunner's works *man* will be left unchanged (with the inclusive German *der Mensch* in mind). Unchanged will also be the biblical and technical term *Son of Man* (*Menschensohn*) when used as correlative to *Son of God*.

3. Brunner, *Wahrheit als Begegnung*, 88–89 (TM); ETR 87–88. This claim is, e.g., backed by Duvall and Hays, *Relational Presence*, 1–6, 10–11, 325, who call it *God's relational presence*, and by Fretheim, *God Enters*, 18.

They too are always seen as acting, and their action—whether sin or faith—is always understood as action in relation to God.[4]

Brunner concludes and gives a brief but very nuanced definition of the relationship between God and humans:

> The event of this relation of God to the human and the event of this relation of the human to God: that is the content of Holy Scripture. . . . But this relationship, although it is a two-sided one, is never an equilateral or reversible one. Rather, it is always one-sensed [*einsinnig*] in this sense: it goes out from God to the human, and only because of it also from the human to God. . . . That is why God's relation to the human is completely different from that of the human to God. God's relation to the human is simply setting, creating, and unconditional. From the human side, there is nothing that could be conditioning God's relation to him. God's relation to the human has no precondition whatsoever in a relation from the human to God. This is the primordial opposition of the biblical to the idealistic, pantheistic, and mystical thought of God. God is simply leading the way. . . . The Bible speaks and teaches about this God and this human and this *irrevocable two-sided, but irreversibly one-sensed [einsinnig] relationship*. God is to be recognized in this, his relation to the human, and also the human should recognize himself in this, his relation to God.[5]

These statements depict Brunner's basic theological understanding of God and humans. However, while already theologically reflected, it is clear that at the core lies an actual, existential interaction, a very real relationship. For him, this is the center; everything else, theology and dogmatics, is only of secondary relevance, a pointer toward Christ himself and one's existential relationship with him.[6] Indeed, theological thinking is only the preface and the epilogue to the actual and existential encounter with the living God.[7] Hence, the question emerges, how Brunner comes to this fundamental conviction.

---

4. Brunner, *Wahrheit als Begegnung*, 89 (TM); ETR 88.

5. Brunner, *Wahrheit als Begegnung*, 89–90 (TM); ETR 89–90.

6. Brunner, *Dogmatics I*, 15, 54; Gloege, "Gläubiges Denken," 59; McKim, "Brunner the Ecumenist," 95; Schmid, *Lehre von Gott*, 131; Altamira, "Offenbarungsgeschehen," 236–38. Similar statements concerning the primary and secondary language of faith can be perceived in other theologians (e.g., Rollefson and Gouwens, *Kierkegaard and Wittgenstein*, 106–7; McFague, *Metaphorical Theology*, 119–21, 130).

7. Altamira, "Offenbarungsgeschehen," 228–29.

One could attempt an answer from two different directions: either from a psychological analysis of Brunner's personality and development or purely from the logic and the biblical foundation of Brunner's thought. Brunner himself would have boycotted the former since he once avoided doing exactly this with Schleiermacher's theology: "As long as we take a person seriously, we do not psycho-analyze them, but try to follow the factual compulsion of their discourse."[8] Brunner's oldest son confirms this in saying that he would have seen such a reduction as a personal "assassination."[9] On the other hand, the latter option also must be rejected since this would lead to an unrealistic conclusion. Brunner himself mentions that biographical influences are apparent and important: "a completely false picture of the person standing behind this theology would arise if the human climate in which this work took place were left unmentioned. Just as the family of my parents had much to do with my theology, so has my own family certainly influenced my activity in the church."[10] He saw that "a relationship of mutual influence exists between [his] theology and [his] life."[11] Consequently, our approach is to trace, even track, Brunner's development towards *Truth as Encounter* in conversation with his biography,[12] without being ignorant of his theological reflections.[13]

a) Existential: Relationship as Praxis

Pietistic Influences: Blumhardt

Brunner clearly and admittedly had pietistic influences in his life.[14] His parents were part of the circle around the Blumhardts in Bad Boll. His

---

8. Brunner, *Mystik und das Wort*, 7 (TM).

9. Brunner, *Mein Vater*, 135 (TM).

10. Brunner, "Intellectual Autobiography," 12.

11. Brunner, "Reply to Interpretation," 326.

12. This is not the place for a biography of any sort or a chronological listing of Brunner's works and accomplishments. That task has already been afforded with aplomb: Frank Jehle's biography is the most comprehensive book on Emil Brunner's life to date.

13. For an example of emphasizing the former over the latter, see Lüdemann, *Denken*, 379.

14. Time and again Brunner refers to that influence and even believes himself to continue the line of Hermann Cremer and Martin Kähler (see, e.g., Althaus et al., *Briefwechsel*, 8).

godfather, Friedrich Zündel, was one of the closest friends of Johann Christoph Blumhardt and became later his biographer. Brunner's wife had a Moravian background (*Herrnhuter*) and her family was also connected with the same Blumhardt circle. Although Brunner was, as a theologian, part of the Reformed tradition, his family background also valued the personal experience of interaction with God.[15] On two occasions Brunner's father took him to meet the younger Blumhardt.[16] All this was to have a definite impact on young Brunner. This influence continued through his later acquaintance with Hermann Kutter and Leonhard Ragaz, about whom Brunner, late in his life, makes the statement that they "kept [his] faith alive."[17] Throughout his school years (*Gymnasium*) his pietistic devotion and religious interest took the background whilst humanism and philosophy the foreground. Only through Hermann Kutter was his interest in God reawakened and his influence caused Brunner to study theology and to become a pastor.[18] During that time one can perceive how Brunner was torn between the two poles of pietism and liberalism. In 1911, Brunner was confronted by one of his professors because "he wanted to be 'exclusively a mystic or a theologian,' not a scientist,"[19] which reflects Brunner's pietistic upbringing. However, after a while, it became obvious that the young theologian was more influenced by the predominant liberal theology of the nineteenth century than he was himself aware.[20] That said, there is little evidence of reflection of this tension between pietism and liberalism during this time of his life. It shows, however, that the praxis of faith has always been a central theme in Brunner's life.

The Praxis of Faith: Ragaz and Kutter

The tension between theory and praxis was a constant in Brunner's life.[21] Theologically he had a clear view that there is no either/or and that the

---

15. Brunner, *Mein Vater*, 61, 92.
16. Jehle, *Emil Brunner*, 24, citing from *Nachlass* 127,3.
17. Brunner, "Intellectual Autobiography," 6.
18. Jehle, *Emil Brunner*, 30–31.
19. Jehle, *Emil Brunner*, 35–36 (TM), citing from *Nachlass* 43.
20. Jehle, *Emil Brunner*, 45–46.
21. See, e.g., Lütz, *Weg zum Glauben*, 47.

one cannot exist without the other.²² Later he emphasized that dogmatics and ethics belong together: "Separating dogmatics from ethics would make dogmatics speculative and ethics morally degenerate."²³ Brunner had a very relational understanding of ethics:²⁴ its foundation is divine grace and out of this "indicative of the divine promise" the imperative grows.²⁵ "The viewpoint that Christian faith involves the whole of life has always been a main emphasis of my whole theological work,"²⁶ Brunner summarizes. As such then, his academic work was consistently a means to a practical end.²⁷ These perceivable fruits of the Spirit were important for Brunner throughout his life and his work:²⁸ "'There is no faith in itself apart from acting.' It degenerates into theory if it is not obedient at the same time."²⁹ Gerhard Ebeling praises Brunner for this focus on the "determined turning to the world of experience" and concludes that the world needs more such people like Emil Brunner.³⁰ Brunner himself saw this, his orientation towards the concrete, as having grown out of the pietistic soil of his youth. Consequently, he dedicated the last part of his *Dogmatics* to Christoph Blumhardt as a role-model.³¹

Brunner's focus on the existential created much strain in Brunner's own life. As a religious socialist, he was caught between his mentors, Leonhard Ragaz and Hermann Kutter, who seemed to embody the two different poles he saw united in Blumhardt: Kutter focused more on being in God, Ragaz emphasized doing for God.³² Back then, Brunner was already drawn to active involvement, while at the same time being fascinated by

---

22. Jehle, *Emil Brunner*, 246. See also Brunner, *Theology of Crisis*, XXI, 2.

23. Brunner, *Gebot und die Ordnungen*, 72 (TM). Also cited in Jehle, *Emil Brunner*, 257–58.

24. See, e.g., Brunner, *Mein Vater*, 208.

25. Brunner, *Gebot und die Ordnungen*, 67, 293 (TM).

26. Brunner, "Reply to Interpretation," 339.

27. Brunner, "Intellectual Autobiography," 8.

28. Ebeling, "Die Beunruhigung der Theologie," 356–57.

29. Ebeling, "Die Beunruhigung der Theologie," 358 (TM), citing from Brunner, *Gebot und die Ordnungen*, 103.

30. Ebeling, "Die Beunruhigung der Theologie," 358, 368 (TM). Also cited in Jehle, *Emil Brunner*, 574–78.

31. Brunner, *Dogmatik III*, 11; ETR 16.

32. Leuenberger, "Theologie als Gespräch," 19. Leuenberger cites one of Brunner's letters.

Kutter's spirituality and simple rest in God's grace.³³ It seems that Brunner never truly found this rest.³⁴ Whether this was due to his pietistic heritage of self-examination or because of his theological emphasis on the responsibility of humans,³⁵ this much is certain: Brunner had high ideals concerning himself. For instance, in 1916 he wrote to Barth that he finds himself "again and again lazy, unfaithful and weak in his faith." This is one part of Brunner's personality that was a constant throughout his life.³⁶ One very poignant example of this can be found in a letter he wrote shortly before a surgical operation in 1948. The letter was labelled "Für den Fall," meaning in case of his death. Next to a beautiful, childlike prayer in Swiss German—which shows Brunner's simple, existential relationship with God—the envelope contains a letter presumably addressed to Brunner's family. He speaks with great thankfulness of his life, his work, and his friends and above all his wife. Brunner even mentions Karl Barth benignly. Yet, in between he mentions himself bitterly, calling himself "unfaithful," feeling "ashamed," "disappointed," and like a "first grader in Christianity" who despite his knowledge as a theologian, as a disciple was rather working backwards than forward.³⁷ Jehle helpfully states: "He knew of his own contradictions and suffered from them. As he perceived himself, he often failed to live up to his high ideal."³⁸ In reading this, one wishes that Brunner himself had heeded more the advice he gave a former student: "We may only look inward for the purpose of seeing the obstacles and letting ourselves be driven to repentance but not to

---

33. See Jehle, *Emil Brunner*, 54, 97.

34. See Brunner, *Mein Vater*, 306.

35. See Part II about *personal correspondence*, especially section 4b and chapter 6.

36. Jehle, *Emil Brunner*, 31 (TM).

37. Brunner, *Für den Fall* (TM). This letter has not yet been published; therefore, we cite this part of the German original typescript: "Bitter bin ich nur gegen mich, dies aber sehr, [sic] tief, und dauernd. Ich bin mir gram, dass ich so untreu war, dass ich es mir so bequem machte im Leben. . . . Ich schäme mich, dass ich noch immer im Christentum ein Etstklässler [sic] bin trotz meiner ungewöhnlich guten Erkenntnis dessen was Christsein bedeutet. Ich bin tief enttäuscht von meinem Lebenslauf-in-persönlichster-Beziehung. Ich hatte wirklich gehofft ich werde es ein wenig weiter bringen als ein Jünger Jesu. Mich dünkt ich habe fast eher rückwärts als vorwärts gemacht seit meiner ersten Pfarrerzeit."

38. Jehle, *Emil Brunner*, 11 (TM). See also Brunner, *Mein Vater*, 306, 364–65; Leuenberger, "Theologie als Gespräch," 26–27; and 63, 92, 95, 111, 173–74, 208 in the same volume by other former students of Brunner's.

measure our level of faith."[39] However, statements made in the last weeks of his life shed further light on Brunner's increased existential focus: he did not regard his theological books as very important anymore, important was only living this relationship with God by setting an example and helping others to do the same (e.g., through preaching).[40]

Experiencing God: The Oxford Group

Within this context, the praxis of faith, the influence of and his involvement with the *Oxford Group* have to be located.[41] This movement fascinated him, while he also perceived and addressed the problematic tendencies and developments in it.[42] Brunner did not identify with the group itself but with its wake-up call that he believed to be crucial for himself and the church in general.[43] There he saw what he had developed theoretically lived out in praxis. He saw the power of the Holy Spirit to change people's lives in action. He believed to witness a realization of something he had been waiting for, something that had been lacking for a long time, and he was not shy to compare it with the renewal around the older Blumhardt.[44] Brunner himself was also changed for the better through his engagement with the Oxford Group as many of his former

39. Caprez-Roffler, "Gebet und Introspektion," 87 (TM).

40. Jehle, *Emil Brunner*, 546. This coincides with a calligraphy that could be found in the Brunner's bedroom saying "Professor in that Christ was crucified" (Spycher, "Miniaturen," 142 [TM]). For this tension between being a theologian and a Christian, see also Leuenberger, "Theologie als Gespräch," 17.

41. This movement, founded by Frank Buchman, later changed its name to *Moral Re-Armament*. Space does not allow us to treat Brunner's ambivalent and somehow complicated relation with this movement in more detail. For a concise treatment of this phase of his life, see Jehle, *Emil Brunner*, 273–91. For a short summary of the group's focus, see Glaw, *Bockmuehl*, 85–86.

42. Hans Heinrich Brunner highlights that his father was always a critical voice within the movement. His main points of criticism were the assumed doubt-free leading of the Spirit and the almost dictatorial leadership resulting from it, the radical call to spiritual surrender, and the resulting pressurizing counselling (Brunner, *Mein Vater*, 73–74). These differences lead 1938 to a friendly dissolution of Brunner's active involvement with the group (Jehle, *Emil Brunner*. 284). Nonetheless, he remained sympathetic towards the positive impact of the movement (see, e.g., Brunner, *Dogmatik III*, 134–35; ETR 111). For another evaluation of the group from one of Brunner's contemporaries, see Bockmühl, "Buchmans Botschaft."

43. Brunner, "Oxforder Gruppenbewegung," 288.

44. Jehle, *Emil Brunner*, 277–78, citing a letter to Eduard Thurneysen.

students testify.⁴⁵ Brunner's friend Thurneysen, however, was very critical of the Oxford Group. He had the impression that all those phenomena could be explained psychologically and that the focus on the experience was a step back from what they had accomplished. He reminded Brunner that he himself had published against such a religion of feelings and experiences.⁴⁶ Yet, Brunner defended his position against Thurneysen and also against Barth and others because he believed to see in those meetings his theory worked out in praxis.⁴⁷ However, the situation exploded when Brunner invited Barth to a meeting of the movement; a final contribution to their definite break-up.⁴⁸ Indeed, it can be said that Brunner's involvement in the Oxford Group did not initiate but rather amplified his focus on an existential, actual and therefore also experiential relationship with God, and the resulting conflict kindled its theological reflection to which we now turn.

b) Epistemological: Relationship as Theological Leitmotif

Brunner's biography clearly shows that the relational theme developed in *Truth as Encounter* is neither sudden nor new in Brunner's life nor his theology. As early as twenty-two years of age the young Brunner defined faith as "like when a mother says to her son, I believe in you."⁴⁹ However, at that time he was still worlds apart from the view he later held. One could simply assume that Brunner's pietistic background was the reason he developed such a pious (*fromm*) focus, but in the following sections we will show that it is not as simple as that and that this would be, as we have already established, a glib and superficial oversimplification. Brunner's personality had no signs of credulity, whatsoever. He was dialectic by nature and he developed his theology by answering different and opposing views, which is evident throughout his life and work.⁵⁰ Therefore,

---

45. See Leuenberger, "Theologie als Gespräch," 21; and in the same volume 86, 97, 121, 131, 148.

46. Jehle, *Emil Brunner*, 296–98. Also Brunner's allies in other respects, e.g., Gogarten, were very critical of his involvement with the group (Barth et al., *Gogartens Briefwechsel*, 369–71). See section 1b for Brunner's critique of psychologism.

47. Brunner, *Mein Vater*, 73–74. Brunner valued the praxis of the group and not its theology (Barth and Brunner, *Briefwechsel*, 220–21).

48. Hart, *Barth vs. Brunner*, 191.

49. Jehle, *Emil Brunner*, 16, citing from *Nachlass* 63,47.

50. See section 2a.

we turn to sketch some of those early battlefields and reflections leading to his relational leitmotif in *Truth as Encounter*.

Dialectic: Intellectualism vs. Psychologism

In his 1913 dissertation, *Das Symbolische in der religiösen Erkenntnis*, Brunner turned against any intellectualism and proposed that human reason was only able to "unlock a limited part of reality," namely "inanimate matter."[51] In this work, it was already apparent what he would later develop in his habilitation *Erlebnis, Erkenntnis und Glaube* and most definitely in *Wahrheit als Begegnung*: a new, comprehensive conception of truth.[52] Between his dissertation and his habilitation he had made himself "a controversial figure at Zurich" because he doubted the intellectual methods of academic theology "focusing especially on epistemological questions, such as the dangers of a false objectification of knowledge."[53] Rather, Brunner was convinced that a non-intellectualistic epistemology was needed which could show that religious knowing is both valid and that it could explain why religion and science are two different epistemic fields.[54] The title of his habilitation in 1921, *Erlebnis, Erkenntnis und Glaube* (experience, knowledge, and faith), already reflects his figure of thinking: not A, not B, but C! This will become especially obvious in *Wahrheit als Begegnung*.[55] As before, he wrote against intellectualism, but now he was even more concerned about a psychologism that would be the main enemy of good theology:[56] not only the American psychology of religion he got to know during his time overseas but also the "humanizing of God-certainty" (*Vermenschlichung der Gottesgewissheit*) in

---

51. Brunner, *Das Symbolische in der Erkenntnis*, 129 (TM). With his thesis Brunner was ahead of his time. He thought about the religious *language game* without using this term. The language of faith is torn between two extremes: the *via negativa* or in danger to be idolized. Brunner brings the *symbol* as a term between the extremes. The symbol is not exactly the same as God, but also not totally different; it is an analogy. In this, he used in advance what later Wittgenstein, Paul Ricoeur or Eberhard Jüngel called a metaphor (see also Jehle, *Emil Brunner*, 64).

52. Jehle, *Emil Brunner*, 50–51.

53. McGrath, *Emil Brunner*, 17.

54. Jehle, *Emil Brunner*, 65–66.

55. Hauge, "Truth as Encounter," 138.

56. Jehle, *Emil Brunner*, 52.

general.⁵⁷ It becomes clear that Brunner was fighting on multiple fronts whilst developing his own unique approach.

> For Brunner, theology had to move on from Schleiermacher and Ritschl, and even more from the trends that he regarded as having so impoverished and misled theology in recent years: its historical relativism, its mysticism, Romanticism, and obsession with the "kingdom of God."⁵⁸

Brunner found, also through his affiliation with Karl Barth and Eduard Thurneysen, a new accentuation of "the 'distance' between God and humanity [and] declared the centrality of the concept of revelation" so typical for the dialectical movement.⁵⁹ Out of this aspect of a distance between God and humanity that cannot be bridged by any intellectual or psychological effort, instead which can only be overcome through God's self-revelation, Brunner birthed in 1924, three years after his habilitation, his Schleiermacher book *Die Mystik und das Wort*. This, Brunner's baby, screamed at the top of its lungs against subjectivism, "when a more scholarly and reflective analysis would have been more productive and persuasive."⁶⁰ In this work, Brunner offers the reader another example of his polemic style of thinking.⁶¹

Again, three years later came what Brunner would call the first monograph of dialectical theology,⁶² *Der Mittler*,⁶³ which presented the doctrine of Christ from this new perspective, clearly focusing the God-human relation on the divine. In the years following, Brunner would become an ambassador of dialectical theology especially to the English-speaking world where it became known as *theology of crisis* with Brunner's *The Mediator* as one of its most important tools. That said, it is important to note McGrath's insight, namely, that Brunner's "theological development was that of independent alignment with the emerging 'dialectical theology' movement, not of being its 'follower.'"⁶⁴ Whilst Brunner was influenced by Barth and Thurneysen, he always had his own accentuation,

---

57. Brunner, *Erlebnis*, 2 (TM).
58. McGrath, *Emil Brunner*, 21.
59. McGrath, *Emil Brunner*, 22.
60. McGrath, *Emil Brunner*, 25, citing Karl Barth.
61. Jehle, *Emil Brunner*, 116.
62. Brunner, "Intellectual Autobiography," 9.
63. Translated as *The Mediator*.
64. McGrath, *Emil Brunner*, 21.

constantly standing his ground that following God's action there was also human re-action,[65] that epistemologically the theo-logical is followed by the anthropo-logical. For Brunner, the human has a role to play and therefore the epistemological question, the question of grasping God's self-disclosure, and consequently the question of impartation, the how of the God-human encounter, is a very real and important issue and so are "pedagogical" considerations.[66] Thus, this is the context where Brunner's debates with Barth about the other task of theology,[67] eristics, the point of contact,[68] and finally the fight about the so-called *natural theology*[69] must be located and where they find their common denominator.[70] With hindsight, it is now possible to see that it was these epistemological aspects, together with Brunner's involvement in the Oxford Group with the corresponding existential questions, represented by Brunner's *Vom Werk des Heiligen Geistes* that would lead to a crisis that would finally cause a break with the other main spokesmen of the theology of crisis. In summary, in between the years 1929–35, Brunner developed and voiced his own position over and against his dialectical colleagues, especially Karl Barth,[71] and it can be assumed that after the break-up he had the necessary distance to articulate his specific concerns in a less pressured and therefore more nuanced and encompassing way; evidence of this is the publication of his massive theological anthropology *Der Mensch im Widerspruch*. While most of the content of his dynamic theological position was already in place at that point, Brunner had not yet found either the right terminology, concept, nor voice to express his concern.

---

65. See, e.g., Jehle, *Emil Brunner*, 168. Brunner's development during his "dialectical phase" can be perceived very well in his letters, e.g., to Gogarten (Barth et al., *Gogartens Briefwechsel*, 355–60, 373). Brunner also reflected this in retrospect in a letter to Barth (Barth and Brunner, *Briefwechsel*, 287).

66. See, e.g., Barth and Brunner, *Briefwechsel*, 236, 455–57. Other theologians who emphasize the "how" are, e.g., Paul Holmer (Rollefson and Gouwens, *Kierkegaard and Wittgenstein*, 98–101, 127) and James Loder (Kovacs, *James E. Loder*, 2–3).

67. Represented by Brunner, "Die andere Aufgabe."

68. Represented by Brunner, "Anknüpfungspunkt."

69. See Brunner, "Natur und Gnade"; Barth and Brunner, *Nein!*

70. See more in section 2b.

71. Evidence of this is unmistakably perceivable in their written correspondence: Barth and Brunner, *Briefwechsel*, especially 210–97.

I-You Relationship: Objectivism vs. Subjectivism

With the publication of *Wahrheit als Begegnung* in 1938 Brunner's main theological development came to a certain completion. As we have already shown, *Truth as Encounter* is like the link that connects his earlier thought with the later "implementation of his theological vision."[72] Now the two poles of tension, the two opponents to fight against, were called objectivism and subjectivism. In *The Divine-Human Encounter* Brunner avoided the general philosophical questions attached to this relation and focused on purpose on its relevance only within the Christian faith and theology.[73] He postulates: "The biblical understanding of truth cannot be grasped by the object-subject contradiction, but is distorted by it."[74] Brunner makes clear that throughout church history until today, people have been drawn to either subjectivism or objectivism. In explicit words, he argues that these tendencies always endanger the church and the Faith.[75] On the one hand, objectivism is a human attempt to control the objective, that cannot be controlled, with "a system of human securities" and belief systems.[76] Subjectivism, on the other hand, often a reaction to objectivism, is the experience of the individual taking center stage.[77] Brunner paints a picture of a see-saw: On the objectivistic side, he locates *classic Catholicism, Orthodoxy* in general and *reformed Orthodoxy* in particular and the so-called *Neo-Orthodoxy* with Barth as its prime proponent.[78] On the subjectivistic side, Brunner perceives *Mysticism, enthusiastic streams, Schleiermacher, Bultmann* and *Pietism*.[79] Brunner, on the other hand, calls for a biblical faith that is beyond Pietism and Orthodoxy that does not view the biblical message through this foreign conception of objectivism and subjectivism. There has to be a third way, not a via media, but rather one that is distinct from the other two and not

---

72. McGrath, *Emil Brunner*, 181.

73. Brunner, *Wahrheit als Begegnung*, 67–68, 112; ETR 65–66, 112.

74. Brunner, *Wahrheit als Begegnung*, 71 (TM); ETR 69. For a similar evaluation of objectivism and subjectivism, see Sanders, *Theology in the Flesh*, 92.

75. Brunner, *Wahrheit als Begegnung*, 72; ETR 70.

76. Brunner, *Wahrheit als Begegnung*, 73 (TM); ETR 71.

77. Brunner, *Wahrheit als Begegnung*, 80–81; ETR 79.

78. Brunner explicitly accuses the emerging dialectic theology to have fallen into the objectivistic trap. Brunner, *Wahrheit als Begegnung*, 83–84; ETR 81–83.

79. Brunner, *Wahrheit als Begegnung*, 72–85; ETR 70–83.

simply the assertion that the truth is found in the middle.[80] This third way is the *I-You*[81] *relationship* between God and humans as subjects.[82] In this relationship, the categories of objective and subjective concerning truth are meaningless since God is not an object one believes in, but a subject, a person, who gives himself, and the human response of trust is something entirely different than subjectivism since it involves the whole person.[83] In short: it is not an I-it relationship but an I-You relationship. Viewed from another angle Brunner can propose:

---

80. Brunner, *Wahrheit als Begegnung*, 86; ETR 84–85.

81. The German *Ich-Du* is always translated as *I-Thou* in the English translations of Brunner's works. Another example would be the title of Martin Buber's famous work *I and Thou* which influenced Brunner's use of this terminology. In this book the translation of *I-You* is preferred over *I-Thou* for the following reasons: First, it reflects the modern-day use of the English language, although *you* is both plural and singular and the German *Du* is specifically singular. Second, *thou* today generally seeks to reproduce archaic language or is used mainly in formal religious contexts as a special reverence in the address of God. Since the German *Ich-Du* does not mirror any of this, *I-You* is chosen. Some further clarification: The modern-day usage is reflected inasmuch that *thou* is ignored on purpose in grammars focusing on present-day English (Huddleston et al., *Cambridge Grammar*, 3). Also, *I-You* is preferred over *I-Thou* in certain contemporary theological works (see, e.g., McGrath, *Christian Theology Reader*, 113). Whilst this is not the place to discuss the whole history of the etymological change from *thou* to *you*, a short outline will shed some further light on the issue. The basic meaning of *thou* in Old English was simply this: *thou* addressed one person, and *ye* more than one. But then in the Middle English period this changed, and *ye* became an address for a superior, later for an equal. *Thou* was not only used for those inferior in status but also for a more intimate, informal address and for private speech. Then, mainly because of the rise of the middle class, the use of *you* spread at the expense of *thou*. The Bible translations in the sixteenth century chose *thou* because it reflected the second person singular of the original texts. "The Authorized Version of the Bible published in 1611 confirmed the usage, by then obviously archaic; and because of its own prestige helped to initiate the association of thou with a 'standardised religious usage'" (Wales, "Thou and You," 120). The conclusion is that the meaning of *thou* was once an intimate address but through the almost exclusively religious usage it became formal in the highest sense and expresses therefore not anymore what it basically should express: the simple second person singular address. For further studies concerning this topic, see also Finkenstaedt, *You und Thou*.

82. Brunner, *Wahrheit als Begegnung*, 88–90, 92–94; ETR 87–89, 91–92. Later many theologians have proposed a "third way" in a very similar manner. See, e.g., Bracken, "Toward a New Philosophical Theology," 719; Cavey, *End of Religion*, 210; Kovacs, *James E. Loder*, 1–3; Peckham, *Love of God*, 15–17, 45, 269, 278.

83. Brunner, *Wahrheit als Begegnung*, 108–9; ETR 108–9. A very similar reasoning can be perceived in Maurer, "Metapher als eigentliche Rede," 33–37.

To put it differently, one cannot defend the so-called objective and the so-called subjective in faith strongly enough. The more one correctly emphasizes the one, the more the other also comes to the fore. But in reality, the formula is wrong. . . . The dichotomy of objective and subjective is not applicable to the Word of God and faith. It is a category of thought that is completely foreign to the Bible, not only in words but also in substance.[84]

The content of this I-You relationship, termed *personal correspondence*, will be unpacked in more depth in Part Two. For now, we hold that Brunner had found a way to connect the seemingly contradictory poles—whatever they were called throughout his development—and the language for his theological leitmotif: the analogy of a close relationship.[85]

Brunner did not shy from admitting the influence of Søren Kierkegaard, Ferdinand Ebner, and Martin Buber on his own conception.[86] While this is not the place to examine Kierkegaard's existential or Ebner's and Buber's so-called I-You philosophy, we cannot avoid taking a short look at their connection to Brunner. Brunner never tired of showing that whilst *Wahrheit als Begegnung* was stimulated by those philosophies, it was never based upon them.[87] Although Kierkegaard is especially close to Brunner's concept,[88] Brunner insists that it does not depend on the validity of the arguments in that philosophy; it merely shows its closeness.[89] Even concerning the I-You or personalist philosophy,[90] Brunner does not

---

84. Brunner, *Wahrheit als Begegnung*, 86 (TM); ETR 84–85.

85. Brunner, *Wahrheit als Begegnung*, 114–15; ETR 114–15; Brunner, *Offenbarung und Vernunft*, 52, 54; ETR 39, 41.

86. Brunner, "Intellectual Autobiography," 11. See also Hauge, "Truth as Encounter," 146.

87. Brunner, *Wahrheit als Begegnung*, 52; ETR 49. This is also one of the reasons for the additional chapter or introduction in the new edition of *Wahrheit als Begegnung* (1963). Brunner does something, he articulates, he has not done so far: he puts his main thought of *truth as encounter* in context with the philosophical question of epistemology. He did not do it so far because he wanted to avoid a misunderstanding of a philosophy that is preceding the Christian faith. Brunner states that the goal of this introduction is to put the Christian concept of truth against the naturalistic-positivistic and the idealistic-speculative. In doing so he wants to illustrate what he proposed in *Offenbarung und Vernunft* (1941) as Christian philosophy (Brunner, *Wahrheit als Begegnung*, 9; ETR 3–4).

88. For a relatively complete overview of the places in Brunner's writings where Kierkegaard is mentioned or used, see Thompson, "Emil Brunner," 77–99.

89. Brunner, *Wahrheit als Begegnung*, 112; ETR 112.

90. For a brief definition of *dialogical personalism*, see McInroy, "Personalist Philosophy," 47.

regard it as a philosophical system, "but rather a signal appearing over and over again that as responsible beings we stand in another dimension than we do as thinkers."[91] He advances repeatedly that the concept is derived from the Bible: "There can hardly be any doubt that the divine 'I' and the address 'thou' characterize the Biblical kerygma just as much as they are unknown to the ontological thought of the Greeks."[92] David Cairns summarizes Brunner's view well: "In this book of Brunner there can be no doubt that the stimulus of Buber has led Brunner to a deeply Christian insight."[93] Brunner confirms: "It is not an I-Thou *philosophy* which is at its base. Far rather does it express the quintessence of the gospel: Grace and *truth came through Jesus Christ* (John 1:17)."[94] To this day, Brunner is accused to have imported extra-biblical, philosophical, personalist categories into theology and thus has built on a shaky foundation. Interestingly Karl Barth is accused of the same, although he criticized Brunner for his use of personalist categories.[95] For this reason, Mark McInroy makes a case for freeing Barth of these seemingly false accusations. Apart from his highly superficial treatment of Brunner, his essay makes an interesting argument not only for Barth against Brunner but for Brunner as well. Thus, the following summary: "Barth maintains that extrabiblical concepts can and often do shed light on certain aspects of Christian theology. The key, however, is that such extrabiblical ideas are critically reconstructed in light of the biblically derived doctrines they approximate."[96] This is precisely what we propose Brunner has done.[97] He was simply more up-front in admitting the stimulus of Ebner

---

91. Brunner, "Reply to Interpretation," 335.

92. Brunner, "Reply to Interpretation," 341. This is a reply to Anders Nygren's criticism that Brunner would base his theology on personalist philosophy (Nygren, "Doctrine of God," 181, 183). Brunner argues that it is, as Nygren's *Eros and Agape*, a "central concept of the Bible" while it does not appear in this exact same form within its pages.

93. Cairns, "Theology of Emil Brunner," 304.

94. Brunner, "Reply to Interpretation," 338. Brunner points out that, although he tried to read Ebner's work before, he did not actually read it until 1935 only to discover that his own path had led him in the same direction and Ebner gave him a terminology to express it (Brunner, "Ferdinand Ebner," 7).

95. McInroy, "Personalist Philosophy," 53; Deddo, *Theology of Relations*, 103.

96. McInroy, "Personalist Philosophy," 58. For the whole argumentation, see 58–63.

97. See also Williams, "Brunner and Barth on Philosophy," 243, 248; Jewett, *Concept of Revelation*, 67; Schmid, *Lehre von Gott*, 20–21; Scheld, *Christologie Emil Brunners*, 201. Leiner calls for a theology based on Martin Buber since he misinterprets

and Buber than Barth.[98] Brunner's appreciation of Buber was as basic and narrow as Barth's and he reinterpreted much of Buber's philosophy in a very similar way. The main difference may well reside in his freer usage and adaption of these categories and terminologies but not in their less critical appropriation.[99] Brunner clothed his biblical theology in these "foreign" terms and thought patterns because they expressed the core of its content in a very suitable and adequate manner:[100] the language and domain of relationships.[101]

Since *Wahrheit als Begegnung*, everything Brunner wrote was written in the light of this relationship focus.[102] Much of Brunner's thinking and work can be illustrated in a figure of concentric rings around a center.[103] In specific contexts, he calls it *the law of relational closeness* (*das Gesetz der Beziehungsnähe*).[104] The center is God's self-disclosure within the wider theme of the existential God-human relationship. Everything else revolves around this center and is in a certain sense relative to it.[105] Brunner puts it thus:

> The closer a subject is to that center of existence where everything is at stake, i.e., the relationship with God and the person's being, the more clearly the Christian view differs from every other, while the farther the object of knowledge is away from the personal center, the more blurred the contrast between Christian and non-Christian becomes.[106]

Brunner at crucial points. We would propose that almost all adaptions he proposes are already accomplished by Brunner (Leiner, *Gottes Gegenwart*, 282–84).

98. See, e.g., Brunner, "Ferdinand Ebner," 7.

99. It can easily be shown, while this is not the place for it, that many of Barth's critical questions concerning Buber's philosophy are reflected in the concrete usage of Brunner's I-You terminology throughout his *Dogmatics I-III*.

100. For a discussion of this, see Jewett, *Concept of Revelation*, 174.

101. Brunner, *Wahrheit als Begegnung*, 114–15; ETR 114–15. See also Dowey, "Redeemer and Redeemed," 190.

102. Brunner, "Intellectual Autobiography," 12.

103. See, e.g., Brunner, *Dogmatics I*, 80–81. See also Brunner, *Revelation and Reason*, 383.

104. See, e.g., Brunner, *Wahrheit als Begegnung*, 134–36; ETR 134–37; Cairns, "Brunner's Conception," 77.

105. Brunner, "Reply to Interpretation," 331. He denies any "expression of relativism," but states that "only the center, but definitely that, is absolute."

106. Brunner, *Wahrheit als Begegnung*, 58 (TM); ETR 54–55. See also Brunner, *Revelation and Reason*, 383.

While in this quote Brunner refers primarily to a potential Christian philosophy with its epistemological questions, as elucidated in *Offenbarung und Vernunft*,[107] it is a conception he repeatedly comes back to in different contexts. Everything was connected with this center of relationship, but not everything had the same relational closeness to it. Thus, when tackling the question of the *ecclesia* as the community of the saints vs. the church as an institution in *Das Missverständnis der Kirche*[108] in 1951, the relation to the center was very close. However, in 1943 when confronting the beast of totalitarianism with a state based on Christian values, in *Gerechtigkeit*,[109] the connection was a little farther. Interestingly, in all of this Brunner did not construct a closed theological system, but rather was guided by his dynamic leitmotif of I-You relationship.[110]

---

107. Translated as *Revelation and Reason*.
108. Translated as Brunner, *The Misunderstanding of the Church*.
109. Translated as Brunner, *Justice and Social Order*.
110. See Brunner, *Wahrheit als Begegnung*, 197–98; ETR 198–99.

2

Why Building on Emil Brunner?

a) Why Not Brunner?

At the time of his death in 1966, Brunner was perceived "as one of the greatest theologians of the twentieth century," wielding a major impact on European and American Christianity and academic theology.[1] However, his theological presence has long since faded.[2] While Cynthia Bennett Brown's and Alister McGrath's recent work demonstrate that the man from Zurich may be ready for a comeback,[3] and we propose below that indeed he is,[4] this section focusses on how the work of a world-renowned, influential theologian could disappear like it did only a short time after his death.[5] How, for example, could his "own" church, the Fraumünster in

---

1. McGrath, *Emil Brunner*, 225. See also Henry and Dockery, *Evangelicalism*, 143–44. Henry perceives Brunner's influence in 1964/1965 greater than Barth's. However, he already points out that Brunner's theology is not taking center stage of the debate anymore.

2. Evidence of this is Brunner's absence in "the lists" of famous theologians, either concerning theological history, accomplishments, influence, or concepts, whereas he would belong there. Due to the lack of space only a few examples are given: Balswick et al., *Reciprocating Self*, 32; Cavey, *End of Religion*, 37; Holtzen, "Dei Fide," 62–63; Rehfeld, "Seinskonstitutive Christusbezogenheit," 71–72, 78–79; Härle, "Relationale Erkenntnistheorie," 15–32.

3. Brown, *Believing Thinking*; McGrath, *Emil Brunner*.

4. See section 2b.

5. McGrath, *Emil Brunner*, 225.

Zurich, reject a memorial service in honor of Brunner's one-hundredth jubilee in 1989 and host a Catholic "hunting service" instead?[6] How was it that within his own homeland the foundation initiated in 1973 to "promote interest in Brunner and his works," was dissolved in November 2011?[7] How can it be that the fiftieth anniversary of Brunner's death in 2016 was almost forgotten? After all, it was only through the reminder from a former pastor of the *Evangelical-Reformed Church of the Canton of Zurich*, Benjamin Stückelberger, and through a meeting with Alister McGrath that the *Studienzentrum für Glaube und Gesellschaft* in Fribourg (CH) organized a convention in honor of Emil Brunner.[8] The speculations are manifold.

Forgotten?

One reason for Brunner's disappearance is given by Mark McKim: whilst Brunner's views influenced many theologians "no specific Brunner school of thought or following developed."[9] Secondly, the rise of the popular theologies of Pannenberg and Moltmann could be blamed in that they seemed to make Brunner obsolete.[10] A third train of thought is that, put bluntly, the time of the "great teacher" is over. Hans Heinrich Brunner proposes that after World War II a change in perception occurred regarding authority figures. In the 1980s he observed that many theology students lost their interest in the great fathers of dogmatics.[11]

---

6. This aired on Swiss radio show, "Regionaljournal ZH/SH," through broadcasting company Schweizer Radio und Fernsehen. Interestingly, Hans ten Doornkaat says in an interview in this radio report that Brunner would be more relevant for today than he was for his own time.

7. McGrath, *Emil Brunner*, x. David Cairns had written in 1948 that "it must be a cause of pride for Switzerland" to have one of the greatest living theologians (Cairns, "Theology of Emil Brunner," 308). This time is long gone.

8. Personal email correspondence with Ralph Kunz from the *Studienzentrum für Glaube und Gesellschaft*, November 2017.

9. McKim, "Brunner the Ecumenist," 91. This is no coincidence but can be perceived as a natural consequence of his "unorthodox" view of theology (Kramer and Sonderegger, *Erinnerung*, 7, 10, 81, 95, 99, 113, 116, 117, 126, 129).

10. Henry and Dockery, *Evangelicalism*, 145–46. Ralph Kunz mentioned the same in a personal email (2017).

11. Brunner, *Mein Vater*, 167, 187. Ralph Kunz makes the same point (see above). He sees the reckoning of the '68 generation with their "fathers" as one of the main reasons and points to Hans H. Brunner's book about his father as proof of this.

Although he surely makes a valid point, it is perhaps too general since not every famous theologian of the twentieth century vanished from center stage; Karl Barth, as an example, raises interest to this day.[12]

This brings us to the fourth and main reason usually mentioned for Brunner's demise: Karl Barth. Whilst Brunner's nemesis at first did not have the same international recognition, he quickly did and soon Brunner became either only a footnote to Barth[13] or mentioned within the context of their war over natural theology. Stanley Grenz and Roger Olson capture this well: "It is not unusual in any field of scholarship to find a true giant overshadowed by the colossi. Emil Brunner's stature and influence in twentieth-century theology would be indisputable were it not for Barth and Bultmann who overshadowed him."[14] Even Frank Jehle, who wrote the most comprehensive biography of Brunner to date, is keen to admit that if he would not have been asked, he would have never thought about writing it because Karl Barth had always been the center of his interest.[15]

A fifth reason follows naturally: Brunner's weaknesses. McKim considers Brunner's theological middle ground as one of the reasons for his vanishing: "His efforts often placed him in the theological center, where there is precious little room in contemporary Protestant thought."[16] Grenz and Olson conclude similarly that whereas "radical originality" is the sign of a "truly great theologian" Brunner was mainly interested in a "contemporary restatement of classical Reformation theology" in between the conservative and liberal extremes.[17] This view of Brunner's theology and approach will be further investigated and defeated below. Whilst being fond of Brunner McGrath identifies several other weaknesses. He

---

12. The fact that there is no street named after Emil Brunner in Switzerland, yet there is a Karl Barth square in Basel and several streets in Germany that bear the name of the theologian from Basel, illustrates well the lack of Brunner's remembrance. Nonetheless, there is a small University in Florida, USA, keeping his memory alive since it is named after him: *Emil Brunner World University* (www.ebwus.com).

13. McEnhill and Newlands, *Fifty Key Christian Thinkers*, 84. Also cited in Brown, *Believing Thinking*, 6.

14. Grenz and Olson, *20th-Century Theology*, 77. Also cited in Brown, *Believing Thinking*, 5.

15. Jehle, *Emil Brunner*, 583. He usually emphasizes that he is not a Brunner student (see Evangelisch-reformiertes Forum, "Emil Brunner," 0:22).

16. McKim, "Brunner the Ecumenist," 91. Also cited in Brown, *Believing Thinking*, 5.

17. Grenz and Olson, *20th-Century Theology*, 85.

mentions three major contributions to Brunner's own eclipse: First, Brunner's lack of exegetical work and therefore shallow engagement with the Bible compared to Barth. Second, that Brunner developed his theology through massive monographs on specific topics in a "not very accessible style." Third, Brunner's tendency to heated dismissal of his opponents, theological categories, and approaches in an often somewhat denigratory and simplistic manner. McGrath concludes: "It is a matter for regret that Brunner seems to have played a significant role in his own decline."[18] Although McGrath emphasizes important aspects, especially with Brunner's lack of explicit exegetical engagement,[19] his style-argument seems superficial since at least for a German-speaking person his writing style is very accessible compared to Barth's.[20] McGrath himself quotes Austin Farrer, who has said that Brunner "is Barth with the rhetoric pulled out and thought inserted in its place."[21] Could it be that it was not mainly Brunner's style but the focus of many of his monographs to be explicitly grounded in a contemporary context that contributed through the years to a perceived loss of relevance of his works?[22] However, this nonetheless appears short-sighted since, although written within a certain context in history, many of Emil Brunner's propositions and insights had an almost prophetic dimension to them.[23]

All of those perceived weaknesses of Brunner lead us to a sixth possibility: Perhaps Brunner was, at best, simply misunderstood or, at worst, ignored on purpose.

---

18. McGrath, *Emil Brunner*, 226–28.

19. Gerhard Gloege condemns Brunner's approach, which often paraphrases instead of showing proper exegesis, as early as 1951 (Gloege, "Gläubiges Denken," 71).

20. Gloege praises Brunner's relaxed writing style as unequaled mastery (Gloege, "Gläubiges Denken," 57). David Clairns means that Brunner's works are "easier to understand . . . and more congenial" than Barth's. He quotes an Anglican theologian who said that Brunner was "more digestible and more reasonable than Barth" and even Barth should have admitted that Brunner has an "uncanny clarity." Cairns, "Theology of Emil Brunner," 306–7.

21. McGrath, *Emil Brunner*, x.

22. Gill, "Teacher and Preacher," 320. McKim calls it his "effort to communicate effectively the ancient faith to modern Western society." McKim, "Brunner the Ecumenist," 91.

23. See Leiner, *Gottes Gegenwart*, 276; Hans ten Doornkaat's statement in a Swiss radio show (1989, see above).

Misunderstood or Ignored?

As has already been shown in the last section, a considered weakness of Brunner was his being a wanderer between theological worlds. While this is apparent, the explanation that he was simply balancing the extremes[24] is superficial and misses Brunner's underlying core concept of *Truth as Encounter* as well as his personality. Hans Heinrich Brunner remembers his father's personality as very competitive, as a fighter in whatever he did, whether it was playing sports with his children or in theological discourse with colleagues.[25] He is remembered as someone who, in a general conversation, "quickly strived to reach the point where clear frontiers arose" so that the "argument could begin."[26] Towards the end of his life Emil Brunner summarized:

> A critical analysis of my own theology has not only been welcome [sic] by me—as all my students would certainly testify—but it has also been a necessity for me. I can develop my own thoughts best in answering different or opposing views, and I am of the conviction that the truth, especially the truth of God's word, can be found only by common effort.[27]

This, "answering different or opposing views," can be observed throughout Brunner's life. For instance, Gloege perceives him as one who was fighting on all kinds of theological and philosophical fronts in order to establish his "basic existential motif."[28] Peter Vogelsanger goes further in commenting that Brunner's theology "always tends to aggressiveness, encounter, criticism, dynamic decision" and it aims to "reveal errors, misunderstandings, hiding places" against true faith.[29] It is clear, then, that Emil Brunner was never tame nor a thinker merely searching for a middle way between the extremes. He was always a fighter—either for or against something.[30] He was passionate and remained so from youth until old age. His son asks rhetorically: "Wouldn't a 'tranquil' [*abgeklärter*]

---

24. Grenz and Olson, *20th-Century Theology*, 85.
25. Brunner, *Mein Vater*, 118–19.
26. Brunner, *Mein Vater*, 275 (TM).
27. Brunner, "Reply to Interpretation," 325.
28. Gloege, "Gläubiges Denken," 63 (TM).
29. Vogelsanger, "Brunner as Apologist," 289.
30. Salakka, *Person und Offenbarung*, 94. See also section 1b.

Emil Brunner have been a contradiction in terms?"[31] It is safe to claim, therefore, that Brunner needed, in his earlier life, something to fight against and through his theological process, he found something worth fighting for: truth as encounter. Hence, McKim clearly and rightly shows in his study that "Brunner did not set out to be some sort of diplomatic theologian, the reconciler of extremes. He would have repudiated any such description of his work, but that is, in fact, what his writings often did, as he combined the best from various schools in creative synthesis."[32] He demonstrates therefore that Gloege's label of Brunner's theology as a problematic mediation-theology (*Vermittlungstheologie*) is wrong.[33] One could note with a wink that Emil Brunner was not very Swiss in this respect, but rather showed an American attitude: to be theologically the "world police."

Grenz and Olson's work *20th-Century Theology: God & the World in a Transitional Age* can be used as a representative case study for this lack of understanding of Brunner's leitmotif. The authors appear to highlight Brunner's concept of I-You relationship:

> However, his contribution to contemporary theology has its positive and original side. This contribution begins with his identification of revelation with the "I-Thou Encounter" between the individual and God. . . . Building from his concept of revelation as I-Thou encounter, Brunner's entire approach to theology has been designated "biblical personalism." He did indeed elevate this insight, and his attempt to center everything around it stands as his greatest contribution to modern theology.[34]

However, in reality, the authors pay lip service to this appraisal because they merely and falsely interpret it as a balancing act. Simultaneously, they somehow seem blind to Brunner's contribution to the declared goal of their volume: a balance between immanence and transcendence.[35]

---

31. Brunner, *Mein Vater*, 308 (TM).

32. McKim, "Brunner the Ecumenist," 104.

33. Gloege, "Gläubiges Denken," 76. Sadly McKim does not emphasize enough that it was exactly Brunner's relationship motif that created this synthesis and the perception of balance (see, e.g., McKim, "Brunner the Ecumenist," 95).

34. Grenz and Olson, *20th-Century Theology*, 79–80.

35. Grenz and Olson, *20th-Century Theology*, 9–12, 311–15. Interestingly Robert Bertram sees Brunner's concept of revelation clearly cast "in terms of transcendence-immanence." Bertram, "Brunner on Revelation," 641. This tension has many similarities to Brunner's depiction of objectivism vs. subjectivism (see section 1b) and is also

They miss that Brunner does not only balance the two but introduces a third option of, as they rightly call it, an I-You encounter. Ironically, Grenz and Olson criticize or praise various theologians throughout the book for their specific one-sided contributions, while Brunner would have brought many of those different approaches together uniquely and elegantly. For example, Karl Barth is praised by the authors, on the one hand, for his "recovery of the transcendence of God" and his focus on God's absolute freedom and, on the other, they critiqued that he "may have sacrificed too much on the human side of the God-world relationship." Also, they point out that Barth may have landed on the other side of Schleiermacher's lopsided focus on humankind.[36] Yet it was Brunner who went against this "A" of objectivism in Barth's Neo-Orthodoxy and Schleiermacher's "B" of subjectivism with his proposed leitmotif "C" of truth as encounter.[37]

Grenz and Olson show that Bultmann's existentialist approach erred in a similar way to Schleiermacher in arguing that "theology becomes the reflection on the experience of the encounter that leads to authentic existence." As such, God somewhat dissolves into the realm of personal faith and loses his ability to work in the world apart from personal relation. The outcome of this injection of transcendence into immanence was the loss of the transcendence.[38] The American authors appear ignorant of Brunner's proposal of an I-You encounter that saves transcendence within the immanence of personal faith while also avoiding a wrong faith-inwardness that lacks any impact on the wider society.[39]

Strangely, the authors praise Reinhold Niebuhr for his attempt to create a balance between transcendence and immanence but fail to do the same with Emil Brunner or draw attention to the many similarities between the two. They conclude that Niebuhr could keep this balance only at a great cost: "Niebuhr's proposal worked to remove the activity of God in history—whether past or future—to a realm beyond history. Thereby he left his followers little hope of finding the transcendent God in actual events, whether in salvation history or the consummation of

---

perceived by others without any reference to Brunner (Duvall and Hays, *Relational Presence*, 7; Fretheim, *God and World*, 23).

36. Grenz and Olson, *20th-Century Theology*, 77.
37. Brunner, *Wahrheit als Begegnung*, 86; ETR 84. See section 1b.
38. Grenz and Olson, *20th-Century Theology*, 96–98.
39. Brunner, *Wahrheit als Begegnung*, 88–90; ETR 87–88.

history."[40] Brunner, on the other hand, did not lose the God who is active within history because this divine action is fundamental and crucial for his concept of personal correspondence.[41]

Finally, Grenz and Olson conclude their work: "As the century has drawn to its close, we have been left wondering if any progress has been made. Rather than create a balanced theology, the efforts of the last decades seem only to have increased the tension between immanence and transcendence."[42] They further lament that "no single signpost pointing the way forward emerged" and that the "greatest lasting legacy of this century of theology is its recovery of the importance of the transcendence theme." They close with the vision of a theology of the future that balances divine immanence with divine transcendence.[43] One has to admit that Brunner at least has been misunderstood, perhaps even ignored.[44] This is unfortunate since he not only created a balance without merely balancing extremes but also introduced a basis that has the potential to be built upon for the challenges of twenty-first century theology. Somehow the authors appear to be missing the importance and centrality of this conception and Brunner as its "signpost."[45]

Another example of misinterpretation of Brunner's leitmotif is found in Gerhard Gloege's reception of *Dogmatik I & II* in 1951. Although Gloege's precision accurately summarizes Brunner's structure and train of thought throughout the volumes and perceives *Wahrheit als*

---

40. Grenz and Olson, *20th-Century Theology*, 99–112.

41. Brunner, *Wahrheit als Begegnung*, 154–59; ETR 155–58.

42. Grenz and Olson, *20th-Century Theology*, 311.

43. Grenz and Olson, *20th-Century Theology*, 311–15.

44. Brown makes a similar point with a different example, although she calls it more mildly "instances of overlooking Brunner." Brown, "Personal Imperative of Revelation," 422.

45. Interestingly, Roger Olson later wrote several web-articles that show his great appreciation of Brunner (see Olson, "Favorite Theologian Revisted" (two parts); Olson, "Gems of Wisdom"). After being asked about this assumed change of mind in personal email correspondence in November 2017, Olson responded that *20th-Century Theology* was his first book and that he "tended to 'bow' to his [Stanley's] thoughts about theologians." Whilst he does not recall who wrote the chapter about Brunner, he says that years later he rediscovered "a whole new Brunner" whom he "had forgotten about or overlooked." Since then, Olson has written *The Journey of Modern Theology* based on and rewritten from *20th-Century Theology*. Sadly, his new chapter on Brunner "got cut in the editorial process." This supports the point being made in this section of a deliberate, since in this case editorial, annexing of Brunner to the theological hinterland.

Begegnung as the foundation which is now explicated dogmatically,[46] Gloege misses the meaning of this core concept. Gloege calls it the "basic existential motif" and questions whether it is strong enough to carry Brunner's dogmatics, pointing out that Brunner has a renewed "synthesis of Pietism and Rationalism" and that everything shows that this leads to an "emotionalizing of thought" (*Emotionalisierung des Denkens*).[47] This is a strange conclusion given this position is exactly what Brunner fought against and explicitly repudiated.[48] Gloege goes on to accuse Brunner of a "theology of experience" (*Erfahrungs-Theologie*), where the last "inappealable instance" is the personal experience.[49] Gloege concludes that the impression given is that Brunner "seems to be able to save himself from oppressive objectivism only by fleeing into the liberating subjectivism of religious experience."[50] He even draws parallels between the approaches of Brunner and Troeltsch.[51] The problem with this critique, however, is not its harshness but its focus on Brunner's subjective experience aspects. Gloege misses the whole point of the concept of personal correspondence, which "blends" objectivity and subjectivity within the leitmotif of relationship. In fact, Gloege appears to have no place for relational categories within theology whatsoever. This basic misinterpretation leads to the misinterpretation of certain dogmatic *topoi* in Brunner, which in return shows that Gloege indeed did not understand the central relational leitmotif.[52]

These examples from Gloege as well as Grenz and Olson do not stand alone. Brunner bewails the fact that even his own students (as Gloege was) did not understand him correctly and that he had to "swim against the current." He believed that with *Wahrheit als Begegnung* only a few had "recognized that something like a breakthrough had happened, which assessed, would bring a radical change to the whole of the theological and

---

46. Gloege, "Gläubiges Denken," 57.
47. Gloege, "Gläubiges Denken," 64 (TM).
48. Brunner, *Wahrheit als Begegnung*, 86; ETR 84–85.
49. Gloege, "Gläubiges Denken," 65 (TM).
50. Gloege, "Gläubiges Denken," 67 (TM).
51. Gloege, "Gläubiges Denken," 77.
52. He questions, e.g., in Brunner's hamartiology its focus on the sinful act instead of the sinful person (Gloege, "Gläubiges Denken," 69), whereas the same passages seen through Brunner's relational lens lead to the exact opposite conclusion (see section 4b).

ecclesiastical enterprise."[53] It would appear that not only did Brunner's students but also his oldest son fall into this category. It is quite normal that a son of a famous theologian has to find his own unique theological path, even going astray, in parts, from his heritage.[54] It is also understandable that those differences lead to conflict, even a sense of betrayal from the viewpoint of the father.[55] However, the baffling point is that the son appears to miss his father's main conception. Although he saw truth as encounter as his father's most profound insight,[56] he did not understand it in the same personal, Jesus-focused way his father proposed. One indicator of this can be found in what he understands as the heart and core of Emil Brunner's heritage: "Herz und Kernstück des väterlichen Erbes ist und bleibt für mich der Gedanke der Verantwortung."[57] With this intentional statement, he changes his father's word construction *Verantwortlichkeit*[58] to the simple *Verantwortung*, which obscures the focus from personal correspondence to an ethical task.[59] In another section, he puts his father in the objectivistic corner of the theology of his time. He makes a case against him with the statement from 1 Corinthians 13 that truth is only perceivable as through a very imperfect mirror.[60] This seems odd since one of Emil Brunner's main achievements with *Truth as Encounter* was to find a third way between objectivism and subjectivism, where truth can only be relatively and relationally perceived and encountered in the person of Jesus Christ. One attempt to explain this redefinition of Brunner's leitmotif by his son[61] could lie in a possible gap between what he saw and what he heard from his father. Could it be that he mainly saw his father's systematic and dialectic nature showing within

---

53. Jehle, *Emil Brunner*, 425 (TM), citing a letter to Huber in August 1941.

54. This is the main reason for the release of Brunner's book about his father (Brunner, *Mein Vater*, 10).

55. Brunner, *Mein Vater*, 302–3, 377.

56. Brunner, *Mein Vater*, 386.

57. "For me, the heart and core of my father's inheritance is and remains the thought of responsibility." Brunner, *Mein Vater*, 345 (TM).

58. See, e.g., Brunner, *Wahrheit als Begegnung*, 35–38; Brunner, *Mensch im Widerspruch*, 88. The closest translation of this German wordplay would be *response-ability* and *responsibility*. See section 4a for more about this difference.

59. It is not only this specific terminology that shows Hans Heinrich Brunner's differing focus. The main difference seems to be his avoidance of the centrality of the I-You relationship between God and humans for everything else.

60. Brunner, *Mein Vater*, 380, 384.

61. See Brunner, *Mein Vater*, 386.

the struggle around seemingly objective truths and fights,[62] instead of hearing his father's proposal of a personalized and therefore more "relaxed" truth? This speculation would fit well into the observation of Emil Brunner's lifelong battle between theory and praxis.[63]

More examples could be given,[64] even from those sympathetic to Brunner. Brown focuses more on Brunner's theological methodology than on his relational leitmotif. Whilst a perfectly valid focus, by underemphasizing his central motif of relationship she gives the impression to understand Brunner as solely balancing the extremes of subjectivity and objectivity. Furthermore, she appears to regard knowledge too much as knowledge about something (e.g., the resurrection) instead of knowledge of someone, which includes knowledge about some things.[65] In one passage she comments, "Brunner cautions, truth as encounter, if isolated, can lead to an exaggerated subjectivism."[66] However, Brunner would hardly put things this way since truth as encounter, rightly understood within personal correspondence, cannot be exaggerated subjectivism; rather, it is its solution. Brown's underexposure of the relational paradigm leads her to write about the balancing of the extremes instead of sticking to Brunner's program—something also reflected in her conclusion about the value of *Truth as Encounter*: First, Brunner's referencing to Scripture as the normative source. Second, "his rejection of the object-subject antithesis." Third, "Brunner's appreciation of dogmatics and his desire to reorientate theology back towards the biblical witness to God's self-communication in Jesus Christ."[67] It appears somewhat programmatic that Brown makes no explicit mention of the relational dimension of personal correspondence, which is omnipresent throughout Brunner's book.

---

62. Brunner, *Mein Vater*, 306.

63. See section 1a.

64. See, e.g., Peckham, *Love of God*, 134, 168; Jewett, *Concept of Revelation*, 177–85; Schirrmacher, "Emil Brunner."

65. Brown, *Believing Thinking*, 19. Footnote 38 is a good example for this observation. She cites Brunner: "You believe in the resurrection, not because it is reported by the apostles but because the resurrected One himself encounters you in a living way as he unites you with God," who explicitly stresses the relational language. But she does not mirror the same relationality in her text, instead changing the focus to "that belief in the resurrection is the first point of commonality that we share with the apostles." For more about this topic, see section 6a.

66. Brown, "Personal Imperative of Revelation," 431. She does not confirm her statement with any concrete reference.

67. Brown, "Personal Imperative of Revelation," 423.

In this respect, Reidar Hauge has correctly pointed out that one cannot isolate "facets of Brunner's understanding of truth unless we examine them in the light of his basic position, namely, personalism."[68] Brunner himself puts it this way: "we can never separate the abstract framework from the personal Presence contained in it, although certainly, we must differentiate them."[69] In summary, this adds to the observation that many theologians have not given due weight to Brunner's central theme of I-You relationship.

This section has sought to show that whilst Brunner may perhaps have been forgotten or his foibles contributed to his demise, the fact remains that his leitmotif of relationship has either not been considered sufficiently, at best, or has been misunderstood or even ignored, at worst. The least that can be said is that the relational aspect of Brunner's central concept of *Truth as Encounter* has not yet received the reception or consideration in theological literature that it deserves. Some would argue that it was precisely because of this focus on a personal relationship that Brunner has even been deliberately ignored in academic circles. Put bluntly, Brunner was simply too *fromm* for academia.[70] The German word *fromm* could be translated as pious or devout, but it does not render the meaning well. The use of this word in this specific context indicates something or someone that is looked down upon by more "sophisticated" theologians or theologies because of its or his simplicity and closeness to the everyday life of faith. Perhaps, however, the time has now come for Brunner to rise out of the ashes like a Phoenix and for his voice to take on contemporary resonance.

b) Why Brunner?

Brunner did not leave a "Brunner School" as his legacy, nor did he create an abstract theological system or framework,[71] and both might have contributed to his decline. Instead, he exposed abstraction as a "bête noire"

---

68. Hauge, "Truth as Encounter," 146.

69. Brunner, *Truth as Encounter*, 79; GR 133. Although this quote is translated badly and taken a bit out of context, as it does not primarily refer to a methodical framework, it reflects Brunner's overall conviction very well.

70. This is anecdotal and has been mentioned in a conversation by Benjamin Stückelberger and in a correspondence by Ralph Kunz. Therefore, it could be at least assumed for the context of the academia of the Reformed Church in Switzerland.

71. Jehle, *Emil Brunner*, 576.

of theology[72] and bequeathed a dynamic leitmotif that is driven by the "person-to-person encounter between human beings as analogy to the person-to-person encounter between God and man."[73] In essence, this intimate combination of the existential God-human relationship and its epistemological and structure-giving ramifications for the task of theology is the main reason for choosing Brunner as the theological springboard for this book and why we believe Brunner should be rediscovered. We are not alone with this assessment.

In a bold statement, McGrath asserts concerning Brunner that "the time has come to reconsider his significance for the challenges facing both the academic discipline of theology and the needs of the churches in the twenty-first century."[74] In conformity with McGrath, McKim points to Brunner's relevance for the twenty-first century as a "way back for Protestant theology, out of the quagmire of division."[75] Olson makes a similar point for evangelicals that Brunner's theology liberates from fundamentalism and saves from liberalism. He calls this "postconservative evangelicalism."[76] McGrath concludes his book on Brunner with the statement that "Brunner needs to be reconsidered and rehabilitated—not in his totality, but certainly in relation to some of his methods and approaches."[77] Brown confirms and makes an important contribution to Brunner's rediscovery by pleading for a renewed attention of the "how" of his theology and his biblical orientation.[78] McGrath, on the other hand, highlights Brunner's "theological angle of approach," his "theological legitimation of apologetics" that is of "landmark importance" and especially his "style of theology that was deeply concerned with analysing relations . . . above all between human beings and God" which "safeguards important theological themes." He confirms our argumentation that Brunner's relational approach offers what he calls an exhaustive theological framework or platform,[79] while we rather speak of a dynamic

---

72. Dowey, "Redeemer and Redeemed," 190.

73. Tillich, "Brunner's Epistemology," 99. The question of the validity of this analogy is the declared aim of Part III.

74. McGrath, *Emil Brunner*, xii.

75. McKim, "Brunner the Ecumenist," 103. For a similar statement, see Swarat, "Gesetz und Evangelium," 203–4.

76. Olson, "Favorite Theologian Revisited (Part Two)."

77. McGrath, *Emil Brunner*, 226.

78. Brown, *Believing Thinking*, x.

79. McGrath, *Emil Brunner*, 229–34. For a similar statement, see Petzoldt, "Wahrheit als Begegnung," 81, 86.

theological leitmotif. According to McGrath, this leads to a theology as "an activity, rather than an outcome," which seeks to communicate the gospel contextualized and relevant for today. He believes that "it would be madness not to make better use of it."[80]

Therefore, after arguing for building on Emil Brunner's legacy we now turn to why a theology of relationship should use Brunner as its trailblazer rather than other relationally oriented theological conceptions and scholars. Gerhard Ebeling once considered three areas of Brunner's theological uniqueness that concur with our observations so far and lead us to three fields of preference of Brunner over and above three major relational approaches. Brunner's "personal encounter-character of theological truth" leads to the following unique theological angles:[81] First, the simplicity of the essential. As such, we will engage some contemporary, so-called relational theologies and question their essential substantiality. Second, the focus on the concrete. In comparison, we will investigate Brunner's potential advantage over explicitly trinitarian theologies and their speculative jeopardy. Third, the "drivenness" to mission that leads us to compare Brunner with Karl Barth's relational emphasis focusing on Barth's indifference to or even refusal of the question of grasping the gospel.

Why Not Relational Theology? Brunner's Simplicity of the Essential

In many respects, Brunner was precocious, and perhaps no more so than in his relational approach. While he earthed his theology in relationship almost a century ago, it has been only in the last two to three decades that the term *relational theology* has emerged. Thus, "Brunner's approach and concerns resonate strongly with more recent theological trends."[82] Yet, what is relational theology? Thomas J. Oord groups all kinds of different theological approaches, out of an Anglo-Saxon perspective, under the umbrella of relational theology: "Missional, Arminian & Holiness, Feminist/Womanist, Open, Trinitarian, Process, Wesleyan, Liberation/Postcolonial, and others." He goes on to explain that some may reject one but embrace an alternative theological direction while others combine

---

80. McGrath, *Emil Brunner*, 237–38.

81. Jehle, *Emil Brunner*, 576 (TM), citing Gerhard Ebeling in a radio speech in 1959, typography in *Nachlass* 128,1.

82. McGrath, *Emil Brunner*, 233.

different traditions.[83] That said, while it would be interesting to evaluate each of these theologies it exceeds by far the scope and goal of this work.[84] However, Oord attempts to define relational theology by the lowest common denominator: "God affects creatures in various ways. . . . Creatures affect God in various ways."[85] In a similar manner Sanders, as an open theist, encloses further by stating that God, whilst being "ontologically distinct from creation (contra process theology) . . . , enters into reciprocal relations with creatures."[86] Hence, it already becomes clear that with these definitions the label *relational theology* is very wide and too diverse to be helpful, which is our first point of critique. William Holtzen agrees that the use of this terminology is very broad and "has yet to be defined in any normative manner." Yet, he agrees with and quotes John Cobb's general definition of *relational* not as a distinct position but as "an adjective highlighting an emphasis on relationality."[87] Still others have defined the common denominator as a relational paradigm.[88] In line with this, we will show in this section that *relational* is used as a broad term that is "filled" differently, does not have to describe an actual relationship between persons or subjects and that there is no agreement on what is even meant by "God." Thus, important issues revolve around the definitions of the terms *relational, relationality* or *relationship* which will be the main

---

83. Oord et al., *Relational Theology*, 3.

84. *Open theism* could have earned a special place among these theologies since it has been at the forefront of the evangelical theological discussion in the last decades in being opposed to *classical theism* and as such claims to be more relational. Since this is not the place to analyze this specific conception in detail and track its origins, we simply refer to Manuel Schmid's superb work, *Gott ist ein Abenteurer*, for an overview and analysis. Schmid shows that *open theism*, while being very close to many aspects in Brunner's, Barth's, Moltmann's and Pannenberg's theology, would do well to "go back" and learn more from these theologians by permeating the larger systematic theological issues instead of focussing on certain minor aspects (186–87). While it would have been interesting to compare open theism with Brunner's approach (for a rudimentary comparison, see 188–222), we have decided to focus on some broad issues with "relational theologies" and propose instead to revisit Brunner as a starting place for a "new" theology of relationship.

85. Oord et al., *Relational Theology*, 2.

86. Sanders, *God Who Risks*, 161–63. He calls this *relational theism* and tries to differentiate it from three alternatives. In a similar manner John Peckham proposes what he calls a *foreconditional-reciprocal* model over and against the alternatives of classical theism (*transcendent-voluntarist*) and process theology (*immanent-experientialist*). Peckham, *Love of God*, 15–17, 45, 269, 278.

87. Holtzen, "Dei Fide," 29–30.

88. See Meyer zu Hörste-Bührer, *Gott und Menschen*, 86–89.

emphasis of Part III. For now, we point to Michael Welker's justified critique that those terms have become buzzwords that try to show "dynamic constellations and illuminating structures" while often being devoid of content. He poses the crucial question: "What is a relationship?"[89] Does it mean something like the relationship between billiard balls, the brief contact in an elevator or the close relationship between lovers? Or does it mean all of it? Herein lies the main problem of the so-called relational theologies and thus leads to our second point of critique. What has been an important shift towards relationality has become unclear and has sometimes even lost the essential: its substance. What we mean by this will be shown by engaging briefly with some relational conceptions.

F. LeRon Shults has proposed a relational theology as opposed to substance metaphysics. This is a common train of thought among relational theologians. After sketching the history of philosophy and the turn to relationality,[90] he claims that "the demise of the substance metaphysics of ancient Greece and early modern science is a happy occasion for theology and for Christian praxis."[91] Up to this point, Brunner has said the same.[92] However, after outlining Robert Kegan's system Shults summarizes his relational approach as one that "requires that one take the relationship itself as prior to its parts. . . . This primacy of relationality is central to the postmodernist fiduciary structure" that he proposes.[93] Shults, at that point in his theological development, still admits that this focus on the relational structure does not make the objects or subjects obsolete,[94] but it is already obvious that he does not perceive the relationship between God and humans as I-You relation between persons as compelling.[95] This is exactly what Maarten Wisse critiques in Shults's approach that the kind of relation would need to be defined further through a focus on its "parts," meaning God and humans:[96] "While the subject

---

89. Welker, "Beziehung," 541, 547 (TM).

90. Shults, *Theological Anthropology*, 11–19. Maarten Wisse questions this popular view of history in his critique of Shults's monograph (Wisse, "Truly Relational Theology," 150).

91. Shults, *Theological Anthropology*, 35.

92. See, e.g., Brunner, *Dogmatics I*, 139–40.

93. Shults, *Theological Anthropology*, 47. For a similar non-theological proposal, see Gergen, *Relational Being*, xxvi, 5, 10, 17, 29, 38, 372–73, 386, 393.

94. Shults, *Theological Anthropology*, 59.

95. Shults, *Theological Anthropology*, 124–25.

96. Wisse, "Truly Relational Theology," 152, 157.

is directed to the other, it remains completely unclear who or what this other is, and how different relationships with different 'others' have to be evaluated."[97] Whilst Shults's focus is on the relational structure and system, in countering substance theology in favor of relationality he loses its substance.[98]

This tendency to relationality as principle can be observed throughout different and less radical forms of so-called relational theologies. Even Oord's conception of a theology of love, although mostly very personalistic, tends to focus on love primarily as a structural principle for theology.[99] Raphaela Meyer zu Hörste-Bührer detects the same tendency within contemporary German theology. After analyzing the conceptions of Wilfried Härle/Eilert Herms,[100] Ingolf Dalferth/Eberhard Jüngel[101] and Christoph Schwöbel[102] she categorizes their approach as a "relational ontology,"[103] whereas others use the term *relationality* for this specific view of reality.[104] While Emil Brunner should be considered an important forerunner of a relational ontology,[105] Meyer zu Hörste-Bührer shows that there are differences between German theological personalism and the more recent relational theologies. She concludes that a major difference is that the former focuses on the relationship *and* the subjects involved while the latter emphasizes relational structures. She summarizes Wilfried Joest in pointing out three essential features of theological personalism: First, the relationality of the content of faith: faith is not about an "it" but about a response to someone. Second, the actuality of the position in faith (*Glaubensstand*): faith is not an objective

---

97. Wisse, "Truly Relational Theology," 157.

98. Shults became an atheist. He argues in one of his later books, *Theology after the Birth of God*, against a God who is a supernatural agent. This seems to be a radical but consequential conclusion of what was already present in seed form in his earlier works.

99. See Oord, "Relational Love." See also Oord, *Uncontrolling Love*, his manifesto for the conception of kenotic love.

100. Härle and Herms, *Rechtfertigung, das Wirklichkeitsverständnis*.

101. Dalferth and Jüngel, "Person und Gottebenbildlichkeit."

102. Schwöbel, *Gott in Beziehung*.

103. Meyer zu Hörste-Bührer, *Gott und Menschen*, 72–73 (TM).

104. For some non-theological approaches see, e.g., Künkler, "Relationalität und relationale Subjektivität," 27–29, 41; Künkler, "Relationalität menschlicher Existenz," 68–70, 76; Krautz, "Relationalität," 16–17.

105. Lütz, *Weg zum Glauben*, 217–18. Brunner's *"relational ontology"* will be depicted and evaluated in chapter 4.

property but an ongoing encounter. Third, the subjective access to faith: faith is the result of an encounter between God and humans.[106] It becomes clear that theological personalism, and Brunner as one of its protagonists, sees relationality primarily as a relationship between actual persons. As in every relationship, the relation is important but only with the actual parties involved.[107] The parties are, so to speak, the essence, the substance of the relation. Colin Gunton says exactly the same when he laments "the syndrome" of having "a particularity without relation and a relationality without particularity." He believes that the time has come to put "substance" back on the table again, or, as he calls it to avoid confusion, "substantiality." One cannot have true relationality without substantiality, "ontology and relation stand or fall together rather than are opposed approaches to the way we understand things." He concludes that "t the heart of the matter, and of immense importance, is the concept of person."[108] As such, Kenneth Kovacs calls Brunner's approach *relational personalism* since it is not simply personalism or relational but a uniting of both.[109] This dual focus is one of the reasons for building this book on Brunner's theology. Could it be that contemporary relational theology has, by and large, deviated from the simple relationship-path of an Emil Brunner and has therefore fallen into the trap of abstraction once again?[110] Johannes Hartl would agree: "Where the persons dissolve, there also the relationship, even love ends."[111] Perhaps it is time to go back to the roots of relational theology and develop a different stream that is simply and essentially about the I-You relationship between God and humans as persons.[112]

---

106. Meyer zu Hörste-Bührer, *Gott und Menschen*, 94–95.

107. Härle calls this equiprimordial, *gleichursprünglich* (Härle, "Relationale Erkenntnistheorie," 29).

108. Gunton, *The One*, 193–96. For further discussions concerning the primacy of relationality or substantiality, see Guthrie, "Anthropomorphism," 39; Krautz, "Relationalität," 18–19; Rabens, *Holy Spirit and Ethics*, vii, 142–43; Oster, *Person-Sein*, 224; Rabens, "Sein und Werden," 113, 116. For a helpful overview of different theological streams concerning these questions, see Wolf, "God as Person," 26–32.

109. Kovacs, *James E. Loder*, 49–50.

110. Bracken, "Toward a New Philosophical Theology," 708–9.

111. Hartl, "Abschied" (TM), a critical response to Richard Rohr's theological development.

112. Wisse makes a related proposal after his critique of Shults's theology (Wisse, "Truly Relational Theology," 159–60).

Why Not Trinitarian Theology? Brunner's Focus on the Concrete

A similar train of thought can be made within trinitarian theology. Here the danger lies not chiefly in the loss of the essential but in abstraction and speculation. Although it seems current to base a relational approach on the Trinity, we will see why Brunner's pull to the concrete has its advantages. In the theological era before Brunner, the dogma of the Trinity had almost become a marginal note. Karl Barth subsequently recentered it in his *Church Dogmatics*.[113] Since then, there has almost been an inflation of *trinitarianism*. Colin Gunton comments ironically: "Suddenly we are all trinitarians, or so it would seem."[114] Andreas Loos observes a "tendency to turn the Trinity into an abstract ideal" and calls it "trinitarian idealism." He defines it as "a theology that employs the triunity of God's being as an a priori principle for constructing a view of this world as God's creation," and believes it "opens the back door for anti-trinitarianism."[115]

To identify Brunner's merit over and against a trinitarian idealism we have to take a brief look at his non-speculative, moderate trinitarian approach.[116] Brunner's center of attention and starting point for everything else is God's self-revelation in Jesus Christ. Only there can we see who God is.[117] Therefore, Brunner refuses to speculate about a "God in himself" that might be different from this historic revelation and calls the doctrine of the Trinity a "safeguarding doctrine" *(Grenz- und Schutzlehre)*[118] but "not a Biblical kerygma."[119] For Brunner, the doctrine of the Trinity is not the presupposition but the outcome of faith.[120] As such, it is important to understand how God's revelation works, as Brown points out:

> Knowledge begins with the man Jesus, and then proceeds to know him as the Son of God, in whom is revealed also the

---

113. See Barth's justification in Meyer zu Hörste-Bührer, *Gott und Menschen*, 304–5. See also Grenz and Olson, *20th-Century Theology*, 72.

114. Gunton, *Promise of Trinitarian Theology*, xv.

115. Loos, "Divine Action," 257.

116. See for helpful summaries of Brunner's view of the Trinity: McGrath, *Emil Brunner*, 235–37; Brown, *Believing Thinking*, 33–34.

117. For a similar reasoning, see Tanner, *Christ the Key*, 207–8, 221–22, 233–34, 243.

118. Brunner, *Wahrheit als Begegnung*, 141 (TM); ETR 141–42.

119. Brunner, *Dogmatics I*, 206; GR 214.

120. McGrath, *Emil Brunner*, 237.

Father and the Spirit. This outline reiterates why Brunner rejects out of hand theological reflection that begins with the invisible divine being or that pursues its study apart from the apostolic witness to Christ.[121]

Brunner thus begins with and focuses on the concrete action of God in history and moves from there to ontology, to God's being. He differentiates between what can be perceived and the reality that still is a mystery:[122]

> From the point of view of *knowledge*, Jesus Christ comes first, and all that we can say about God is secondary, yet actually God, the Three in One, comes first, and the Incarnate Son, Jesus Christ, comes second. When this distinction between the *ratio cognoscendi* and the *ratio essendi* is misunderstood, it necessarily leads to speculation and fantasy.[123]

Brunner thus advocates something similar to what has been called *economic Trinity* that can be characterized with the following sentences: One can only perceive God in what he has done. The person gets revealed through the work. The substantive noun needs replacement by the verb and the static by the dynamic.[124] "Anything to do with metaphysical being and substance is the background, not the foreground, of the message of the New Testament."[125] But at the same time, he makes it perfectly clear that from this historical happening, this establishing of a relationship in time and space, "we can better see into the realm of the Transcendent": "This does not mean that the doctrine of an 'economic' Trinity is played off against that of an 'immanent' doctrine. We have no desire to lay exclusive emphasis upon the historical as such, and to ignore the background of eternity."[126]

Exactly this is what Loos and Gunton, too, have called for in current trinitarian theology: "a movement in thought from the dynamic of the divine involvement in space and time to the implications of such an

---

121. Brown, *Believing Thinking*, 54.

122. Brunner, *Dogmatics I*, 225; GR 239.

123. Brunner, *Dogmatics II*, 239; GR 257. Loos comes to the same conclusion and calls it the *noetic* and the *ontic* level. Loos, "Die Krise der Trinitätslehre," 229–30.

124. See Brunner, "Reply to Interpretation," 343–44.

125. Dowey, "Redeemer and Redeemed," 198.

126. Brunner, *Dogmatics I*, 223–24; GR 238.

involvement for an understanding of the eternal dynamic of deity."[127] This is what Loos observes within Adolf Schlatter's theology, calling it "an applied Trinitarian theology" with the following features that should be adapted in twenty-first century theology: First, the doctrine of the Trinity has to be grounded "in the concrete and particular actions through which God reveals himself in this world." Second, this grounding is not a sign of "an epistemological lack of a better foundation but rather of taking God's being in action seriously at the ontological level." Third, "the theological interrelation of God's being and action" has to be "centred around Christ." This way one can avoid that the doctrine of the Trinity becomes an abstract principle instead of communicating us something about God: his nature of love in being for us.[128] Loos believes that an approach like this would lead to a fresh turning to the Bible with a comeback of a biblical language that would generate a renewed attention of the Trinity within the church.[129]

In essence, Brunner appears to be in line with Gunton and Loos with their call for a new and more moderate trinitarian theology. Nonetheless, there are differences. The main question Emil Brunner would ask them is this: what is the gain of starting with the economy but then moving to the immanent Trinity in order to use it as a foundation for analogical statements about the world's ontology,[130] while it is possible and less speculative to derive those analogical statements directly from the "economic Trinity?" Brunner already calls some of the statements about the inner workings of the Trinity "speculations," despite them being derived from God's action towards the world and he even warns that these are unnecessary speculations that are out of bounds.[131] For Brunner, it is important that God's relational acting in this world is an expression of his relational being; however, he makes a case for focusing on the concrete instead of "transferring the interest from the real of salvation to that of

---

127. Gunton, *The One*, 163. See also Loos, "Die Krise der Trinitätslehre," 229; Loos, "Divine Action," 259–60.

128. Loos, "Divine Action," 276–77. He calls this reading of Schlatter also an "*analogia operationis* [that] immediately gives rise therefore to an *analogia relationis*" (272–73). In a personal conversation with Loos in December 2017 he confirmed that the case made here can also be adapted for Brunner's doctrine of the Trinity.

129. Loos, "Die Krise der Trinitätslehre," 222, 228–29.

130. See Gunton's train of thought in *The One*, 165, 230.

131. See Brunner, *Dogmatics I*, 225; GR 239.

transcendental speculation."[132] For him, God's revelatory acting in this world in the Son, through the Spirit, both revealing the Father is a sufficient base for his leitmotif of I-You relationship. Although this somewhat radical view against any speculation can be and has been questioned,[133] it might be precisely the approach to take to be able to communicate the gospel intelligibly to religiously critical people of the twenty-first century.[134] Which leads us to the third and last of Brunner's advantages: his drivenness to mission and Karl Barth.

Why Not Karl Barth? Brunner's Drivenness to Mission

Karl Barth articulated not only a very relational theological approach[135] but one that has also been said to be personalist.[136] In fact, Brunner could well be the author of this statement by Barth: "For me, the relation of this God and this person, the relation of this person and this God, is, in a nutshell, the theme of the Bible and the totality of philosophy."[137] Meyer zu Hörste-Bührer explicates different aspects of Barth's theology concerning the relationship between God and humans. Many of them are similar to Brunner's approach, as the following summarizing, based on Meyer zu Hörste-Bührer, shows. Without Jesus Christ, God has no face for us. It is not merely about the right searching for God; rather, it is about a real encounter with him. Any human searching would not make sense without God's showing Godself. True theology, then, only emerges from an encounter with God. For Barth theology is an act of faith, it happens only in the context of prayer. Barth resists any abstract talk about God; indeed, his epistemology, rather than being founded on a subject-object-structure, assumes already that God reveals himself to humans. God is always a "you" for us and never an "it." Relationship for

---

132. Brunner, *Dogmatics I*, 238; GR 253. For an example of basing an argument on what Brunner would have called "speculation," see Balswick et al., *Reciprocating Self*, 36–37, 41.

133. See, e.g., Cairns, "Theology of Emil Brunner," 305; Nygren, "Doctrine of God," 186.

134. See McGrath, *Emil Brunner*, 237.

135. See, e.g., Deddo, *Theology of Relations*; Meyer zu Hörste-Bührer, *Gott und Menschen*.

136. See the short discussion in section 1b.

137. McGrath, *Emil Brunner*, 16, citing from the preface to the second edition of Barth's Romans commentary. See also Meyer zu Hörste-Bührer, *Gott und Menschen*, 106.

Barth, therefore, is not some relational state of being but rather a dynamic movement and interaction that must happen within concrete history. As such, it is not anthropomorphic categories that are a projection on God but, rather, the other way around: our relational orientation is analogous to God's being in relationship. God's relationship with humans is asymmetric, starts one-sided with God but focuses on answer and reciprocity. Thus, as a human being, Jesus Christ shows that he is God-for-humans and the human-for-God. And, because God is in relation with humans in Jesus Christ he is affected by the fate of humanity.[138] As a result, we can see that Barth's dogmatic leitmotif of covenant is per se relational.[139] Meyer zu Hörste-Bührer concludes that Barth has a logic of relation (*Relationslogik*) because aspects of his writing only make sense within the reality of relationships (*Beziehungswirklichkeit*).[140] Indeed, Barth even talks about a close, intimate relationship between God and humans.[141]

Perhaps, then, one has to ask, after all being said, why Brunner has been chosen over Barth as the focus of this book? After all, Barth is much more "present" in contemporary theology. The first significant reason for building on Brunner's work is that he was quite candid about his leitmotif of relationship, while Barth often secretly wove it into the fabric of his *Church Dogmatics*.[142] Secondly, there is the specter of Barth's objectivism or what some might even call a form of monergism.[143] Whilst it is not the place here to analyze this aspect of Barth's theology, this verdict is, to some extent, an oversimplification. That said, there is validity in it since Barth tended to focus more on the objective side of the revelation, hereby underexposing the human side. This is the reason why Brunner was welcoming what he perceived as a "new Barth" in *Church Dogmatics III* and his presumably new-found acceptance of the human responsibility in this

---

138. Meyer zu Hörste-Bührer, *Gott und Menschen*, 114–26.

139. Meyer zu Hörste-Bührer, *Gott und Menschen*, 289; Deddo, *Theology of Relations*, 81–83.

140. Meyer zu Hörste-Bührer, *Gott und Menschen*, 317.

141. Meyer zu Hörste-Bührer, *Gott und Menschen*, 403; Deddo, *Theology of Relations*, 81–83.

142. As has already been shown in section 1b, Brunner was also more generous in revealing his inspiration through the I-You philosophy. Barth was either not aware of it, as Shults suggests (Shults, *Theological Anthropology*, 118), or he just did "little by way of indicating [his personalist] sources" (McInroy, "Personalist Philosophy," 50).

143. Olson, "Gems of Wisdom."

I-You relationship.¹⁴⁴ It even would appear that by the end of their respective theological works, and after *Church Dogmatics IV*, this aspect of the content of their theology was not so different after all and that Brunner had only illuminated it earlier.¹⁴⁵

Finally, the main reason of difference between Barth and Brunner, and thus also the reason for choosing Brunner over Barth for this book, lies in their different take on the actual task of theology. Whilst Brunner posed the epistemic question and asked not only what but how God's self-disclosure and the corresponding faith-answer can be grasped,¹⁴⁶ Barth was not only disinterested in this question but was even opposed to it.¹⁴⁷ The different terms Brunner uses, depending on the context,¹⁴⁸ are *the other task of theology, missionary theology, eristics* or *the point of contact*, and all lead to this same fundamental conviction: that humans can be addressed and challenged and, this being so, it matters how this communication occurs and can be perceived.¹⁴⁹ Looking back, one has to conclude that this was also the main point of difference or misunderstanding in the so-called Barth-Brunner "natural theology" debate.¹⁵⁰ Barth's weakness is seen in what has also been considered one of his greatest strengths:

---

144. Brunner, "New Barth," 127. This, Brunner's view of a "new Barth" has been questioned. Although John McDowell makes some valid observations, he interprets Brunner's theology too strongly only in reaction to Barth (McDowell, "Subjectivity of the Object," 27). Shults on the other hand, argues strongly for a change in Barth (Shults, *Theological Anthropology*, 120–22).

145. While the two theologians both proposed *relationship* as a central category of the Bible and theology they differed for long periods in its existential perception concerning the "fruit of the Spirit" (see section 1a). However, in *Church Dogmatics IV*, Barth can be perceived to have made a *turn* towards the human's responsibility. Klaus Bockmühl locates this *turn* from the middle of *Church Dogmatics IV/2* onwards and even speaks of Barth's self-correction by highlighting the second half of the whole picture (Bockmühl, "Wende im Spätwerk").

146. See, e.g., Barth and Brunner, *Briefwechsel*, 455–57; Brunner, "Anknüpfungspunkt," 239, 243, 247, 266–67; Brunner, "Natur und Gnade," 373; Kramer, "Aufgabe," 363–79, 366; Brunner, *Dogmatics I*, 69; Schmid, *Lehre von Gott*, 108.

147. This development and dichotomy between Barth and Brunner can clearly be perceived in their correspondence (Barth and Brunner, *Briefwechsel*, 210–14).

148. Brunner's changing terminology will be investigated in more detail in section 3a.

149. See, e.g., Brunner, "Intellectual Autobiography," 19; Kramer, "Aufgabe," 363–64, 366; Leipold, *Missionarische Theologie*, 286–89.

150. As already noted, this is not the place to unfold the details of this debate. For further studies see, e.g., McGrath, *Emil Brunner*, 90–133; Hart, *Barth vs. Brunner*; Jehle, *Emil Brunner*, 293–321.

The extreme to which he takes theological autonomy. His refusal of every kind of rational justification of the truth of revelation leads theology beyond autonomy into isolation. If there are no intelligible bridges connecting theology with other disciplines or with common human experience, how can Christian belief appear to outsiders as anything but esoteric?[151]

Grenz and Olson go as far as accusing Barth of having "effectively removed God from the realm of everyday life."[152] Brunner, on the other hand, believed that a theological description of the Faith that approves itself is needed, instead of merely proving a point as in classic apologetics.[153] He was certain to have the responsibility to communicate with the recipients in mind[154] since God did the same in and through Jesus Christ.[155] There one has to locate his speech about the point of contact (*Anknüpfungspunkt*) that every human being possesses.[156] Brunner, after his missionary experience in Asia, feels vindicated and affirms again the importance of this concept of the other task of theology.[157] In *Dogmatics I*, he summarizes well, not only missionary theology but his broader concern and intention:

> Missionary theology is an intellectual presentation of the Gospel of Jesus Christ, which starts from the spiritual situation of the hearer, and is addressed to it. As dogmatics is necessarily deductive, missionary theology is equally necessarily inductive. . . .

151. Grenz and Olson, *20th-Century Theology*, 75.

152. Grenz and Olson, *20th-Century Theology*, 156.

153. Gill, "Teacher and Preacher," 317. See also Schrotenboer, *New Apologetics*, 148.

154. Brunner, "Missionary Theology," 816.

155. Brunner, *Offenbarung und Vernunft*, 449–51; ETR 413–15. See also Scheld, *Christologie Emil Brunners*, 215, 220.

156. The German *Anknüpfungspunkt* has a slightly, but important, different meaning than the English term "point of contact." Point of contact paints a picture of two entities moving towards each other until they make contact. *Anknüpfungspunkt* on the other hand renders one party active in movement towards the other, while the other is passive. Like a ship's rope attached to an iron ring on land. This metaphor helps to understand the intended meaning of Brunner. This understanding is perceivable in Brunner's own definition (Brunner, *Mensch im Widerspruch*, 549; see also Leipold, *Missionarische Theologie*, 120, 213–14). Maybe this translation has contributed to some of the misunderstandings among English-speaking theologians. For a wrong interpretation of Brunner's point of contact, see Smedes, "Emil Brunner Revisited," 202. For a brief treatment of *the point of contact* in light of Brunner's *imago Dei* interpretation, see chapter 4.

157. Brunner, "Intellectual Autobiography," 19.

Missionary theology takes the form of a conversation between a Christian believer and an unbeliever. The Christian believer enters into the questions raised by the unbeliever; he gives full weight to all the truth and insight the unbeliever already possesses. But he shows also how his knowledge, and therefore also his questions, ignore the very thing which brings light and true knowledge. Missionary theology is, so to say, pastoral work in the form of reflection, just as dogmatics is witness in the form of reflection.[158]

This is also what Brunner's *eristics* means and seeks to accomplish: "It is the reverse side of the dogmatic task. Whoever approves of this one and takes it seriously finds himself confronted at the same time with the other one."[159] It becomes clear that this eristic approach is not only directed towards the world and other religions but also has to happen within the church when there is a false, although Christian, religion.[160] "This means that the missionary task of the church is not an after-thought or a peripheral interest for the theologian but a primary responsibility."[161] Thus, Brunner's evaluation that Barth is "a churchman for the church" whilst he is "a missionary"[162] might be misleading since the wider question for Brunner was epistemic and not merely concerning the mission field.[163]

---

158. Brunner, *Dogmatics I*, 102–3; GR 110. McDowell and Hart believe that Brunner's approach did "instrumentalize the non-Christian" and that Brunner "only engaged them to defeat them." They point out that in praxis Barth was much more apt to learn from others (McDowell, "Subjectivity of the Object," 33). While this might very well have been the case it does not reflect Brunner's definition of *missionary theology* but might only proof our point made in section 1a of Brunner's struggle between theory and praxis.

159. Vogelsanger, "Brunner as Apologist," 293 (TM). See also Rössler, *Person und Glaube*, 44–50; Lütz, *Weg zum Glauben*, 224–25.

160. See Brunner, *Revelation and Reason*, 272. See also White, "Missionary Theology," 69; Müller, "Church in Action," 43–44, 48.

161. White, "Missionary Theology," 56. However, Brunner made it very clear that it is primary not in the sense that it is more important than the dogmatic task. Earlier, he proposed the epistemic as the *second* question (Brunner, "Anknüpfungspunkt," 239) but one might argue that later, with his relational leitmotif in place, he saw it as intrinsically intertwined, since language always brings form and content together (241–42).

162. Brunner, "Missionary Theology," 817.

163. See, e.g., Vogelsanger, "Brunner as Apologist," 294–96; McGrath, *Emil Brunner*, 172. Consequently, it is no coincidence that Brunner's popular booklet *Unser Glaube: Eine christliche Unterweisung* was published during those years of struggle with Barth as an adaption of Brunner's academic work for "normal" people within and outside of the church.

However, Brunner was not primarily interested in general epistemological questions but in the question of grasping God's revelation.[164] His law of relational closeness, that has already been briefly introduced,[165] with its depiction in concentric rings, sheds further light on Brunner's thinking. Whereas the primary task of theology is concerned with the center of God's self-disclosure and the corresponding actual and existential relationship with humanity, the very "next ring" consequentially must be devoted to grasping, communication, and embodiment of those matters.[166] Thus, Rössler appears to be right in concluding that *eristics* was Brunner's theological program with *truth as encounter* as its basic category.[167] Ebeling points out that as such theology becomes, in a sense, more "secular," that is, more attentive to the people it serves, at the same time it is also more "spiritual" by corresponding to its God-intended purpose.[168] Finally, for Brunner, this "bidirectional" task of theology was simply a form of love[169] and a logical consequence of truth as encounter.

Precisely this bidirectionality is the reason why Brunner is preferred over Barth for this book since the analogy of relationship was not only his leitmotif for the content of dogmatic reflection but also its form. We believe that the late Barth, while proposing a very relational theology by giving due dogmatic weight to the anthropological side of the relationship, still ignored its epistemological ramifications.[170] Put differently, when there is a concern about the dogmatic content (what) then the concern of the communicative form and cognitive reception (how) comes along with it. We agree, then, with McGrath that "[Brunner's] importance lies more in the theological angle of approach that he advocates"

164. Brunner, "Reply to Interpretation," 333–34.

165. See section 1b.

166. See, e.g., Brunner, *Offenbarung und Vernunft*, 452, 454; ETR 416, 418. For further details concerning the role of the church, see section 5b. One of his students shares a metaphor from Brunner's classroom where he compared teaching with a piece of cake where the center has to be connected with the peripheral and vice versa (Ernst, "Anekdoten," 163).

167. Rössler, *Person und Glaube*, 42.

168. Ebeling, "Die Beunruhigung der Theologie," 361.

169. Brunner, "Anknüpfungspunkt," 248; Lütz, *Glauben*, 176. Graham McFarlane makes a similar point and calls it being *bilingual*. McFarlane, *Evangelical Theology*, 12.

170. See for example Barth's concept of *content* and *form* of relations (e.g., Deddo, *Theology of Relations*, 84–85, 94–95, 131–39). This is very similar to our proposal of the *existential* and *epistemological* dimension in Brunner (chapter 1) with the exception of an epistemic reflection in Barth.

and that "Barth's weakness in this area indicates the need for alternative approaches."[171] Brunner himself sees this, his drivenness to mission, also as the prime distinction between his own and Barth's thought and adds: "But I am aware that I have only begun this task. . . . I shall have to entrust its continuation to the younger generation."[172] We gladly pick up this baton handed to us. Frank Jehle's words resonate with the goal of this present work: "The encounter with Emil Brunner is stimulating and fascinating. He has given a lot to his own time. Still not all his visions have been realized; some of them have even been forgotten."[173] We believe that Brunner's leitmotif of the I-You relationship is one of those forgotten and waiting to be realized visions and that precisely this leitmotif is central and crucial to fulfilling the task of theology as dogmatics *and* communication well. Brunner presents a theology of relationship in content and in form due to the central and existential nature of an actual God-human relationship, which is depicted by analogy with human relationships. Therefore, we turn now to investigate this core of Brunner's theology in more depth.

---

171. McGrath, *Emil Brunner*, 229.

172. Brunner, "Missionary Theology," 817. See also White, "Missionary Theology," 55.

173. Jehle, *Emil Brunner*, 18 (TM).

II

Personal Correspondence
Emil Brunner's Leitmotif

BRUNNER'S LEITMOTIF OF RELATIONSHIP clothed in the technical term *personal correspondence* has already been sketched,[1] whereas the goal of this part is to gain a deeper understanding of Brunner's leitmotif and bring his sometimes scattered, often misunderstood and over time evolving considerations in one coherent flow. Simultaneously, the dogmatic and systematic ramifications of his leitmotif will surface at least in their main features. In other words, we will see Brunner's relational leitmotif "in action." However, before we start explicating personal correspondence as the lost ontic basis, and move to its restoration, first from God's and, secondly, from the human point of view, some preliminary considerations should be made. Three areas require attention at this point since they impact not only the way the subject will be treated but potentially also its content. Firstly, there is Brunner's handling of words in general and technical terms in particular. Secondly, there is the temptation of further systematizing Brunner's conception and closely connected with that, thirdly, the question of structuring the following chapters.

---

1. See the introduction in Part I.

3

Personal Correspondence
Preliminary Considerations

a) Brunner's Evolving Terminology

THE BASIC THEME OF Brunner's theology, as already discussed, is an I-You relationship between God and humans.[1] Various aspects of this relationship have been termed differently, but they all mean the same leitmotif. As such, Brunner's approach has been called *theological* or *biblical personalism*,[2] which focuses primarily on the parties involved and those as persons. Brunner calls God's part within the relationship *revelation* or preferably *self-disclosure* (*Selbst-Mitteilung*).[3] For the human aspect, Brunner often uses the general technical term *responsive actuality* or simply names it the response of faith or sin. While the terminology, *truth as encounter*, focuses on the epistemic dimension as a whole, Brunner gives the existential reality of the God-human relationship the technical term *personal correspondence*.[4] This "primordial relation" (*Urrelation*) is for Brunner identical with the whole of the content of the Bible[5] and becomes

---

1. See section 1b.
2. Brunner rarely uses this terminology for his theological program. The reason for this avoidance appears to be not wanting to base his theology on a certain stream of philosophy. See the brief discussion in section 2b.
3. Rössler, *Person und Glaube*, 79.
4. Rössler, *Person und Glaube*, 17, 96.
5. Brunner, *Wahrheit als Begegnung*, 102; ETR 102.

the guiding term for the whole of the relation (*Beziehungsgeschehen*).⁶ The point here is that all these different technical terms stand for different theological aspects of the one simple leitmotif within Brunner's theology: relationship.⁷ Depending on the context, Brunner calls all of the aspects mentioned above *the main theme of the Bible*, which can be confusing, but as different viewpoints of the same relationship, this seems intelligible.

Nevertheless, Brunner's use of terms requires further attention. As has already been shown, *personal correspondence* is the main technical term throughout *Truth as Encounter* and stands for the whole of Brunner's theological conception.⁸ Yet, as Reidar Hauge points out, Brunner uses this term rarely thereafter:⁹ In *Offenbarung und Vernunft*, published only three years after *Wahrheit als Begegnung*, it is absent. In his *Dogmatics I* the term appears only twice and not as a technical term.¹⁰ *Dogmatics II* shows no use of *personal correspondence* at all and in the almost five hundred pages of *Dogmatics III*, it can be found eleven times, presumably only due to the fact that this volume has a similar focus as *Truth as Encounter*. That said, in *Truth as Encounter* this terminology can be found forty-nine times on only ninety-six pages after its first introduction. What can be made of this? Could it be that Brunner shifted his focus or changed his mind? Not at all, but it does point to an important observation: Brunner's almost "unbearable ease" in the use of theological terms. Thus, Dietmar Lütz rightly concludes that whilst Brunner's train of thought was always very clear, the same cannot be said regarding the consistency of his terminology.¹¹ Words were only a tool for the actual content and meaning. This inconsistent use of terms is constant throughout Brunner's wider thought. Firstly, as early as his dissertation, Brunner developed a view of words as symbols merely pointing to the actual

---

6. Rössler, *Person und Glaube*, 95.

7. Rössler, *Person und Glaube*, 96.

8. Brunner, *Wahrheit als Begegnung*, 102; ETR 102. Brunner gives a concentrate of his theological leitmotif and introduces the term *personal correspondence* for the first time in this work and presumably in general. Interestingly, Deddo mentions *correspondence* as one of the central terms for Barth in *Church Dogmatics III* as well and it can only be speculated whether Brunner had indirectly influenced this (Deddo, *Theology of Relations*, 412–14, 419).

9. Hauge, "Truth as Encounter," 136.

10. Brunner, *Dogmatics I*, 260, 269.

11. Lütz, *Weg zum Glauben*, 29–30.

thing.[12] In this, he preempted Ludwig Wittgenstein who later postulated: "The meaning of a word is its use in the language."[13] In light of this, it becomes clear why Brunner often only gives "quasi definitions" of terms, as Daniel Williams has pointed out in frustration.[14] Brunner rather concentrates on "filling" those words and creating meaning within the person addressed.[15] This leads to the second constant in Brunner's theology, namely his efforts to communicate understandably and intelligibly to a contemporary audience.[16] Consequently, his terminology changed with the evolving use of language and, even more importantly, with his evolving understanding of theological matters.[17] As such, his use of language became, through the years, intentionally less academic and more understandable to laypeople.[18] Clarice Bowman summarizes this approach well in stating that "meaning does not travel across" only because of the use of a certain word but that it needs to be "awakened *within* a person."[19] It is to Brunner's credit that he was well aware of the danger of triggering a wrong and biased meaning with an otherwise correct term. All of this explains the change and evolution of Brunner's terminology and, in part, the vanishing of the technical term *personal correspondence*, while at the same time preserving its content.[20] However, one can only speculate whether or not Brunner created new terms to say the same thing, such

12. See the brief discussion in section 1b. See also Lütz, *Weg zum Glauben*, 104. Lütz highlights in this context one of Brunner's main terms *word* and points out that time and again it has been misunderstood as simply meaning *words* whereas it has a much richer dimension. Inexplicably Fred Berthold accuses Brunner of the exact opposite and of an almost magical use of language. He therefore wrongly utilizes Wittgenstein against Brunner (Berthold, "Objectivity and Personal Encounter," 40–41).

13. Wittgenstein, *Philosophical Investigations*, §43. See also Schulte, *Wittgenstein*, 170.

14. Williams, "Brunner and Barth on Philosophy," 243.

15. Brunner, *Truth as Encounter*, 86; GR, 87. See also Altamira, "Offenbarungsgeschehen," 203.

16. See section 2b.

17. See also Altamira, "Offenbarungsgeschehen," 11, 255.

18. Brunner sometimes points to this audience of "interested laypeople" in his preface. See, e.g., *Dogmatics I* and *Revelation and Reason*. Althaus also emphasizes this concerning *Dogmatics III* in one of his letters (Althaus et al., *Briefwechsel*, 169).

19. Bowman, "Can Theologies Communicate?," 293.

20. Lütz welcomes this disappearance since it was too abstract for his taste (Lütz, *Weg zum Glauben*, 226). While he might be right in pointing out that Brunner would applaud an avoidance of this term, his argumentation, his favoring *pistis*, and his own construction misses the mark.

as *Theanthropozentrismus*,[21] or whether he avoided technical terms more and more in favor of explaining and painting word-pictures.

Some additional examples of Brunner's evolving terminology might further the point being made. For instance, it is obvious that Brunner moved from the term *revelation*, which is prevalent in *Truth as Encounter* and *Revelation and Reason* to *self-disclosure* as the leading term in his *Dogmatics I–III* that even structures those works. Admittedly, *self-disclosure* can already be found in his earlier writings, but it becomes increasingly evident that for Brunner it means more than revelation and therefore marks a shift in his terminology.[22] Brunner also clarifies the difference between the two and points to the "evolved" aspects in the theology of his later writings.[23] Closely connected with this terminology is the decrease of *word* as one of Brunner's main terms.[24] God communicates more than words: he discloses himself.[25] Those aspects will be further developed below,[26] but for now, it simply shows Brunner's flexibility with terms. One could also point to a certain evolution from *eristic* to *missionary theology*.[27] Other examples for Brunner's wrestling for the right understanding of common words become obvious with *faith*[28] and *church*.[29] In both cases, Brunner prefers to work with the transcribed Greek terms *pistis*[30] and *ecclesia*[31] by re-filling and illustrating them with the intended meaning. This observation of Brunner's freedom of terminology, only serving the central leitmotif of I-You relationship (personal correspondence), leads us to the next preparatory consideration.

---

21. Brunner, *Dogmatik III*, 490; ETR 438.

22. For a more comprehensive overview, see Rössler, *Person und Glaube*, 79. See also McGrath, *Emil Brunner*, 171.

23. See, e.g., Brunner, *Dogmatik III*, 201, 231, 256; ETR 172, 199, 224.

24. Hauge, "Truth as Encounter," 141. In 1931 it is apparent that *word* is still one of Brunner's central terms (Brunner, *Word and World*, 26).

25. See, e.g., Brunner, *Dogmatics I*, 24–26.

26. See section 5a.

27. See the discussion in section 2b and also Leipold, *Missionarische Theologie*, 206.

28. See chapter 6.

29. See section 5b.

30. See, e.g., Brunner, *Dogmatik III*, 205; ETR 176.

31. See, e.g., the preface in Brunner, *Misunderstanding of the Church*, 5–6.

b) The Problem of Systematizing Personal Correspondence

As already noted, Brunner has often been misunderstood by scholars.[32] One reason and difficulty could be his inconsistent terminology. Another reason might be found in the very essence of his relational leitmotif: Brunner's avoidance of abstraction.[33] He is highly critical of any systematization, although admitting that it is to a certain degree unavoidable because it moves away from the simple *Heilsgeschichte* (salvation history) in the Bible.[34] Brunner attempts and advises not to move too far away from the first-person language of the I-You relationship even in theological reflection and doctrine. The well-meaning effort to be "accurate and precise," or scientific and academic, runs the danger of losing the fluidity of relational encounter in becoming hard and a systematic stony building built for eternity. "Above all," Brunner says, "the personal categories are smothered by impersonal objective categories."[35] He concludes, according to his already discussed law of relational closeness, with a proportional statement: "The more that reflection, exact definition, strictly logical argument, reasoned classification, method and system predominate in Christian doctrine, the more 'scientific' it becomes, and the further it moves from the original truth of faith from which it proceeds, and to which it must continually refer."[36] With other words, whilst abstract terms and systems might seem more precise, it is exactly this precision that endangers the actual biblical content and truth and therefore does not reach the desired accuracy at all. For this reason, Brunner did not create an encompassing theological system[37] but rather proposed a dynamic, relational leitmotif.[38]

Brunner's approach has not been easily digested by other theologians.[39] Consequently, it appears obvious that scholars try to further

---

32. See section 2a.

33. As has already been shown in section 2b.

34. Brunner, *Truth as Encounter*, 177–78; GR 177–78. See also Altamira, "Offenbarungsgeschehen," 242.

35. Brunner, *Dogmatics I*, 62. See also 38–39 and 124–26.

36. Brunner, *Dogmatics I*, 64. See also Altamira, "Offenbarungsgeschehen," 243.

37. Brunner, *Offenbarung und Vernunft*, 222–23; ETR 201. See also Altamira, *Offenbarungsgeschehen*, 11.

38. This has been shown in Part I.

39. Berthold, as an extreme example, countered that a theologian has to use

systematize Brunner's "fluid" conception. In doing so, not only do they step into the very trap that Brunner has "prophesied," but they hereby are also altering and misinterpreting Brunner's theology. To show this danger of further systematizing personal correspondence, two examples will be briefly investigated.

Roman Rössler shows in *Person und Glaube* the ability and the understanding to summarize Brunner's central theological conception well and compactly.[40] However, at the same time he feels the urge to become more systematic and abstract and in this he falls out of the "frame" Brunner has given and moves too far from the relational center. Rössler states the necessity to "thingify" the personal categories into impersonal ones to be able to grasp and present the Faith. In doing this, he believes falsely to be in line with Brunner's concern.[41] Indeed, Rössler even admits that Brunner did not explicitly systematize his relational conception in this way, but he nonetheless believes it to reveal unequivocally the same.[42] Although Rössler's analysis of Brunner is impressive and indeed even helpful in extracting the different aspects of Brunner's leitmotif,[43] by pushing Brunner's almost simple relationship conception into his own, more abstract, categories, in the end, he misinterprets important parts of Brunner's theology as a whole and defines *faith* as Brunner's central term.[44] Consequently, Rössler ends up critiquing Brunner for his actualism, existentialism and hereby lack of "substance" (this is his main point of concern).[45] Furthermore, he questions whether Brunner's *personal correspondence* shows the uniqueness of the God-human relation enough but fails to differentiate it from *responsory actuality*.[46] In conclusion, Rössler proposes his own hypotheses which are strangely, on the whole,

---

"highly abstract and technical language" and that one should "lay down [ones] pen" if one objects to this. Berthold, "Objectivity and Personal Encounter," 40–41.

40. Rössler, *Person und Glaube*, 140–41, 142–43.

41. Rössler, *Person und Glaube*, 17–18.

42. Rössler, *Person und Glaube*, 72.

43. See Rössler, *Person und Glaube*, 58–59, 96, 116–17. In the whole first part of his valuable study (44–136) Roman Rössler attempts to further categorize and structure Brunner's concept and terminology.

44. Rössler, *Person und Glaube*, 42, 67, 114. Possible reasons for this will be further discussed below in section 3c.

45. Rössler, *Person und Glaube*, 148–54.

46. Rössler, *Person und Glaube*, 155–60. This topic will be further explored in chapter 4.

how Brunner wanted to be and should be understood.[47] The bottom line is that Rössler falsely critiques Brunner based on the "foreign" system he superimposed on him.

A second example, although less grave, is made by Dietmar Lütz in *Der Weg zum Glauben*. As the title suggests, Lütz interprets Brunner through the lens of *Glaubenswerdung* (becoming of faith).[48] With this move, he makes a similar mistake as Rössler in reading Brunner through his own superimposed or at least one-sided conception. Lütz tries to further categorize Brunner's approach on this basis and introduces his own categories: the question of *meaning, guilt* and *power*.[49] Again, the debunking statement can be observed that Brunner did not say it this way, but it nonetheless would be a helpful differentiation.[50] What follows is a foreign or at least lopsided conception as a hermeneutical lens for Brunner's work.[51] Interestingly Lütz concludes that Brunner was right in not further systematizing the *Glaubenswerdung*, yet Lütz goes on to attempt just that.[52] Admittedly, Lütz's terminology is less abstract than Rössler's but he still obscures Brunner's central concern of relationship with his own superimposed "framework."

These two examples should suffice, while others could be mentioned,[53] to initiate the last preliminary consideration: how to avoid making the same mistake.

c) The Question of Structuring Personal Correspondence

The statement made at the beginning of Part II is, as we have now seen, dangerous: "The goal . . . is to gain a deeper understanding of Brunner's leitmotif and bring his sometimes scattered, often misunderstood and over time evolving considerations in one coherent flow." This is not an

---

47. Rössler, *Person und Glaube*, 160–74.

48. Lütz, *Weg zum Glauben*, 46.

49. Lütz, *Weg zum Glauben*, 42–45. Lütz proposes that this structure is inherent in Brunner's conception, but that Brunner himself was not aware of this.

50. Lütz, *Weg zum Glauben*, 208.

51. Lütz, *Weg zum Glauben*, 208, 215, 217, 222, 231.

52. Lütz, *Weg zum Glauben*, 248.

53. See, e.g., Schrotenboer, *New Apologetics*, 205; Lüdemann, *Denken*, 271; Scheld, *Christologie Emil Brunners*, 319. Interestingly, Lüdemann and Scheld both (mis)use Brunner for their own conception, one more on the subjectivistic, the other more on the objectivistic end.

easy task to accomplish without changing Brunner's central meaning and focus; nonetheless, it is necessary. Why? Rössler's mistaken critique of Brunner appears to be programmatic: time and again Brunner has been misunderstood as an existentialist, actualist, or even subjectivist proponent.[54] Admittedly, Brunner did contribute to this misinterpretation and, accordingly, this leads to the first major critique of Brunner in this book. In Brunner's later writings, at least from *Truth as Encounter* onwards, his focus was on the existential, actual encounter of God and humans. Even in the more "objective" parts of *Dogmatics I* and *II*[55] the "subjective" appropriation is omnipresent, while only in *Dogmatics III* it becomes one of the "official" subjects.[56] Clearly, for Brunner this was the main achievement of his work, namely, to bring those two aspects, the objective and the subjective, together in the I-You relationship; and rightly so.[57] On the other hand, this personal correspondence between the divine and the human gives sometimes the impression of a disproportionate and undue focus on the human part in the relationship. Many of Brunner's formulations could easily be interpreted as such:

> It is not as if this response, this answer to the word of God, were something secondary and additional—as someone has said, "a thousand meters lower" than that which God has done in Jesus Christ; but faith is spoken of on precisely the same level as Jesus Christ—so much so that Paul uses the two expressions "righteousness of God" and "righteousness of faith" interchangeably.[58]

In this case, Brunner clarifies only one page later that this does not mean any equality, but God remains primary and the human answer

---

54. See, e.g., Berthold, "Objectivity and Personal Encounter," 42–44. See also the examples in sections 1b and 2a.

55. The title of part one, *The Eternal Foundation of the Divine Self-Communication*, and part two, *The Historical Realization of the Divine Self-Communication*, point to this.

56. Part three is titled *God's Self-Communication as his Self-Representation through the Holy Spirit*.

57. See section 1b.

58. Brunner, *Truth as Encounter*, 160; GR 160. Similar formulations are in Brunner, *Dogmatik III*, 202–3; ETR 173–74. In those passages Brunner proposes that the whole of revelation and faith-response biblically can be termed *the Faith*.

second.[59] Nonetheless, Brunner's phrasing is not very clarifying. He uses, for example, the word *coincidence* and *identity* interchangeably:

> The peculiarity of the justifying faith is precisely the coincidence of the self-communication of God and the self-understanding of man, the identity of the objective-historical of revelation and the existential-subjective of self-understanding.[60]

This coupling is confusing since *coincidence* (a coming together of two events) and *identity* (sameness) are not synonyms.[61] Only a couple pages later Brunner paraphrases this identity again: "By seeing that God's self-communication achieves its goal in faith, faith is put into one [*in eins gesetzt*] with the justifying verdict of God."[62] These observations point to another possibly bewildering example: Brunner's statement that revelation is only revelation when it is received.[63] Can revelation not be revelation without being perceived as such? Can God not reveal himself and still be misunderstood? Can God not love the human creature without being loved back? If Brunner were to answer these questions in the negative, he would indeed be on dangerous ground. Whilst his wording can be interpreted this way, it becomes clear that his point is an entirely different one: God's self-revelation and God's love only reach their goal when received and only then God's will is fulfilled.[64] Even so, one has to criticize Brunner for not being clear at this point and it becomes comprehensible why it has been asked whether Brunner has changed "the vertical into the horizontal" and the theological into the anthropological, even into a mere inner-anthropological dialectic.[65] This popular accusation of Brunner, perceiving an increasing anthropological bias, was refuted by him multiple times and finally encapsulated through the invention of the term *theanthropocentrism*, a *theocentrism* that is at the same time the

---

59. Brunner, *Truth as Encounter*, 161; GR 161.

60. Brunner, *Dogmatik III*, 242 (TM); ETR 210.

61. For a further discussion of this topic, see Kanzian, "Koinzidenz."

62. Brunner, *Dogmatik III*, 256 (TM); ETR 224.

63. Brunner, *Dogmatics I*, 19.

64. Brunner, *Truth as Encounter*, 101, 122; GR 101;122; Brunner, *Offenbarung und Vernunft*, 45–46; ETR 32–33; Brunner, *Dogmatik III*, 464–65; ETR 415–16. For an example where Brunner has been misunderstood, see Leiner, *Gottes Gegenwart*, 273. For a contemporary discussion of the conditionality of God's love in the context of relationship that has the same ambiguous feel to it, see Peckham, *Love of God*, 41, 96, 124, 160, 193–94, 203, 213–14, 242.

65. Rössler, *Person und Glaube*, 41.

fulfilment and the true calling of the *anthropos*.⁶⁶ Stefan Scheld proposes that this close connection of theology, even Christology, and anthropology in Brunner has not been recognized enough in academia. He praises Brunner for having "prepared the way" in the first half of the twentieth century with this intimate conjunction.⁶⁷ For Brunner, it was of utmost importance, also for epistemological reasons, that God always has to be known as *God-towards-human* and the human as *human-from-God*.⁶⁸ Lütz calls this Brunner's purposefully chosen inductive way, and we want to add that this was exactly the reason for the dismantlement of the object-subject contradiction in *Truth as Encounter*. However, all of Brunner's seemingly problematic statements have to be perceived as part of his ever-increasing focus on the *actuality*⁶⁹ of the I-You relationship between God and humans and its existential relevance. This, as we have already seen, is an expression of Brunner's avoidance of objectivism and should at the same time not be misunderstood as subjectivism.⁷⁰

In addition, it should be made clear, that Brunner gives a proper and important place for the objectives of faith:

> In any case, faith in Christ is, first and foremost, the true opposite of mysticism as it is *and remains* [spaced type] faith in a historical person, a historical fact and a written word standing opposite of us. . . . Communion with God exists only through

---

66. Brunner, *Dogmatik III*, 490–95; ETR 438–42. See also Schrotenboer, *New Apologetics*, 61, 87, 95.

67. Scheld, *Christologie Emil Brunners*, 2–3.

68. Brunner, *Wahrheit als Begegnung*, 102 (TM); ETR, 102.

69. Alfredo Altamira's valuable study is one of the few works that analyzes an actualistic misinterpretation of Brunner (Altamira, "Offenbarungsgeschehen," 2–6, 179–81, 183, 192, 244). He shows that Brunner must be read and understood within his own terms and that it has to be avoided to read a general understanding of *actuality* into him. Altamira points to the difference between *actualism* and Brunner's use of *actuality*: "Actualism rejects the permanent, persistent subject, whereas actuality wants to emphasize the subject's character of reality and activity" (5 [TM]). He shows that Brunner knows mere *actualism* and speaks against it, while meaning something entirely different with his use of *actuality* (179–81, 244). *Actuality* for Brunner is not without objectives or a subject, if anything, it is its activity and manifestation, its actual being (183). This also sheds further light on our discussion about relational theologies in section 2b. For an actualistic misunderstanding of Brunner, see Schrotenboer, *New Apologetics*, 66.

70. See section 1b.

this fact; the immediate urge of mysticism is *and remains* [spaced type] broken by the connection to the historical mediator.[71]

It is crucial to keep in mind that the same person who has written *Wahrheit als Begegnung* has also written, a decade earlier, *Der Mittler*,[72] and while Brunner's perspective on God's historical self-revelation in Jesus Christ might have slightly changed, he did not revise the importance of the incarnation as a historical, "objective" event. Altamira notes that Brunner developed his theology of revelation between 1924–30 and his theology of faith between 1932–37,[73] which appears accurate;[74] besides, as has been shown in Part One, around 1937 he explicated and combined the two in his leitmotif of I-You relationship. Yet, importantly, both parts, the revelation and the faith-answer are not dissolved in any form of "mystical union," but rather have to be seen in terms of a "double actuality of God and humans."[75] The individual subjects in this relationship are of utmost importance.[76]

Consequently, Part II is structured in such a way as to depict Brunner's personal correspondence, which partly takes apart what Brunner laboriously has brought together. We are aware of the possible danger this "separation" inheres, yet at the same time it reflects Brunner's overall intention, namely giving revelation and faith its right weight, more accurately and systematically and without a "foreign" systematization.[77] We agree with Altamira: "God and man, each according to the irreversible

---

71. Brunner, *Werk des heiligen Geistes*, 34 (TM). See also Brunner, *Wahrheit als Begegnung*, 26–27, 159, 174–75; ETR 21–22, 159, 174–75; Brunner, *Faith, Hope, and Love*, 17–18, 20, 22; Brunner, *Offenbarung und Vernunft*, 309, 433; ETR 281–82, 399; Scheld, *Christologie Emil Brunners*, 210. Against Henry and others who believe Brunner dismisses the historical foundation of Christian faith, see Henry and Dockery, *Evangelicalism*, 180.

72. The same point is being made by Leipold, *Missionarische Theologie*, 105. For the context of *Der Mittler*, see the short treatment in section 1b.

73. Altamira, "Offenbarungsgeschehen," 254.

74. See chapter 1.

75. Altamira, "Offenbarungsgeschehen," preface. See also Brunner, *Dogmatik III*, 25; ETR 11. For a similar reasoning inspired by Brunner, see also James Loder (Kovacs, *James E. Loder*, 24). For an argument to keep God's action and human action separate even in the context of relationship, see Kevin Vanhoozer's statements in Holtzen, *God Who Trusts*, 65–67, 83.

76. See also our discussion in section 2b.

77. Prior to *Wahrheit als Begegnung*, Brunner proposed the same "split structure" (Brunner, *Word and World*, 28–29).

order, are the subjects of events [*Geschehenssubjekte*], so it is advisable to look at the events themselves once from God's, then from man's point of view."[78] Hence, we need to address first God's self-disclosure in Jesus Christ and only then investigate the human response of faith. Yet, both come together through the actual work of the Holy Spirit, mediated through the church, which is the existential initiation of the restoration of personal correspondence and as such part of God's revelation. This "hinge" is crucial if we are to do justice to Brunner's structure of personal correspondence. However, before we can turn to the question of restoration of this relationship, we have to understand its ontic foundation according to Brunner and out of this derive the characteristics of personal correspondence.

---

78. Altamira, "Offenbarungsgeschehen," 206 (TM).

4

Personal Correspondence as Ontic Basis

To speak about the ontic basis of personal correspondence is not the same as considering Brunner's entire theological approach as being relational ontology; this simply would be wrong.¹ Nonetheless, Carlton Andersen rightly calls Brunner's *imago Dei* doctrine, the foundation of the relationship between God and humans, a relational ontology. He fails, however, to give sufficient weight to Brunner's fundamental distinction of the *true* and the *real* human.² Brunner has presented this dual mode of humanity's being in his theological anthropology *Man in Revolt*:³ it is the distinction of the human as he is intended to be, *true* (*wahr*), and as he actually is, *real* (*wirklich*).⁴ According to Brunner the correct understanding

1. See section 2b.
2. Andersen, "Theological Anthropology," 36, 291.
3. The English title does not render the German original *Der Mensch im Widerspruch* well, although it has been chosen by Brunner himself (see translator's note, 13). *Widerspruch* has a double meaning of *revolt* and *contradiction* and as such reveals that through the human revolt humanity lives in contradiction with itself, with its nature. Concerning the translation issues of this title, see also Andersen, "Theological Anthropology," 29.
4. Brunner, *Man in Revolt*, 114; GR, 116. The German subtitle, *Die christliche Lehre vom wahren und vom wirklichen* Menschen, highlights this fundamental distinction better than the English version. Altamira points to the importance the term *true* (*wahr*) has for the hermeneutics of Brunner and how it denotes, depending on the context, a categorical or a qualitative difference (Altamira, "Offenbarungsgeschehen," 223). The same can be proposed for the opposite term *real* (*wirklich*). It should also be considered whether for Brunner it is not always a fundamentally qualitative *and* as

of this distinction is the indispensable "pre-supposition for the message itself," namely the gospel, the restoration of personal correspondence.[5] As such, this also has to be a dual presupposition: a negative and a positive. Negatively, the gospel message has to presuppose the *status corruptus*, the human in his actual, sinful, contradictory-rebelling stateitively, this *status corruptus* has to be the "perversion of an original *status integratis*," which was the primary state of humanity in a positive relation to God.[6] Consequently, we will explore the ontic basis first as original, positive, primordial relationship, namely personal correspondence, and only then as corrupted relation, as mere responsory actuality.

a) Personal Correspondence as Primordial Relationship

The technical term Brunner uses for the relationship humans were created in and for is *personal correspondence*:

> So God is the God-towards-human [*Gott-zum-Menschen-hin*], and the human is the human-from-God [*Mensch-von-Gott-her*] that God's will is fulfilled in a recognition and free love of the human and that the human's true life is realized in the free recognition and affirmation of divine action and will. And this two-sided but one-sensed [*einsinnig*] relationship, this God-given presence of the dependent-independent creature, is the basic category of the Bible within which everything else it tells us is said and must be understood. Everything that the Bible says about God's nature and work, about time and eternity, about counsel and creation, about sin and redemption, about grace and works, about faith and repentance, about church and sacrament, is always said within this primordial order and characterizes this primordial relationship in a certain way. And that is why everything that theology says must remain within this primordial order and everything that contradicts this basic presupposition must be rejected and fought against as unbiblical, contra-biblical speculative aberration or other corrupt doctrine.

---

such also a categorical difference, as we will show below. It is worth noting that Barth also used these terms but filled them conversely (Deddo, *Theology of Relations*, 88–89) which might have added to their misunderstanding.

5. Brunner, *Man in Revolt*, 478–79. It is worth noting that Brunner consequently focuses on this presupposition and, save for this part and the last chapter of the book, does not cross the line of how humanity can become true humanity again.

6. Brunner, *Revelation and Reason*, 52; see also 26.

> We call this formal primordial relation, which is identical to the cause of the Bible, the relation of *personal correspondence*.⁷

This personal correspondence depicts an originally intended and positive relation between God and humans. As such, it is not a neutral or merely formal term. At first, this seems to run contrary to what Brunner stated above in calling it a "formal primordial relation" but from the wider context it becomes apparent that, in this case, he is not contrasting *formal* with *material* (which will be explored further below).⁸ For Brunner, personal correspondence is the primordial, ontological category in the Bible,⁹ yet much more than a category: this transcendental relationship is the meaning of the existence of each and every human and hence the ontic basis of their being. As Hermann Volk puts it: "It is therefore not animal rationale that is the starting point of theological anthropology, but the essence of the human as being destined for God."¹⁰

It's All about Love

Consequently, it comes by no surprise that love is the decisive term in Brunner's definition of the human nature to which he comes back time and again throughout his works: "responsibility from love, in love, for love."¹¹ Out of love, God creates humanity and thus the life of the human is existence in this love. This love *from* God and this being *in* the love of God is the foundation, the primary, the first. "The Primal Word is not an imperative, but it is the indicative of the Divine love: 'Thou art mine.'"¹² Brunner stresses that it is, first of all, a gift, life, grace, and self-communication from God and not a demand of the human in the form of a task or a law.¹³ Indeed, this is meant by Brunner's expression *God-towards-human* and *human-from-God*, yet one more thing needs to be considered before this relation can be called personal correspondence:

---

7. Brunner, *Wahrheit als Begegnung*, 102 (TM); ETR, 102.
8. See section 4b.
9. Lütz, *Weg zum Glauben*, 209.
10. Volk, *Lehre von dem Sünder*, 33 (TM).
11. Brunner, *Man in Revolt*, 99. Brunner sometimes also uses the expression "through the word, in the word and for the word" interchangeably instead of love (e.g., Brunner, *Dogmatics II*, 73).
12. Brunner, *Man in Revolt*, 98.
13. See also Volk, *Lehre von dem Sünder*, 35.

the human is not only created *from* and *in* love, but also *for* love. This being *for* love is the decisive difference between humans and the rest of creation.[14] While humans are on the same level as all of creation as being created and as *creatures* and they are placed at an unbridgeable distance from God their *Creator*,[15] humans are the only creatures that are created *for* love. Accordingly, one of Brunner's former students reflects his teacher's anthropology: "The being-for-love is not an attribute of being human alongside others, but it is being human itself."[16] This *being-for-love* is the human assignment in this relationship between Creator and creature, the human answer to the creating word of God and as such the uniqueness of humanity. This response-ability and thus responsibility is not any unique substance inherent in human beings, such as the "possession of reason or a 'rational nature' existing in its own right," but humanity's unique relation: personal correspondence.[17] Brown summarizes well: "This divine-human love encounter is not an additional element to God's will but identical to it."[18]

Response-Ability in Freedom: The *imago Dei*

Precisely because of this particular will of God, Brunner claims, God created a true counterpart (*Gegenüber*) to himself. The human's being is not independent, yet it is a being *himself* vis-à-vis of God.[19] The difference to all other creatures is the human's "being-in-self-knowledge and a being-in-self-determination," based on being known and determined. As such, in contrast to the divine being, the being of the human is "not actus purus, not a being which arises out of itself, not one which originally posits itself, but is responsive being."[20] Nonetheless, to be able to respond

14. Others have made a similar point: Holtzen, *God Who Trusts*, 5–9; Oster, *Person-Sein*, 91.

15. Brunner, *Man in Revolt*, 90–91.

16. Klein, "Tradition," 227 (TM). See also Knauer, "Ontología Relacional," 1, 5. Interestingly, Knauer's relational ontology was influenced by Ebeling who was a student of Brunner (Knauer, "Ontología Relacional," 6, 9–10).

17. Brunner, *Dogmatics II*, 77–78. See also Gloege, "Gläubiges Denken," 60; Brown, *Believing Thinking*, 49; Andersen, "Theological Anthropology," 12; Volk, *Lehre von dem Sünder*, 36.

18. Brown, "Personal Imperative of Revelation," 434.

19. Brunner, *Wahrheit als Begegnung*, 92–94; ETR 91–93.

20. Brunner, *Man in Revolt*, 97–98. See also Dietrich, "Responsive Anthropologie," 152–53.

to God's love with love the human has to be an "I," a person, because only an "I" is able to truly answer a "You" and not merely react like an animal. Again, this human response-ability is not any form of substance, yet it is being a "substantial" subject that is in relation with its Creator.[21] This is precisely how Brunner defines the *imago Dei*, the analogy between humans and God. Andersen summarizes well:

> By analogy here Brunner does not mean an analogia entis in the sense of a pre-established ontic orientation of human creation towards divine fulfillment, but rather a positive similarity between God and the human creature as Persons. The human being is the creature of God specifically intended as a being-for-love in personal correspondence to his or her Creator, and the creature called in his or her radical otherness to respond to God's Word as a summons to fellowship.[22]

Consequently, the *imago Dei* is not pure actuality or mere relation, as we have already discussed,[23] but a human person, a subject, an "I" in actual relationship with God.[24] As such, as a true subject and person, the human has to be free. Again, Brunner does not define this freedom as independence but as the freedom to decide: "The freedom from which, in which and for which man has been created is freedom-in-responsibility, freedom-in-and-for-love."[25] Brunner even calls it a "necessity for decision," which is the "distinguishing feature of man,"[26] and as such, this decision is an actualization of his being a person, his being-in-self-determination[27] and at the same time an actualization of his relation to God. The first is God's grace and love, yet he does not force them on his

---

21. Brunner, *Dogmatics II*, 55–56, 59. See also O'Donovan, "Image of God," 450. Others have given a similar definition of the *imago Dei*: Fretheim, *God and World*, 298 (referring to Moltmann); Tanner, *Christ the Key*, 2–13; Brümmer, *Model of Love*, 234–36, 243–44; Duvall and Hays, *Relational Presence*, 17; Urban, *Das Menschenbild*, 447–49, 457–58; Balswick et al., *Reciprocating Self*, 26–27, 41, 44–45, 73; Meyer zu Hörste-Bührer and Bührer, "Bindeglied zwischen Exegese und systematischer Theologie," 5 (referring to Dalferth, Jüngel, Härle, Helms).

22. Andersen, "Theological Anthropology," 12.

23. See section 3b.

24. Therefore, *person* appears to be a better fitting term than *agent*, which is used in many contemporary theological enterprises, since *person* depicts more than simply doing or causing something (see, e.g., Smedes, "Emil Brunner Revisited," 203).

25. Brunner, *Man in Revolt*, 262.

26. Brunner, *Man in Revolt*, 98.

27. See also Altamira, "Offenbarungsgeschehen," 163, 170.

human counterpart: the human is free to choose, to accept this love with counter-love.[28] This responsibility from love, in love and also for love is what being the image of God all is about.[29] *Imago Dei*, understood in this way and, according to Brunner, delineated as such in the New Testament, is a very fitting term to express what personal correspondence means.[30] Only from this primordial relationship everything else can be understood, or, as Salakka puts it: "If this original relationship between God and the human could have existed de facto, there would be no metaphysical and even less an epistemological problem."[31] However, because of humanity's misuse of freedom the original *status integratis* does—de facto—not exist anymore but has been perverted into the *status corruptus*[32] and as such everything has become more complicated. The following section seeks to shed some light on Brunner's term *responsory actuality* and his concept of a *formal* and *material imago Dei* as a solution to this complication.

b) Responsory Actuality as Actual Relation

As true as humanity was created for this love-relationship with its Creator, as equally real is humanity's current being apart from it. There is a contradiction (*Widerspruch*) between the original creation of the human and the human as he currently is.[33] According to Brunner "this contradiction is not 'something in' the actual man; it is himself."[34] Hence, this real humanity belongs as much to the ontic basis as the true humanity,[35] although the former is only the renunciation of the latter and as such less fundamental.[36] Consequently, before we turn to Brunner's depiction of the human's contradiction (*Widerspruch*) within himself, we need to

---

28. Brunner, *Wahrheit als Begegnung*, 146–47; ETR 146–48.
29. Brunner, *Man in Revolt*, 99. See also Fretheim, *God and World*, 278.
30. Brunner, *Wahrheit als Begegnung*, 149; ETR 149–50.
31. Salakka, *Person und Offenbarung*, 186 (TM).
32. Brunner, *Revelation and Reason*, 52.
33. See Brunner, *Man in Revolt*, 114.
34. Brunner, *Man in Revolt*, 478–79. And this contradiction (*Widerspruch*) is the declared topic of Brunner's book.
35. See also Andersen, "Theological Anthropology," 8.
36. Brunner, *Wahrheit als Begegnung*, 110; ETR 110. See also Brunner, *Dogmatics II*, 91–92.

understand the human's revolt (*Widerspruch*), which the Bible calls sin,[37] that leads to this contradiction.[38]

Sin, the Human Revolt

It should be clear from our exploration of the original personal correspondence and *imago Dei* that for Brunner sin is also relational by nature and not primarily about vice or virtue.[39] Sin is not a "not yet," on the contrary, it is a "no longer" because it is apostasy and rebellion against the original being created in the love of God.[40] Sin, therefore, is not simply something negative, but a negation of the positive, a "positive negation," as Brunner calls it. As such, sin is closely connected to the original positive: the human as person, personal correspondence, and responsibility. Sin would not be possible without this precondition.[41] Free humans were destined to say "yes," but they chose to say "no" instead; they were destined for love, but they fell away from love through their own decision. Brunner calls this the "mystery of man."[42] The human's calling is in being a true opposite to God, but he turned it into opposition and became an opposer. The human is created to answer God, but he has answered against (*widersprechen*) his Creator and became a contradictor. The human is destined for greatness as ruler of the earth but chose the delusion of grandeur (*Grössenwahn*) and, as a result, turned into a megalomaniac.[43] Thus, as Brunner puts it, our true (*wahrhaft*) humanity

---

37. This is not the place to explore Brunner's hamartiology in detail; we rather trace his fundamental, his structural, and relational understanding of sin.

38. Lüdemann, in his reception of Brunner, wants to reverse this order. He criticizes Brunner for focusing on revolt (*Widerstand*) rather than existential contradiction (*Widerspruch*). In changing this order and with his one-sided perception of *Widerspruch*, Lüdemann misinterprets Brunner in other areas as well. See Lüdemann, *Denken*, 60, 259–60, 300, 309, 378.

39. Brunner, *Dogmatics II*, 106. For sin as broken relationship, see also Meyer zu Hörste-Bührer and Bührer, "Bindeglied zwischen Exegese und systematischer Theologie," 6 (referring to Dalferth, Jüngel, Härle, Herms); Duvall and Hays, *Relational Presence*, 20; Wright, *Revolution*, 68, 85–100.

40. Brunner, *Dogmatics II*, 91–92.

41. Brunner, *Man in Revolt*, 129; Brunner, *Offenbarung und Vernunft*, 37, 67; ETR 25–26, 53; Brunner, *Wahrheit als Begegnung*, 149–50; ETR 150. See also Oord, *Uncontrolling Love*, 60.

42. Brunner, *Man in Revolt*, 134; Brunner, *Our Faith*, 37–39.

43. See also Brunner, *Man in Revolt*, 170–71.

has turned into delusional (*wahnhaft*) humanity.⁴⁴ Consequently, this leads us to an important observation: sin, according to Brunner, is always an act, never a "quality" or substance, never simply a predicate. "Being a sinner" is by no means the same as an "elephant being a mammal": sin is act, yet, what Brunner calls a *total act*, since the human is involved as whole person. Hence, this acting, through its continual repetition, alters and perverts human nature itself⁴⁵ and is preserved and cemented through the fact that each individual human is always part of humanity as a community of sinners.⁴⁶ This doing that becomes each human's being is our actuality.⁴⁷ As such, and this is crucial for Brunner's understanding, this actuality is always an actuality in relation to God: "Sin is indeed ungodliness [*Gottlosigkeit*]—not in the sense that man is free from God [*Gott los*], but that he would like to be free from him."⁴⁸ Consequently, this rebellion is a failed revolt, because human beings cannot get rid of God; instead, they still live in responsive or responsory actuality,⁴⁹ albeit a negative one.

The *imago Dei* in Its Contradiction

Based on what has been said concerning sin it becomes clear that this condition leads to a contradiction within each human, "a contradiction

---

44. Brunner, *Dogmatik III*, 172; ETR 145.

45. Brunner, *Man in Revolt*, 148–50; Lütz, *Weg zum Glauben*, 210.

46. Brunner, *Man in Revolt*, 140–41.

47. Against Schroetenboer, Brunner made this point as early as *The Mediator* (142–46, 148). For further clarification on Brunner's connection of sinful act and being and the terminology of actuality, see Altamira, "Offenbarungsgeschehen," 158–59, 183, 245–46. For a similar point, see Bracken, "Toward a New Philosophical Theology," 719.

48. Brunner, *Truth as Encounter*, 150; GR 150. The original German wordplay cannot accurately be translated into English. See also Brunner, *Our Faith*, 52. Barth makes a very similar point (Deddo, *Theology of Relations*, 80). For a resemblant conception of dependent freedom in pedagogy, see Krautz, "Relationalität," 19.

49. The technical term *responsorische Aktualität* and its corresponding concept first appears in Brunner, *Mensch im Widerspruch*, 88; ETR 97–98. In *Wahrheit als Begegnung* it is used throughout, yet much less than *personal correspondence*. It appears also in his *Dogmatics*, but not frequently, which might point to Brunner's avoidance of technical terminology (see section 3a). The English translations use *responsive actuality*, which can have a positive undertone and therefore we have chosen the more neutral translation *responsory actuality*.

of the whole man against the whole man,"⁵⁰ hence, to understand the human correctly he needs to be seen in this, his responsory actuality.⁵¹ If the human is created in and for the love of God, as seen above, then consequently, in rebelling against this, he lives in contradiction, in conflict, not only with God but also with himself and as a result with his fellow humans and all of creation.⁵² Volk concludes: "Sin affects the overall reality of the human and his world in the disintegration of the true and the real human."⁵³ The split is not only within the relationship with God, but it goes right through the human person since it has its being in and for this relationship.⁵⁴ Accordingly, this split affects the *imago Dei* and Brunner's adjustment of the original *status integratis* is the differentiation between the formal and the material image of God. Admittedly, this formulation appears to be wooden, ambiguous and not very relational.⁵⁵ It also caused much critique and confusion,⁵⁶ not least from Barth in his debate with Brunner about natural theology.⁵⁷ Volk gives a short overview how Brunner adapted this already existing terminology and perceives a development in how Brunner fills those terms:⁵⁸ First, in *Die Frage nach dem Anknüpfungspunkt* (1932), then, in *Natur und Gnade* (1934), only to be banned reluctantly from the foreground in *Der Mensch im Widerspruch* (1937) due to Barth's and other's critique.⁵⁹ This reluctance might have been the reason that the terminology reappears in *Offenbarung und*

50. Brunner, *Man in Revolt*, 118.

51. Brunner, *Man in Revolt*, 172.

52. See also Sonderegger, "Pfarramt," 133–34; Lüdemann, *Denken*, 60. Interestingly, "rockstar" psychologist Jordan Peterson points in the same direction. Peterson, *12 Rules for Life*, 57, 218, 229.

53. Volk, *Lehre von dem Sünder*, 170 (TM).

54. Brunner, *Man in Revolt*, 204. See also Lüdemann, *Denken*, 299; Schrotenboer, *Apologetics*, 168. Schrotenboer helpfully points out that the focus on this split *within* the human person can only be perceived in Brunner's later writings. In his earlier, dialectic writings, Brunner saw the split mainly between the transcendental reality and human experience.

55. See, e.g., McGrath, *Emil Brunner*, 146.

56. Also from Pannenberg and Moltmann (Andersen, "Theological Anthropology," 20–21).

57. See section 2b.

58. Volk, *Lehre von dem Sünder*, 159–67.

59. Brunner, *Man in Revolt*, 513. One of Brunner's former students also remembers that Brunner avoided those terms in the classroom (1948) due to a potential misunderstanding with Greek philosophy (Mielke, "Doctrine of Imago Dei," 116–17).

Vernunft (1941) and his *Dogmatics* (1946, 1950, 1960). It is important to note that Brunner uses *formal* and *material* in the opposite sense than it has been normally used in scholastic theology.[60] Also, Brunner's conception appears to be similar to the catholic *similitudo* terminology yet turns out to be something entirely different.[61] What then does Brunner want to indicate with the differentiation between a formal and a material *imago Dei*? Formally it is simply this: "that even the unbeliever is still related to God, and therefore that he is responsible"[62] and response-able. It is his being *for* the love of God. In turn, the material *imago* is simply the positive relationship with God, the human's being *in* the love of God, which has been entirely lost through sin.[63] Hence, again, it is not about substance, but about relationship since only a relationship can be negated without the loss of the structural "being related."[64] It is obvious, then, that the formal relation and the ability for relationship are always determined by their material "filling," the actual relationship, whether it is positive or negative.[65] As such, concerning the *imago Dei*, there is no neutral, pure formal aspect to it: it is always either positive or negative, *status integratis* or *corruptus*, the true human or the real human that lives in *Widerspruch* (revolt and contradiction).[66] The real human, then, is contra-personal

---

60. See, e.g., Volken, *Glaube bei Emil Brunner*, 38; Altamira, "Offenbarungsgeschehen," 175.

61. See, e.g., Brunner, *Man in Revolt*, 513; Schmid, *Lehre von Gott*, 112.

62. Brunner, *Man in Revolt*, 11. See also Leipold, *Missionarische Theologie*, 197; Salakka, *Person und Offenbarung*, 187.

63. See Brunner, *Dogmatics II*, 77–78; Leipold, *Missionarische Theologie*, 194–95; Salakka, *Person und Offenbarung*, 153–55 (although Salakka wrongly perceives a contradiction in Brunner).

64. Volk, *Lehre von dem Sünder*, 143. Leipold points out that Brunner uses *structural* exchangeable with *formal* in his later works (Leipold, *Missionarische Theologie*, 194–95). Interestingly, the sociologist Rosa makes a similar point: Rosa, *Resonanz*, 305, 447.

65. Volk, *Lehre von dem Sünder*, 166.

66. Leipold rightly asks the question whether Brunner's *formal* is truly *only formal* and reminds of Barth's corresponding critique. He negates and points out that this was never Brunner's intention. According to Leipold, Brunner's formal terminology was never "empty"; it always had a certain direction, a goal: the love-relationship (Leipold, *Missionarische Theologie*, 197–205). O'Donovan on the other hand accuses Brunner of having separated form and content and that he hereby runs into ethical difficulties (which certainly would need further attention). Yet, his examples are the same that Leipold rightly uses to show that form and content are not separated (O'Donovan, "Image of God," 457–58).

person, with an un-natural nature.⁶⁷ However confusing or controversial Brunner's conception of the formal and material imago might be, two things are decisive for its correct understanding: first, its unity and secondly, its relationality. Only the split that has come to pass through sin makes a split understanding of the imago necessary. There is only one *imago Dei*, yet through human corruption, one has to understand two aspects of it.⁶⁸ Those two aspects are only intelligible as unity when perceived through the lens of Brunner's leitmotif of I-You-relationship,⁶⁹ which leads us to the second.

Since only a relational explication of the imago makes sense, it is regrettable that Brunner used such abstract language. As we have already shown, Brunner did not abandon this terminology entirely,⁷⁰ possibly because his position on this only changed impalpably through the years. Nonetheless, Brunner, in *Truth as Encounter*, would have had a technical terminology in place that reflected the relational nature of this matter perfectly. Perhaps he did not identify this as such consciously himself. However, Brunner scholarship for sure has not yet depicted it accordingly:⁷¹ Brunner's use of *responsory actuality* matches the *formal imago Dei*, and *personal correspondence* matches the *material imago Dei*. Personal correspondence is, as we have seen,⁷² always the positive, "original" and "integral" relationship with God and as such includes responsory actuality (the formal). This is important, because, contrary to Rössler, responsory actuality is not the ontological prerequisite for personal correspondence,⁷³

67. Brunner, *Man in Revolt*, 94, 386. See also Altamira, "Offenbarungsgeschehen," 178; Salakka, *Person und Offenbarung*, 169–70. These statements do shed some light on Martin Leiner's question whether Brunner perceives humans as real persons apart from faith (Leiner, *Gottes Gegenwart*, 273–74). The answer must be a clear "yes," but a person in contradiction.

68. See also Andersen, "Theological Anthropology," 23; Altamira, "Offenbarungsgeschehen," 175–78. Altamira rightly states that Volken, Rössler, and Salakka all agree on this.

69. The lack of this consistent understanding appears to be the main reason why scholars struggled with Brunner's imago conception. Leipold mentions in a footnote among those scholars Volk, Salakka, and Rössler (Leipold, *Missionarische Theologie*, 205); O'Donovan would have to be added as well.

70. McGrath perceives too big a change in Brunner's terminology at this point (McGrath, *Emil Brunner*, 146).

71. Only Leipold appears to point in this direction in a footnote (Leipold, *Missionarische Theologie*, 222).

72. See section 4a.

73. Rössler, *Person und Glaube*, 89. See also Cairns, "Brunner's Conception," 83–84.

it is the other way around. In essence, responsory actuality both as a term and a differentiation has only become necessary because of sin (as with the formal imago). Therefore, Altamira, otherwise a very good source for the study of Brunner, wrongly treats responsory actuality and personal correspondence as basically the same.[74] Responsory actuality points to the fact, even better than the formal imago, that human beings, since they cannot be not in relation to God, always have to decide, to answer, and to actualize. Even in being passive, in their non-decision, they decide, since they actualize only their current status in being turned away from God.[75] Thus, as soon as responsory actuality is fulfilled in an actual positive relationship with God it becomes personal correspondence; apart from this it is always "filled" with the contradiction of the original intention. In other words: relation to God (*Gottbezogenheit*) without the I-You relationship with God (*Gottesbeziehung*)[76] always misses its mark and as such is sin, is being under the law and wrath of God. Indeed, this is the actual relation and being of real humanity until it is restored through Jesus Christ to its true humanity.[77] This restoration of personal correspondence will be explored in the following two chapters.

c) Conclusions and Outlook

This chapter on the ontic basis of Brunner's theological anthropology, or his "theanthropology,"[78] concludes with a summary of his various con-

---

74. Altamira, "Offenbarungsgeschehen," 194.

75. Brunner, *Man in Revolt*, 262–65; Altamira, "Offenbarungsgeschehen," 170; Schrotenboer, *New Apologetics*, 79–80. Smedes comes to a similar observation yet draws the wrong conclusion. In his view, Brunner wants to say that humans are always in relationship with God and as such are "natural born believers unless they decide to be otherwise." Smedes, "Emil Brunner Revisited," 197. The problem is that Smedes does not give due weight to the fact that the human's reality is not the positive personal correspondence anymore but only the negation of it as responsory actuality in revolt. This is another example for the impact of the misinterpretation of the difference between personal correspondence and responsory actuality.

76. Leipold, *Missionarische Theologie*, 197–205.

77. See, e.g., Brunner, *Offenbarung und Vernunft*, 90; ETR 74; Brunner, *Truth as Encounter*, 147–48; Brunner, *Man in Revolt*, 478–95; Brunner, *Dogmatics II*, 73; Leipold, *Missionarische Theologie*, 217.

78. This is a word creation based on Brunner's usage of *theanthropocentrism* (Brunner, *Dogmatik III*, 490, 493; ETR 438, 440).

cepts. As we have already noted, concerning Brunner's terminology,[79] the boundaries of his different terms and concepts are blurry and evolved over the course of his career, understandably. Nonetheless, driven by his relational leitmotif and his overall conception there is also a striking consistency of basic lines of thought wherein the different aspects and terms find their common denominator and are sometimes even synonymous. An overview in tabular form will concentrate the themes explored so far:

true human		real human
responsory actuality		
personal correspondence		responsory actuality in revolt
material *imago Dei*	formal *imago Dei*	lost material *imago Dei*
being-in-and-for-love	being-for-love	being-in-contradiction-to-love
I-You relationship with God (and other humans) responsiveness self-disclosure	in relation to God (and other humans) reciprocity asymmetry	I-it relationship with God (and other humans)
freedom in the "yes" to God	*freedom* to say "yes" or "no"	unfreedom in the "no" to God
fellowship with God	response-ability, responsibility	sin, under the law and wrath of God
	"positive" point of contact	"negative" point of contact

Table 1: Overview of Brunner's "theathropology." The dotted line at the top illustrates the relationality of the human's nature. The dotted lines in between the columns illustrate that responsory actuality is formal or structural and therefore included in both of the qualitative expressions of the relationship.

Love has been the central motif of the original divine-human relationship, also in its corrupted state. However, love as a term is too broad to further define this relational dynamic[80] and thus we will extract

---

79. See section 3a.
80. See, e.g., Gergen, *Relational Being*, 43; Welker, "Romantic Love," 128.

a taxonomy from its already explored ontic foundation to specify this love-dynamic of personal correspondence:[81] First, *reciprocity* is the goal of God's love and only as such leads to an I-You relationship. Second, *asymmetry* is the nature of this reciprocity since the Creator loves his creature and love begins with God, who is love in person. Accordingly, we have to speak about an *asymmetric reciprocity*. Third, *freedom* is decisive for love; hence, humans were created out of, in and for freedom. After those rather structural classifications, comes fourth, *responsiveness*, which depicts loving address and reaction between true counterparts.[82] Finally, *self-disclosure* as an expression of love, which will become especially relevant in the restoration of the relationship. Personal correspondence, according to Brunner, includes *all* of those five classifications.[83] This taxonomy will help us throughout the following two restoration-chapters to connect and compare the divine and the human sides of the relationship while keeping its ontic basis in sight, thus staying true to Brunner's own conception and terminology without introducing a foreign systematization.[84] The term *restoration* points to the fact that something original has been destroyed. This primordial relationship, personal correspondence, has been explicated; accordingly, the restoration of this relationship is deeply connected with its ontic basis.[85] Yet, Brunner makes clear that this restoration is even more than a simple restoration because humans not only find God's love again but God's love for his rebellious creatures.[86] That said, we turn first to revelation history (*Offenbarungsgeschichte*)

---

81. For similar categorizations, see Fretheim, *God and World*, 19–22; Holtzen, *God Who Trusts*, 67–68; Peckham, *Love of God*, 66, 219–31, 264, 277; Deddo, *Theology of Relations*, 104–7 (concerning Barth).

82. For a similar qualitative definition of responsiveness, see Rabens, "Sein und Werden," 133.

83. John Barclay comes to similar conclusions by engaging the meaning of the central term *grace* and gift-language within Pauline theology (Romans and Galatians) and Second Temple Judaism. He proposes six "perfections" of grace (superabundance, singularity, priority, incongruity, efficacy and non-circularity) that have the same general intention as our taxonomy. See, e.g., Barclay, *Paul and the Gift*, 70–74.

84. See section 3c. Paul K. Jewett also uses Brunner's own terminology (eight terms) to systematize his conception, yet he does not focus solely on personal correspondence and thus is too general to be truly helpful. See Jewett, *Concept of Revelation*, 50–62.

85. Interestingly, Rosa points to the same fundamental human tension calling it the search for *Heimat* (home) but as a sociologist leaves God out of the equation. Rosa, *Resonanz*, 603–6, 740.

86. Brunner, *Offenbarung und Vernunft*, 41; ETR 29–30.

and only then to salvation history (*Heilsgeschichte*), which, according to Brunner, is the same "story" seen from two different perspectives.[87] Existentially, revelation is truth as encounter, while faith is knowledge as encounter, both showing two sides of the same happening.[88] God's being for and toward human beings has to become one with their being for and toward God in order to reach the divine goal to be "fulfilled";[89] nonetheless, we look at each movement separately,[90] interconnected through our taxonomy.

---

87. Brunner, *Offenbarung und Vernunft*, 18; ETR 8.
88. Brunner, *Revelation and Reason*, 9.
89. Brunner, *Dogmatik III*, 200–201; ETR 171–72.
90. See section 3c for justification.

5

God-Towards-Human
The Call to Restoration of Personal Correspondence

BRUNNER NEVER REVISED HIS position which he defended as early as *Die Mystik und das Wort*: the God-human relationship "either begins with humanity and reaches out to God, which Brunner holds to be the way of philosophy; or it begins with God, who reaches out to humanity, which is the way of revelation."[1] The primary is always God's coming to his human creation, his coming near, and hereby bridging the distance.[2] God only must *come*, because the relationship between God and humans, that ought to be close, has been broken and is now distanced.[3] Yet God only *must* come in the sense that humans "cannot possibly move towards God."[4] According to Brunner, the decisive biblical characteristic is that in God-human interaction the initiative is God's.[5] Hence, God is the one that calls; humans only answer to this call.[6] Humans, says Brunner, can only grasp the world and since God is not the world he stands outside of human grasping and knowledge and can only be perceived in his revelation.[7] In other words: "the rational God is the God whom I construct for

---

1. McGrath, *Emil Brunner*, 26.
2. Brunner, *Dogmatics I*, 258–60.
3. Brunner, *The Mediator*, 314.
4. Brunner, *The Mediator*, 291.
5. Brunner, *The Mediator*, 294.
6. Brunner, *Man in Revolt*, 97.
7. Brunner, *Dogmatics I*, 14; Brunner, *The Mediator*, 296.

myself; the revealed God is the God who speaks to me."[8] Brunner never changed this revelation-focus and in this sense, he always did theology "from above," similar to Barth, to safeguard the sovereignty, the "wholly-otherness" of God and to fight against any human ability and control to perceive the true God.[9] Brunner, therefore, admits that objectivism, also Barth's objectivism, rightly perceives that in the God-human relationship God is always the first—independent of any human answer or doing.[10] True, the God-human relation is a relationship of reciprocity since God created humans as true counterpart and he is therefore never all-causal.[11] However, at the same time Brunner stresses the fact that it is reciprocity in asymmetry, as he writes in one of his most illuminating passages in *Truth as Encounter*:

> But this relationship, although it is a two-sided one, is never an equilateral or reversible one. Rather, it is always one-sensed [*einsinnig*] in this sense: it goes out from God to the human, and only because of it also from the human to God. . . . That is why God's relation to the human is completely different from that of the human to God. God's relation to the human is simply setting, creating and unconditional. From the human side, there is nothing that could be conditioning God's relation to him. God's relation to the human has no precondition whatsoever in a relation from the human to God. This is the primordial opposition of the biblical to the idealistic, pantheistic, and mystical thought of God. God is simply leading the way. . . . God is always and irreversibly the first.[12]

This asymmetric reciprocity in Brunner's conception of the I-You relationship between God and humans is perceived by almost all the scholars;[13] furthermore, it is a decisive difference from Buber's under-

---

8. Brunner, *Man in Revolt*, 243. Boyd says similarly citing an unknown author: "God created man in his own image, and man, being a gentleman, returned the favor." Boyd, *Cross Vision*, 101.

9. See the discussion on Barth and Brunner in section 2b. For a discussion of similarities between Brunner and the late Barth and Pannenberg concerning a theology "from above" or "from below," see Shults, *Reforming Theological Anthropology*, 120–22.

10. Brunner, *Wahrheit als Begegnung*, 174; ETR 174.

11. See Lüdemann, *Denken*, 306.

12. Brunner, *Wahrheit als Begegnung*, 89–90 (TM); ETR 89.

13. See, e.g., McGrath, *Emil Brunner*, 168; Altamira, "Offenbarungsgeschehen," 217–18, 223–24, 225–26, 227, 230; Volk, *Lehre von dem Sünder*, 35; Bertram, "Brunner on Revelation," 626; Rössler, *Person und Glaube*, 156; Brown, *Believing Thinking*,

standing of this relation.¹⁴ Consequently, this asymmetry leads to another characteristic of personal correspondence: God's absolute freedom in loving and moving towards humanity.¹⁵ The Creator must not move toward and does not have to love his creature; his love is always a free gift because God's love is giving love (*agape*) and not coveting love (*eros*). God loves because he wants to love.¹⁶ In this sense the movement of God is not caused by humanity, but "God is in Himself motion because in His very Nature He is Love."¹⁷ God's revelation is based on the absolute freedom of his nature that is love;¹⁸ with other words, God reveals himself because he wants to.

This revelation, this movement of God towards humankind has its unquestioned climax in the incarnation of the word, Jesus Christ; climax in the sense that there is a progressive revelation throughout the Old Testament until the definite revelation in Christ.¹⁹ Yet, it is more than the highlight, the pinnacle of revelation; the incarnation is also its center and Jesus Christ its unity. From him, we look back to the primordial revelation

---

62; Lüdemann, *Denken*, 58–59, 308 (although negative). For a similar view on *asymmetric reciprocity*, see Gunton, *The One*, 225–26; Hartenstein, "Relationalität als Schlüssel," 171, 174; Sattler, *Beziehungsdenken*, 177–78, 324–25, 424, 457, 472, 476, 486; Peckham, *Love of God*, 255–58; Boschki, *Religionspädagogik*, 283–88; Rehfeld, "Seinskonstitutive Christusbezogenheit," 82–85; DesCamp and Sweetser, "Metaphors for God," 233–34; Balswick et al., *Reciprocating Self*, 347–48.

14. See, e.g., Andersen, "Theological Anthropology," 41–42 ("a concretization of the intersubjective by informing its *between* with a specific vertically established content"); Leiner, *Gottes Gegenwart*, 274, 279–81 (although he perceives Brunner too theocratic and too unilateral); Lüdemann, *Denken*, 58–59 (although he perceives Brunner's conception wrongly as a monologue).

15. See, e.g., Brunner, *Wahrheit als Begegnung*, 149, 174; ETR 149–50, 174.

16. Brunner, *Offenbarung und Vernunft*, 41; ETR 29–30; Brunner, *Dogmatics I*, 185–88. Brunner often comes back to the difference between *eros* and *agape*, hereby referring to Nygren. Yet, he does not do it in an undifferentiated manner (Brunner, "Reply to Interpretation," 341).

17. Brunner, *The Mediator*, 285.

18. Contemporary theology sometimes challenges this sovereignty with the notion that God is not free to love (or not love) since his very nature is love (see, e.g., Oord, *Uncontrolling Love*, 158–62). Admittedly, this is an interesting thought experiment, yet Brunner's notion of freedom in this context targets something entirely different, highlighting God's absolute freedom by comparison to humanity's dependent freedom (see section 4a). Perhaps Brunner makes a similar point by postulating that the Bible knows no God-in-himself but only God-towards-man, yet he does that without questioning his freedom or sovereignty (Brunner, *Wahrheit als Begegnung*, 88; ETR 87).

19. Brunner, *Dogmatics II*, 199–200.

in creation and perceive the old covenant as a preliminary revelation. In turn, we catch sight from the incarnation of the last and complete revelation when we will see God face-to-face.[20] Thus, the incarnation of the Son of God "does not stand at the beginning of all things," but is, rather, the center of all, dividing "history into two parts: ante and post Christum natum."[21] As such, the connection between the Old and New Testament is that of promise and fulfilment[22] and the connection between the incarnation of Christ and the eschaton is that of beginning and fulfilling, believing and seeing, already and not-yet.[23] This "looking back" and "looking forward" from the "middle" is according to Brunner the decisive element of biblical revelation.[24] The continuity in this revelation revolves around personal correspondence, the restoration of I-You relationship.[25] This interconnection around a center is the reason why we will focus in the following sections on God's central revelation in Jesus Christ and bypass by and large the question of Old Testament revelation and eschatology without ignoring it. This central revelation of the mediator, Jesus Christ, does for Brunner, as we will see in the corresponding sections, necessarily include the immediate testimony of the Holy Spirit as its actualization and its mediation through the church.[26] By focusing on the central motif of personal correspondence we will also have to neglect detailed

---

20. Brunner, *Offenbarung und Vernunft*, 219; ETR 198.

21. Brunner, *Dogmatics II*, 239. See also Dowey, "Redeemer and Redeemed," 197.

22. See, e.g., Brunner, *Offenbarung und Vernunft*, 113, 116–17, 121–22, 126; ETR 95, 89–99, 104, 108.

23. See, e.g., Brunner, *Dogmatik III*, 492–93, 497; ETR 440, 444; Brunner, *Werk des heiligen Geistes*, 58–73. Volk perceives a development in Brunner that started with *Vom Werk des Heiligen Geistes* that the "already" truly is an experiential *reality* and not only a theoretical factor only pointing to the "not yet." Volk, *Lehre von dem Sünder*, 182–83. Brunner's involvement and his experiences in the Oxford Group probably were key to this development (see also section 1a).

24. Brunner, *Offenbarung und Vernunft*, 73–74; ETR 58–59. In *Faith, Hope, and Love*, Brunner has a similar, yet adapted triad concerning the revelation in Christ: "we live in the past by faith; we live in the future by hope; we live in the present by love." Brunner, *Faith, Hope, and Love*, 13.

25. See Schuurman, *Creation*, 28–29. While admitting this continuity, Schuurman wrongly believes that Brunner cannot consequently hold on to it with his "idea of the community of persons" (76–77).

26. Brunner, *Offenbarung und Vernunft*, 32–33; ETR 21–22; Brunner, *Dogmatics I*, 20–21. See also Gloege, "Gläubiges Denken," 58; Brown, *Believing Thinking*, 23–25, 54; Schmid, *Lehre von Gott*, 115–16.

explorations of dogmatic *topoi* such as atonement-theology, pneumatology, or ecclesiology.

a) The Mediator: Jesus Christ, the Incarnated Word

God's absolute freedom and the asymmetry of the relation to humans, as already explored, point to the fact that he is the sovereign Lord, the "Wholly Other" Creator, and the Holy One. Yet, God as the "Wholly Other" would only be an abstract "it" to us, not a true subject, an "I," without his revealing himself *to* the world and *within* the world as Creator and Lord *of* the world.[27] Indeed, God is the Lord per se, the absolute subject, who freely reveals himself and comes into this world as its Lord and Creator *because* he loves and to show *that* he loves. According to Brunner, there is no difference between holiness and love, although the two need to be perceived separately, since in the God-with-us, Emmanuel, they are identical. The Lord-God is the loving one and the "Wholly Other"-God is the one who wants to give himself to his creature. As such, "the pathos of absolute distance, the awe, passes into the pathos of complete communion, into cordial trust and love." In this love, God reveals his nature through the incarnated son, yet at the same time, he stays mysterious in his unfathomable love.[28] This unfathomable love shows itself in the unthinkable act that the Lord-God, the king, comes into this world as a beggar "to persuade the beggar that He wishes to be his Friend." This self-emptying alone shows the depths of His love, and it might be said that he "gives Himself away."[29] Indeed, first, God's condescension is necessary to reveal himself "according to the mode of the perceiver,"[30] so that humans have any chance at grasping the "Wholly Other." Secondly, God's self-emptying is necessary so that his creature can freely love him

---

27. Brunner, *Dogmatics I*, 158.

28. Brunner, *Offenbarung und Vernunft*, 57, 60–61 (TM); ETR 43, 46. See also Brunner, *Dogmatics I*, 190; Brunner, *Dogmatik III*, 367–68, 373–74; ETR 327, 332–33; Boschki, *Religionspädagogik*, 305–6, 325; Bracken, "Toward a New Philosophical Theology," 710–11. This is also what Gunton was calling for with the crucial and healthy tension between relatedness and genuine otherness (Gunton, *The One*, 6). Schrotenboer wrongly depicts Brunner's concept of revelation as revealing everything (Schrotenboer, *New Apologetics*, 92–93) since Brunner explicitly states that a mystery still remains while at the same time God is no other than he has revealed.

29. Brunner, *The Mediator*, 297–98. See also Smith, *Speech and Theology*, 55.

30. For this terminology, see Smith, *Speech and Theology*, 160, 165. See also Oei, "Impassible God," 243–44.

back and not only obey him as the Lord.³¹ God freely wills the human to be a genuine counterpart.³² Consequently, his will is not to overwhelm and crush but that his "sovereignty is freely accepted by man"; despite the asymmetry of this relationship God wills true reciprocity.³³ These "conditions" God meets and fulfils by coming as a servant king, a human, the incarnated Word and the mediator and as such he shows his loving responsiveness towards the human condition.

God's Personal Word-Act: Self-Disclosure in Responsiveness

This responsiveness is the reason why *the word* is such an important term for Brunner, "for the word is the way in which spirit discloses to spirit, subject to subject, will to will. . . . Through the Word the mystery of the person, both the addressing and the addressed one, is revealed."³⁴ However, Brunner's last sentence already points to the fact that he means much more by the term *word* than simply words; he refers to *the Word* (John 1) which is the incarnated Word, Jesus Christ.³⁵ As already

---

31. Brunner, *Wahrheit als Begegnung*, 98; ETR 97–98.

32. See section 4a.

33. Brunner, *Dogmatics II*, 216; Brunner, *Wahrheit als Begegnung*, 98–99; ETR 97–98. For a similar point, see Welker, "Romantic Love," 134–35; Moltmann, "God's Kenosis," 145–48; Peckham, *Love of God*, 255–58; Polkinghorne, "Kenotic Creation," 102; Schmid, *Lehre von Gott*, 77, 78, 86, 88 (concerning Jüngel). That *reciprocity* was unthinkable in classical theism is pointed out by Bracken, "Toward a New Philosophical Theology," 712.

34. Brunner, *Wahrheit als Begegnung*, 103–4 (TM); ETR 102–3. Bertram adds that revelation as word points to the fact that "it is not a meaningless experience, but rather it makes sense, it has understandable significance." Bertram, "Brunner on Revelation," 626. While this observation is important, it might at the same time obscure the non-accessibility of the revelation without the Holy Spirit (see section 5b below).

35. Wendell Johnson attempts to instrumentalize Walter J. Ong's differentiation of oral and literary cultures for Brunner's depiction of the I-You encounter and his focus on the term *word*. While he might have a valid point in localizing it in the context of orality, it appears to be an oversimplification and reduction (Johnson, "Soteriology," 250–51). Lütz perceives an ignorance in Brunner scholarship concerning the depth of Brunner's usage of this term (Lütz, *Der Weg zum Glauben*, 104). He also proposes that Brunner gained this depth through the rediscovery of the Hebrew meaning of truth with its central usage of *dabar*, the Hebrew word for *word* (221). Yet, he does not include any reference for this assertion. Brown highlights the important fact that for Brunner also the words used in theology are but mere pointers to the ultimate Word, who is Jesus Christ (Brown, *Believing Thinking*, 20).

mentioned,³⁶ there is a development in Brunner's use of the term *word* and a decrease in its usage in his later writings.³⁷ The reason may be localized in Brunner's view of the human limitation in the usage of words since human words are always only a sign pointing to the actual thing. Contrary, God's Word is the "thing itself"; more correctly it is himself, it is his self-disclosure, finally in the person, incarnation, and story of his son.³⁸ This self-disclosure is so much more than mere communication, hence, it is also fundamentally different from God's communication through the words of the prophets in the Old Testament.³⁹ Jesus Christ, as the ultimate Word of God, is more than a prophet and absolutely unique since in him the word and the person have become one and the same. Consequently, through his person, speech and action God speaks, acts, and discloses himself.⁴⁰

Indeed, *self-disclosure* becomes Brunner's main term for revelation.⁴¹ The original German word *Selbstmitteilung* unites communicating and sharing of oneself with another person and therefore *self-disclosure* reflects this dual meaning much better then *self-communication*, which is primarily used in English translations of Brunner's works.⁴² It is of utmost importance for Brunner that God gives not *something* but he gives *himself* and that this self-disclosure is at the same time self-dedication (*Selbsthingabe*) and is one with the act of giving oneself away (*Selbstpreisgabe*).⁴³

36. See section 3a.

37. Hauge, "Truth as Encounter," 141.

38. Brunner, *Offenbarung und Vernunft*, 138–39; ETR 119–20; Brunner, *Wahrheit als Begegnung*, 132; ETR 132. This is also the reason why Brunner rejects a simple identification of the *word of the Bible* (*Bibelwort*) with the *word of God* (*Gotteswort*).

39. Brunner, *The Mediator*, 297; Brunner, *Wahrheit als Begegnung*, 157; ETR 157; Brunner, *Dogmatics II*, 254. See also Boyd, *Cross Vision*, 20–24; Cavey, *End of Religion*, 137, 146.

40. Brunner, *Dogmatics II*, 254, 333, 335. By extension, Brunner mentions also the importance of the communication of God's name as *self-disclosure* and the beginning of a personal relationship (Brunner, *Dogmatics I*, 122–23). See also Hilberath et al., *Communicative Theology*, 47; Cavey, *End of Religion*, 43; McFarlane, *Evangelical Theology*, 56.

41. See section 3a. The predominance of the term *revelation* in *Revelation and Reason* can be explained by the specific epistemological and philosophical focus of the monograph.

42. Brunner sometimes differentiates between *Selbstkundgebung* and *Selbstmitteilung*, the former reflecting closer the meaning of self-communication (Brunner, *Dogmatik III*, 201; ETR 172).

43. Brunner, *Wahrheit als Begegnung*, 27–28; ETR 23–24. See also Brunner, *The Mediator*, 297–98; McGrath, *Emil Brunner*, 170; Rössler, *Person und Glaube*, 79.

This unconditional self-giving, as we have already explored,[44] is identical with God's love, his *agape*.[45] Consequently, Brunner makes a bold statement: this self-disclosure as love is at the same time God's reconciliation with humanity.[46] In the person and through the whole life of Jesus Christ God once and for all reconciles human beings to himself.[47] That said, Brunner rightly asks the question whether the cross then is superfluous and answers passionately that the cross is only intelligible through the person of the mediator. The incarnation and the cross form an "indissoluble unity. The first is fulfilled in the second, just as the second begins in the first." Reconciliation is constituted by "Jesus Christ Himself, That HE IS WHO HE IS" and this, his self-disclosure, culminates on the cross.[48] Only there, the radicality of God's love, his will for communion and his lordship can be perceived[49] and thus, only there the inauguration of the kingdom of God finds its ultimate manifestation in conquering the hostile forces by a "complete deprivation of power and glory."[50]

Accordingly, God is known first and foremost by his actions in Jesus Christ, by what he has done for us as humans. Through his coming, his becoming human, his miracles and exorcisms, his words, and finally his

---

44. See the introduction to chapter 5.

45. See Brunner, *Dogmatics I*, 184–85; Brunner, *Dogmatics II*, 257; Brown, *Believing Thinking*, 42; Schmid, *Lehre von Gott*, 113–14. See also Sanders, *God Who Risks*, 115–16.

46. See Brunner, *The Mediator*, 296; Brunner, *Offenbarung und Vernunft*, 261; ETR 236; Brunner, *Dogmatik III*, 234; ETR 202; Hauge, "Truth as Encounter," 145, 153.

47. Brunner, *Dogmatics II*, 281. See also Rehfeld, "Seinskonstitutive Christusbezogenheit," 81.

48. Brunner, *The Mediator*, 492–93; Brunner, *Dogmatics II*, 281. See also Wright, *Revolution*, 194.

49. Brunner, *Wahrheit als Begegnung*, 159; ETR 159. See also Boyd, *Cross Vision*, 36–37, 53, 55; Holtzen, *God Who Trusts*, 82.

50. Brunner, *Dogmatics II*, 299. Brunner elucidates different meanings of the death of Christ on the cross and concludes that all of them are interwoven and blended in the New Testament (286–87) to show, first of all, the "incomprehensible, unconditional love of God" (295). This diversity is important over and against curtailed views of the atonement, especially Anselm's theory of satisfaction (objectivistic), but also Abelard's (subjectivistic) view (291–95). Although this is not the place to expound Brunner's view of the atonement it is interesting to note that he objects to penal substitution since it is not God who *gets* reconciled, but he *reconciles* himself (Brunner, *Wahrheit als Begegnung*, 158; ETR 158). Despite the differences, Johnson rightly perceives similarities between the *Christus Victor* model of atonement and Brunner's approach (Johnson, "Soteriology," 200–203).

death and resurrection we perceive the God-for-us, Emmanuel.[51] His actions are his responsiveness and this, his responsiveness, points to his very nature as love. In this sense, Jesus's acts and words also communicate *something* about God, in order to reveal, to disclose, who he truly *is*.[52] "He *is* what He does and He *does* what He is."[53] That God *is* love, Brunner argues, is the most audacious claim of personalism. "Hence, the word, personal being [*Personhaftigkeit*], and love belong together."[54] According to Brunner, those three things have only come together once in history, citing Mark 10:45, when the Son of God came to serve, not being served, and to give his life as a ransom for many.[55] Brunner summarizes the things said so far:

> Now let us sum up: Only the true personal presence of God, only the Incarnation of the Word, and the coming "in the form of a servant" of Him who was in divine form, can establish the rule of the Holy Lord, and create communion with Him who is love; only God truly present. Himself in Person, can truly reveal God to us, and truly reconcile us to Him. The revelation in the "Word-about-Him" is not able to do this. The Prophet as person is not the presence of God, and the Prophetic Word is not the presence of God in person. Only the identity of the Revealer with that which is revealed, of the "Bearer" with that which He "bears," can do this. . . . Only the personal Presence of God, speaking and acting, is the perfect revelation and reconciliation. And this has taken place in Jesus Christ.[56]

---

51. See, Brunner, *Wahrheit als Begegnung*, 154–56; ETR 154–56; Brunner, *The Mediator*, 409–10; Brunner, *Dogmatics I*, 191–92; Brunner, *Dogmatics II*, 271; Brunner, "Reply to Interpretation," 343–44.

52. Therefore Schrotenboer's critique that in Brunner's personalist conception God *cannot* "reveal this or that," only himself, since it would be impersonal, shows his misinterpretation of Brunner's I-You and I-it "contradiction." Schrotenboer, *New Apologetics*, 208–9.

53. Brunner, *The Mediator*, 490–91. Brunner sometimes seems to highlight the being of Christ above his doing in *The Mediator*, but he simply wants to point to the fact that Jesus can only be the mediator because he *is* also the Christ, the Son of God (404–7). Although Brunner himself critiques his focus in *The Mediator* on the *being* of Christ (Brunner, *Wahrheit als Begegnung*, 154–56; ETR 154–56), Muller's critique that Brunner's later concept of revelation does not point to the transcendent reality behind it anymore is simply wrong (Muller, "Brunner and Reformed Orthodoxy," 314, 316, 318).

54. Brunner, *Wahrheit als Begegnung*, 30–32 (TM); ETR 26–27.

55. Brunner, *Wahrheit als Begegnung*, 28; ETR 24.

56. Brunner, *Dogmatics I*, 219. For a very similar conclusion, see Wright, *Revolution*, 332–40.

God's Veiled Self-Disclosure

These reflections on the incarnation lead us to one final consideration and problem: "The divine self-manifestation is enclosed within a real historical human life. This human life is the place in which God wills to meet man."[57] For Brunner everything depends on this external historical fact that is absolutely unique within human history and its "once-and-for-allness" is exactly why it so offensive to the human mind.[58] Not only is the historical fact of Jesus of Nazareth decisive, but that through this man God himself is incarnated, that he truly is the Christ.[59] There is no abstraction: the transcendent has become immanent and the suprahistorical has entered history. This is the true and unique miracle of the incarnation and as such God's self-disclosure, which is absolutely decisive and creates at the same time the absolute place of decision.[60] Yet, God's self-revelation through the historical, human person of Jesus is also a veiling and concealment and as such a paradox. God chose an indirect self-disclosure.[61] The reason for this is twofold: First, it is, again, his responsiveness, his grace, so that the human is not overpowered by God's unveiled presence but given room to actually decide.[62] Second, "that even where He is most fully present we have not the power simply to take hold of Him without further ado." In other words: to perceive Jesus as God incarnate is not a human ability.[63] Citing Kierkegaard, Brunner

---

57. Brunner, *The Mediator*, 354.

58. Brunner, *Wahrheit als Begegnung*, 26–27; ETR 21–22; Brunner, *The Mediator*, 153–54, 201; Brunner, *Werk des heiligen Geistes*, 34; Brunner, *Offenbarung und Vernunft*, 43, 309, 433; ETR 31, 281–82, 399; McKim, "Brunner the Ecumenist," 98.

59. Brunner, *Offenbarung und Vernunft*, 126; ETR 108.

60. Brunner, *The Mediator*, 303, 306, 308; Brunner, *Offenbarung und Vernunft*, 323, 334; ETR 294–95, 306; McGrath, *Emil Brunner*, 43–44, 117–22; Lüdemann, *Denken*, 309.

61. This Kierkegaardian terminology of *indirect communication* used sometimes by Brunner can also be overstrained and consequently be utilized in a sense that is foreign to Brunner (see, e.g., Jewett, *Concept of Revelation*, 54–56).

62. See also Boyd, *Cross Vision*, 108; Ward, "Cosmos and Kenosis," 158; Fretheim, *God Enters*, 82.

63. Brunner, *The Mediator*, 330, 334–35, 337–38, 340. Salakka wrongly speaks of a Brunnerian separation of the human and divine in the nature of Christ and that the divine person cannot be perceived in the historical person of Jesus in *The Mediator* (Salakka, *Person und Offenbarung*, 126–27). As has been shown, this is a distorted picture of Brunner's Christology.

says that only an indirect communication through the incognito of the Son of Man makes faith in the Son of God possible.[64]

> Thus two events had to take place before the mysterious, unknown God could be revealed as the Father: He had to come forth from His Mystery, enter into history, and "show" Himself as Father in the form of man, in the Son; and He had to enlighten the darkened heart of men through the Holy Spirit, that in the form of the Man Jesus we might be able to see the Son, and in the Son the Father.[65]

Therefore, God can only be known through Christ *in* the flesh, in this objective historical fact, yet at the same time, he cannot be known *after* the flesh, as a mere human being, but needs to be revealed subjectively as the God-with-us, Emmanuel.[66] There is no either/or, but both have to come together within an encounter of the Holy Spirit as the existential initiation of the restoration of personal correspondence. Indeed, God comes to humanity not through a medium, nor an intermediary, but in the mediator,[67] Jesus Christ, "immediated"[68] by the Holy Spirit, mediated through the church.

---

64. Brunner, *Offenbarung und Vernunft*, 206–7; ETR 186–87. It is important to note that Brunner not only highlighted the veiling of God in *The Mediator* but continued to do so in *Revelation and Reason* as well as in his *Dogmatics*. There is a certain development towards an emphasis of an actual self-disclosure from the early to the late Brunner and Scheld perceives that this development has started in and even within *The Mediator* and has not been considered enough in Brunner scholarship. Yet, we cannot follow Scheld's conclusion that this depiction of the incarnation is incongruent with that presented in *Truth as Encounter* and that Brunner himself should have said so (Scheld, *Christologie Emil Brunners*, 198–202). Brunner critiqued that he did primarily focus on Christ's *being* and not enough on Christ's *work* in *The Mediator* (Brunner, *Wahrheit*, 154–56; ETR 154–56), while still underlining the importance of a certain concealing of Christ.

65. Brunner, *Dogmatics I*, 209.

66. Brunner, *The Mediator*, 156–60, 309, 346, 355, 416.

67. White, "Missionary Theology," 61.

68. This word-invention is very suitable because it combines an adjective with the dynamic and power of a verb. For a defense of such a usage, see Barber, "When Adjectives Become Verbs."

b) Immediated by the Holy Spirit, Mediated through the Church

Now, we are at the point where the historical and "objective" fact becomes existential and actual, where God meets the human, where God meets us. According to Brunner, this has to be seen as truth as encounter, as one happening and therefore this part of the movement from God-towards-human and human-towards-God should be treated as one. Yet, for reasons already explored, we cautiously separate what actually and existentially belongs together.[69] Hence, we are still focusing in the following section on God's "call" and not yet the human "answer." However, we are facing another structural challenge: according to Brunner, God's self-disclosure through the Holy Spirit *and* the church are intimately interwoven and cannot be treated in separate sections.[70] Consequently, although this section will be quite comprehensive, what follows will not be a thorough treatment of Brunner's pneumatology or ecclesiology. The aim, rather, still is to trace the restoration of personal correspondence. Whether one must begin with the church or with the work of the Spirit might be a matter of intention and therefore discussion. Brunner usually starts with the church, the testimony of the apostles, yet he puts this in the "brackets" of the Holy Spirit since the movement of the Spirit is the prerequisite for everything else what the church is and does, the all-encompassing and all-permeating.[71] However, in this section we will first look at the Spirit's work of unveiling Jesus as the Christ, closely followed by, as second, the testimony of the apostles becoming the New Testament. Third, we will explore that by the Spirit the historical becomes actual and, fourth, what role the church occupies in this. Those four points already lead us to the first important observation: the Holy Spirit does his work primarily through the agency of humans, hereby also using human means.[72] This will be further explored throughout this section.

69. See section 3c.

70. See Brunner, *Dogmatik III*, 22; ETR 8; Brown, *Thinking*, 83.

71. See, e.g., Brunner's structure of *Dogmatics III*, which has the title *God's Self Communication as His Self-Representation through the Holy Spirit*. Yet, the first section of this part is *Ekklesia and Church*, which precisely reflects the challenge we try to manage and points to the Spirit as "bracket" around everything else. See also Lütz, *Weg zum Glauben*, 227.

72. Brunner, *Man in Revolt*, 534–35. Right after this Brunner writes about the point of contact which is simply what God "apprehends in man." The following statement can also be generalized for our purpose: "He only apprehends what He has

The Spirit's Work of Unveiling Jesus as the Christ

The work of the Holy Spirit is already present and observable in the disciples of Jesus since he takes the initiative to reveal Jesus *in* the flesh as Jesus the Christ, the Son of God. Brunner hereby points to 2 Corinthians 5:16, where Paul expresses that we know Jesus not anymore *after* the flesh.[73] One of the decisive passages for Brunner is Peter's confession "You are the Christ, the son of the living God" and Jesus's response, namely, that this knowledge was not revealed by flesh and blood (Matt 16:15–17 NKJV). According to Brunner, in this moment revelation occurred and did so through the work of the Holy Spirit, although Jesus in person was standing right in front of Peter. This, Peter's confession of faith, which will be discussed in the next chapter, was only possible through the revealing work of the Holy Spirit.[74] Hence, not only had God to disclose himself in the human Jesus but he also had to illuminate the darkened human heart for the fact that in him truly the living God was encountered.[75] Through the resurrection of Jesus, this lifting of the incognito of Christ was finally and fully confirmed.[76] This first historical and personal enlightenment of the apostles, this first confession of faith as I-You encounter, prayer, became *witness* through these same apostles since they turned to other people and told them; Brunner speaks of a "quarter-turn."[77] This witness contains both *narration*, a record of the things that happened, and the *teaching* that confirms that this Jesus truly is the Christ.[78] The attempt to separate the two, the historical Jesus and the believing witness of the apostles, is according to Brunner a misguided and arrogant attempt of liberalism because the apostles did only point to Jesus as he truly is.[79] Consequently, "God's revelation in Christ is not a historic fact in the secular sense; rather, it is the reality of Jesus seen through the open eyes

---

already created." See also Müller, "The Church in Action," 46. For the general appropriation of human means by God see, e.g., Brunner, *Offenbarung und Vernunft*, 26; ETR 15–16.

73. Brunner, *The Mediator*, 156–60, 309, 346, 355, 416.

74. See especially Brunner, *Offenbarung und Vernunft*, 47, 167–70, 189–94; ETR 34, 148–50, 169–74.

75. Brunner, *Dogmatics I*, 209. See also Brown, *Believing Thinking*, 23–25, 54.

76. Brunner, *Offenbarung und Vernunft*, 333–34; ETR 305–6; Brunner, *The Mediator*, 428, 431, 433.

77. Brunner, *Offenbarung und Vernunft*, 139–40, 167–68; ETR 120–21, 147–48.

78. Brunner, *Dogmatik III*, 208–13; ETR 178–83.

79. Brunner, *Dogmatics II*, 251–52, 258.

of faith, Jesus witnessed to as the Christ, the Son of God."[80] Only because of this witness the following generations and we today, who are not eyewitnesses, came to know of this once-and-for-all event and the person of Jesus Christ.[81]

The Testimony of the Apostles Becoming the New Testament

Thus, God's self-disclosure happens not only through the historical Jesus, although it can never be apart from it, but also through the testimony of the Spirit *and* the kerygma[82] of the apostles which eventually became, in its written form, the New Testament. As such, the Bible is also revelation.[83] According to Brunner this written form was not a mistake but necessary to highlight the uniqueness of the word of the apostles as the foundation of every other spoken word and doctrine of the church. Accordingly, the church is based on the word of the apostles and prophets (Eph 2:20), yet at the same time, there is no word of the apostle or a New Testament without the church.[84] By extension, we perceive a certain over-and-againstness of the Bible and through it an asymmetry, a primary role of the Bible within the restoration of personal correspondence. As a result, Brunner can argue that Christian faith is Bible-faith (*Bibelglaube*) and that both, the Bible and faith, stand or fall together.[85] However, it must not be forgotten that the Bible "is not the object of faith, but the means by which God creates faith."[86] Brunner is entirely clear on

---

80. Brunner, *Faith, Hope, and Love*, 24; see also 17–22; Brunner, *The Mediator*, 159; Brown, *Believing Thinking*, 57.

81. Brunner, *Dogmatics I*, 18. See also Brown, *Believing Thinking*, 83.

82. For Brunner's view of kerygma as *sui generis* and its differentiation from teaching and doctrine, see Brunner, *Dogmatik III*, 215–16; ETR 190.

83. Brunner, *Offenbarung und Vernunft*, 32–33; ETR 21–22.

84. Brunner, *Offenbarung und Vernunft*, 141–42, 145–46, 149, 154–55, 158–59; ETR 122–23, 126–27, 130, 135–36, 139. Brunner uses the picture of concentric rings (similar to the *law of relational closeness*) to illustrate the interplay between apostolic witness/scripture and the dogma/theology of the church (Brunner, *Dogmatics I*, 80–81; Brunner, *Wahrheit als Begegnung*, 137; ETR 137–38). A good term (wordplay) for what Brunner means gives Rehfeld, "Seinskonstitutive Christusbezogenheit," 70: the Bible as *Ur-Kunde* (primordial message). Since this specific topic is not part of our aim, we point to Cynthia Brown's excellent work for an in-depth study.

85. Brunner, *Offenbarung und Vernunft*, 300; ETR 273.

86. McGrath, *Emil Brunner*, 166. See also Brunner, *Dogmatik III*, 273–75, 280–81; ETR 239–41, 246–47. Here Brunner states that "believing the Bible" means something

this: it is never faith in something, but someone; it is never Bible orthodoxy or fundamentalism.[87] Precisely in this misunderstanding of truth, he perceived one of the main problems in church history,[88] as we have already treated in the exploration of objectivism vs. subjectivism.[89] Nevertheless, only through the Bible, through human language, and through an imperfect vessel, can we know God's self-revelation in Jesus Christ and hear the "master's voice."[90] "The Bible is a human witness to God, yet it is also something human through which God reveals himself."[91] Hence, the Bible did not fall from heaven and is not written in angelic tongues, but rather God's self-disclosure is again "incarnated" to be responsive and to be perceived in freedom. In this sense, the Bible not only reveals and discloses but also encloses and veils the "word of God"—not *from* us, but *for* us. This view of the Bible shows the dialectic that comes with the work of the Holy Spirit: he uses something that is not actually himself but encounters us actually through it and in turn, he "supernaturalizes" something human. In other words, through this book, the Spirit speaks to us as he has spoken to the apostles.

The Spirit Makes the Historical Actual

According to Brunner, we do not believe in Jesus Christ because of the Bible. The Bible is the means through which we encounter Jesus (and we could not encounter him without it).[92] Hence, our faith is not based on

---

entirely different than biblical faith. "The Bible is not 'in itself' God's word, just as faith is not 'in itself' faith" (TM). Yet, he goes as far as to say that the Bible *alone* is the place where God speaks to us. Understood in the wider context of Brunner's writings he cannot mean that God *only* speaks through the Bible but that only through the Bible we get to know the true word of God, Jesus Christ.

87. See also section 6a.

88. Brunner, *Wahrheit als Begegnung*, 164–65.

89. See section 1b.

90. For Brunner's famous metaphor of Caruso's record and the Bible, see Brunner, *Our Faith*, 10.

91. McGrath, *Emil Brunner*, 37, citing Brunner, *Philosophy*, 155. For an evangelical, even a biblicist critique of Brunner's understanding of the Bible, see Schirrmacher, "Missverständnis des Emil Brunner." For a riposte and evangelical appraisal of Brunner's bibliology, see Uwe Swarat's short foreword to the 2007 reprint of Brunner, *Offenbarung und Vernunft*. For a similar view, see Boyd, *Cross Vision*, 56–60, 69; Grenz and Olson, *20th-Century Theology*, 71 (concerning Barth).

92. Brunner, *Dogmatics II*, 342.

the witness of the apostles, but their witness is the means by which we *ourselves* encounter the Lord *himself* and therefore we stand on the same basis as they did.[93] In this sense, Peter's encounter is repeated time and again within history until today.[94] The main question is not "who was Jesus," but "who is Jesus."[95] Brunner argues that in one sense God's self-disclosure is historical truth but at the same time, it is not: "It is by present inspiration that past incarnation becomes truth to me."[96] Even more, the incarnated truth in person encounters us through the Holy Spirit. According to Brunner, the Gospel of John especially shows that Jesus and the Spirit are one and that through the Spirit the Father's self-disclosure in his Son continues.[97] The Holy Spirit immediates the mediator, Jesus the Christ, to us. Brunner does not use this exact word-creation, nonetheless, it combines perfectly what he wants to say: the Spirit's word is the same word spoken in Christ, yet it is a present and not a past word. As such, the mediated You coincides and becomes immediate with the I in this actual I-You encounter.[98] The existential-subjective becomes one with the objective-historical.[99] As early as *The Mediator* Brunner formulated what he would later explicate in *Truth as Encounter*: "Complete immediacy in the midst of complete mediacy: this is the paradox of reconciliation, of justification, of faith."[100]

The Church as Imperfect Embodiment and Medium

How, then, does the Holy Spirit disclose himself, the person of Jesus, and through him the Father? By what means does this encounter actually happen? First of all, again, as with the incarnation of Christ, the movement

93. Brunner, *Dogmatik III*, 230; ETR 198.

94. Brunner, *Offenbarung und Vernunft*, 189–94, 200; ETR 169–74, 180.

95. Brunner, *Our Faith*, 64.

96. Brunner, *Christianity and Civilisation*, 40.

97. Brunner, *Dogmatik III*, 26; ETR 12. See also Hilberath et al., *Communicative Theology*, 63; Kovacs, *James E. Loder*, 99, 102–3, 105–6, 109; Cavey, *End of Religion*, 254.

98. Brunner, *Werk des heiligen Geistes*, 1, 13–14, 27, 30–31; Altamira, "Offenbarungsgeschehen," 256–57.

99. Brunner, *Dogmatik III*, 31, 33, 204; ETR 16–17, 18, 174–75. For Brunner's critique of a subjectivism without historical foundation, see Brunner, *Wahrheit als Begegnung*, 76; ETR 74–75. See also Lütz, *Weg zum Glauben*, 220.

100. Brunner, *The Mediator*, 526.

of God is towards the human and not the other way around. He takes, again, the initiative, and as such the encounter is asymmetric. And, again, he encounters humans in a way they can grasp and understand; he is responsive. Brunner asks: "Is there a point of identity between the revelation of the Person and the word in human speech?" He answers with a yes. "It is *the witness of the Holy Spirit*."[101] As we have already explored in the last section, Brunner understands this witness not merely or even primarily as words, but as personal presence. Yet, his remark that to communicate someone you also have to communicate something is likewise valid in this case. Brunner often speaks of the signs that point to the real "thing."[102] Those signs can be words, but they clearly can be more than words. In his works around the time of *Truth as Encounter* Brunner often refers to the sacraments as a different mode of communication that does not come "with many words, but in an intelligible act."[103] Yet, it appears that Brunner perceived the ministry and witness of the Spirit increasingly also in powerful action and the miraculous giving the *dynamis* and the para-logical more room.[104] Brunner bemoans in *Dogmatics III* that usually in theological reflection the work of the Spirit has only been relevant for the disclosure of teaching and understanding but not for the things that hardly can be taught or put into words. For Brunner, this ignorance of the dynamic workings of the Spirit is one of the main reasons for the theological intellectualism of the churches in the West. By contrast, this Spirit-dynamism cannot or should not be exiled into the time of Jesus and the apostles.[105] However, Brunner "preaches to the choir" in this passage since he himself had a long and progressive journey towards this understanding and, until the end, it is not always clear how he understands the dynamism of the Spirit within the church and mission.[106]

101. Brunner, *Dogmatics I*, 28–29.

102. Brunner, *Wahrheit als Begegnung*, 131–34; ETR 130–33. In this context he speaks about the interplay between truth and doctrine, yet by implication, it is also valid for the communication of the Spirit in general. See also McGrath, *Emil Brunner*, 170–71.

103. See, e.g., Brunner, *Our Faith*, 128–30.

104. Ebeling, "Die Beunruhigung der Theologie," 358.

105. Brunner, *Dogmatik III*, 30–31; ETR 15–16. This statement alone should leave us puzzled how and why Brunner's son could doubt whether his father knew the dimension of non-verbal communication (Brunner, *Mein Vater*, 37, 103).

106. It is safe to say that this process was nurtured, if not initiated, by Brunner's involvement with the Oxford Group (see section 1a and Brunner, "Oxforder Gruppenbewegung," 276–77, 285). Brunner's development in this area can be perceived in

When saying "Holy Spirit," according to Brunner, the next one has to say is "church." Where the concrete works of the Spirit are, there is church, *ecclesia*, and where there is *ecclesia*, there is the work of the Holy Spirit. The community and love that can be found within the *ecclesia* is part of the supra-logical power of the Spirit and as such makes him visible.[107] The neglect of this dynamic work of the Holy Spirit within the church as the continuity and reflection of the love and community of God himself has led the church to become an institution rather than a dynamic community of believers.[108] As a result, Brunner differentiates between *church* and *ecclesia*. This distinction often has been misunderstood. Brunner was no romantic wanting to go back to the primal, perfect form of the church in the New Testament; he simply wanted to clarify the terminology.[109] *Ecclesia* stands for the community of the saints, whereas *church* depicts the historically grown form, the "shell" in which the true *ecclesia* lives. Accordingly, the function of the church is to facilitate and promote the life of the *ecclesia*.[110] Hence, Brunner is not against the organized form of church, rather he deems it necessary, whilst at the same time he speaks against the church as a mere institution that becomes static and finally dead.[111] Brunner concludes: "The 'church' as an institution is not the 'visible' one, and the church in the personal sense is not the 'invisible' one."[112]

---

the following passages: Brunner, *Our Faith*, 86–87, 117; Brunner, *Werk des heiligen Geistes*, 24, 53, 55, 56, 57; Brunner, *Wahrheit als Begegnung*, 180–81, 190–91; Brunner, *Offenbarung und Vernunft*, 138–39, 180–82; ETR 119–20, 161–63; Brunner, *Eternal Hope*, 64; Brunner, *The Misunderstanding of the Church*, 47–49, 51–53, 124; Brunner, *Dogmatics II*, 169; Brunner, *Dogmatik III*, 30–31, 406; ETR 15–16, 363.

107. Brunner, *Misunderstanding of the Church*, 108–9.

108. Brunner, *Wahrheit als Begegnung*, 168–69; ETR 168–69.

109. See section 3a.

110. See, e.g., the summary of Brunner's ecclesiology in Schirrmacher, "Missverständnis des Emil Brunner," 293–94, 300–301.

111. Brunner, "Reply to Interpretation," 347. This, Brunner's view, was, according to his son, by no means a "turn" or a new development but a summary of what he lived and taught all his live (Brunner, *Mein Vater*, 247). McGrath rightly points to Brunner's involvement with para-church organizations since he believed them to have, in many cases, a more lively form than the official protestant churches of Switzerland (McGrath, *Emil Brunner*, 201–4). Yet, Jehle shows that Brunner perceived those organizations, as well as the free churches (e.g., in the USA), also in permanent danger of obscuring and hindering the true *ecclesia* (Jehle, *Emil Brunner*, 133–34, 508–11).

112. Brunner, *Wahrheit als Begegnung*, 186; ETR 187.

Therefore, the *ecclesia* is the body of Christ, extending God's call to the I-You relationship into the world.[113] The *ecclesia* is "the historical actualization of the past self-disclosure of God."[114] With other words, the *ecclesia* is the embodiment, the continuing "incarnation" of God through the Spirit and as such it is not only built through faith but also built to generate faith. It is not only the community of the saved but at the same time, the divine means to bring, to mediate, salvation to the world.[115] Hence, the church has a twofold witness and mission: to embody, to re-present Christ through its being and to mediate, to present Christ, like a sign pointing to him. Consequently, the church is an end in itself (*Selbstzweck*) and at the same time, a means to an end (*Mittel zum Zweck*), which is the kingdom, the lordship, the love-rule of God.[116] As such, Brunner's famous quote has to be understood: "The Church exists by mission, just as a fire exists by burning. Where there is no mission, there is no Church; and where there is neither Church nor mission, there is no faith."[117] This mission of the church happens through the immediate work and power of the Holy Spirit and, consequently, as we have already shown above, it also consists of more than words and preaching.[118] As such, the *ecclesia* is "the present reality of the future and the transformation of the idea of revolution."[119] In essence, this means two things: First, the embodiment of Christ in the church is real, yet at the same time veiled. The rule of God, his kingdom is already present, but at the same time not yet fully here.[120] The future

---

113. Brunner, *Wahrheit als Begegnung*, 169–70; ETR 169–70.

114. This is the title of a chapter in Brunner, *Dogmatik III*, 17–18 (TM); ETR 4–5.

115. Brunner, *Offenbarung und Vernunft*, 157–58, 166–67; ETR 137–38, 147–48.

116. Brunner, *Dogmatik III*, 124–25, 159–60, 162; ETR 102, 134, 137.

117. Brunner, *Word and World*, 108. Interestingly, this small book has never been translated into German and accordingly this quote is mainly famous in the English-speaking world. Yet, as White has pointed out, Brunner's conviction that "the missionary task of the church is not an after-thought" but primary is evident throughout his works. White, "Missionary Theology," 55–56, 61–62, 64. See also section 2b.

118. In addition to our discussion above, Brunner appears to have moved from *sacrament* as supplement to *words* towards *example and power* by the end of his life (Brunner, *Dogmatik III*, 162; ETR 137). Therefore, Lüdemann's monograph appears to miss Brunner's point in merely interpreting this mission in the context of preaching, whereas Brunner's vision was much more encompassing (Lüdemann, *Denken*, 271–74, 385).

119. This is the title of a chapter in Brunner, *Eternal Hope*, 59.

120. Brunner, *Wahrheit als Begegnung*, 171–72; ETR 171–72.

has become present, the *ecclesia* is "messianic" or "eschatological" existence, nonetheless, it is still a hidden, veiled existence.[121] Again, God discloses himself through imperfect humans and he shows his Spirit's power within broken vessels.[122] This leads us to the second: the continuation of God's revolution of love is intimately connected with the church's commitment to this mission. The calling of the church is to be a sign, pointing to the risen Jesus Christ, yet, Brunner asks the unpleasant question, whether it lives up to this task. Mere words do not help, it is the lived example, the reflection of Christ in the power of the Spirit that matters.[123] The church is faced with the decision whether or not it will co-operate within this divine revolution and,[124] by extension, one could say the answer distinguishes between the real and the true church.[125] Consequently, it becomes evident why Brunner left the following generation of theologians missionary theology as a central task to develop.[126] This demonstrates that God wants real reciprocity with humans in his mission, an asymmetric reciprocity nonetheless, since he initiates and drives his mission forward (*missio Dei*). This corporate relationship of the church with God forestalls aspects of what we will explore in more detail as the individual's answer of faith in the next chapter. Indeed, theologically it is crucial for Brunner's understanding of the I-You relationship with God that it is never individualistic but always only part of and in relation to the actual *ecclesia*.[127] While this

121. Brunner, *Dogmatik III*, 459; ETR 411. Jehle proposes that Moltmann was influenced by Brunner's ecclesiology since he continued using the term *messianic existence* (Jehle, *Emil Brunner*, 512).

122. The church mediates the mediator, yet it is not the mediator itself. The *ecclesia* embodies Christ, yet Christ still is the head. This dialectic differentiation of the church's *being* and yet at the same time *not being* leads, consequently, to a view of the church (as well as the Scriptures) that cannot be the final authority but only Jesus Christ himself (Brunner, *Offenbarung und Vernunft*, 202–3; ETR 183). This discussion is especially perceivable in the final chapter of the catholic theologian Volken, *Glaube bei Emil Brunner*, 207–23. For a similar point, see Fretheim, *God Enters*, 96.

123. See, e.g., Brunner, *Wahrheit als Begegnung*, 148, 197; ETR 148, 197; Brunner, *Misunderstanding of the Church*, 115. See also Ebeling's appraisal in "Die Beunruhigung der Theologie," 354–68. For Brunner's personal struggle with this topic, see section 1a.

124. Brunner, *Eternal Hope*, 61–62.

125. The analogy to Brunner's depiction of the real and true human (see chapter 4) is intended, although Brunner has not put it that way.

126. Brunner, "Missionary Theology," 817–18.

127. Brunner, *Word and World*, 107. Brunner calls it "communionistic personalism"

corporate dimension is fundamental and is primary, Brunner never dissolves the individual's responsibility and response to the call of God within it, since existentially the individual's decision also precedes its being part of the body of Christ. To this movement from human-towards-God we turn now.

---

or "personal communionism." Brunner, "Missionary Theology," 817–18. However, McGrath rightly critiques that Brunner did not develop the church's corporate relationship with God enough (taken from a personal conversation at the University of Fribourg in 2018).

6

Human-Towards-God

The Answer to Restoration of Personal Correspondence

BEFORE WE TURN TO the details of this chapter, two preliminary remarks are expedient. First, faith has been perceived by many scholars to be Brunner's central leitmotif.[1] As we have shown, this is simply wrong since faith, for Brunner, is only one side of the coin: faith "is a correlative of revelation."[2] Faith simply is the positive human *answer* to the divine *call*, yet as such an all-important part for the restoration of personal correspondence and the reason for structuring this corresponding chapter separately.[3] Second, faith is the non-individualistic, positive reaction of an individual to the action of God. As we have already explored, it is non-individualistic since it grows in the soil of the church and also as part of the church. Faith without the church is, according to Brunner,

---

1. See section 3b. If Brunner would encapsulate everything within *faith*, Volken would rightly criticize him for such an expansion of the term (Volken, *Glaube bei Emil Brunner*, 185–86). Yet, this is a misinterpretation of Brunner's relational leitmotif where faith is only the human part. The only passage where Brunner does stretch *the Faith* towards meaning the whole of the Christian message is in Brunner, *Dogmatik III*, 202–3; ETR 173–74. Admittedly, Brunner's argumentation around Galatians 3:23 is ambiguous and might contribute to a misunderstanding of the term faith; although Brunner wants to avoid it (see 205–8). Yet, the point he is making is an entirely different one, namely that the prominence and weight of *faith* in the New Testament does not promote humans unduly.

2. McGrath, *Emil Brunner*, 33.

3. See section 3c.

impossible: "Christian individualism is a contradiction in itself."[4] Consequently, this chapter must be read permanently with its ecclesial context in mind.[5] Nonetheless, it is an individual that acts, more precisely, re-acts to God's action. The general processes of this individual human answer will be explored in the following sections as *asymmetric, reciprocal, free, self-disclosing* and *responsive*. However, we first need to turn to the human misunderstanding of faith.

a) The Turning from Faith as Believing Something

Faith is an ambivalent term for Brunner. On the one hand, it is central to his understanding of the gospel, yet on the other, he perceives that its contemporary use in the language has changed its biblical meaning.[6] Again, Wittgenstein's saying comes to mind that "the meaning of a word is its use in the language."[7] Therefore, Brunner often uses the Greek *pistis* as a replacement and aims at re-filling it with its originally intended sense. Brunner's primary "bête noire" is that faith has become first and foremost faith in *something* instead of faith in *someone*. For him it leads not only in the wrong direction to perceive faith as believing something, a mere object of faith, he even believes true faith to be "the most radical opposite to everything that could be called object or objective."[8] If faith were something one thinks or believes, humans would remain trapped in a monologue and miss the true answer to a real call.[9] The entire development throughout church history to perceive faith as believing something (*Fürwahrhalten*), be it revealed truth, a dogma, or even the Bible,[10] is for Brunner the gravest misunderstanding: the personal has been replaced

---

4. Brunner, *Dogmatik III*, 35, 164; ETR 20, 138. See also Brunner, *Word and World*, 107; Brunner, *Ewige*, 41; Brunner, *Offenbarung und Vernunft*, 157–58, 166–67; ETR 137–38, 147–48.

5. For this reasoning, see also the opening chapter of the faith-section (II) in Brunner's *Dogmatics III* titled *The Ekklesia as Presupposition of Faith*.

6. See the brief treatment in section 3a. See also Brunner, *Dogmatik III*, 205; ETR 176–79 for his analysis of the changed meaning of *faith* in different languages (Latin, English and German).

7. Wittgenstein, *Philosophical Investigations*, §43.

8. Brunner, *Wahrheit als Begegnung*, 108–9 (TM); ETR 108–9. See also section 1b for a treatment of Brunner's overcoming the object-subject dichotomy.

9. See, e.g., White, "Missionary Theology," 60–61.

10. See section 5b.

by the intellectual.[11] While revelation is truth as encounter, faith, as its correlate, is knowledge as encounter.[12] Now, the mistake has been made to take Brunner as being against the value of any belief in something,[13] yet he is by no means as lopsided. Brunner is not against knowledge per se; he simply refutes a faith where knowledge does not lead to encounter. Knowledge, believing something, without the encounter of someone, namely Jesus, cannot and should not be called faith. In essence, this would simply be head-knowledge that bears no existential fruit.[14] However, there is a place for the revelation and believing of something but only as a means that leads to a personal encounter. In this sense, it-truth is closely connected to personal You-truth and it is not possible to have You-truth without a certain amount of it-truth.[15] In other words, the knowledge *about* someone has to lead to the knowledge *of* someone.[16] Consequently, belief in doctrine is "the vehicle for faith but not faith itself."[17] Reason and faith are interconnected, yet two entirely different domains;[18] the problem only arises when the two are mixed up.[19] Accordingly, what faith grasps is not always comprehensible by reason[20] and therefore faith cannot be proved.[21]

---

11. Brunner, *Wahrheit als Begegnung*, 138–39; 164–65; ETR 138–39, 164–65; McGrath, *Emil Brunner*, 77; Bertram, "Brunner on Revelation," 633.

12. Brunner, *Revelation and Reason*, 9.

13. See Volken, *Glaube bei Emil Brunner*, 153, 181, 185, 199–200; Schrotenboer, *New Apologetics*, 215–16; Jewett, *Concept of Revelation*, 152–53, 169; Henry and Dockery, *Evangelicalism*, 180.

14. Brunner, *Werk des heiligen Geistes*, 28–29.

15. Brunner, *Wahrheit als Begegnung*, 131–34; ETR 132–34.

16. See, e.g., Brunner, *Offenbarung und Vernunft*, 48–49, 51; ETR 35–36, 38. For a similar view of faith, see Anderson, *Living Waters*, 19–21; Cavey, *End of Religion*, 214; Holtzen, *God Who Trusts*, 28, 56–59; Rabens, "Sein und Werden," 102, 119–20; Eckstein, *Gerechte*, 11–15.

17. McKim, "Brunner the Ecumenist," 95. A similar argumentation can be observed in Paul L. Homer (see, e.g., Rollefson and Gouwens, *Kierkegaard and Wittgenstein*, 81–82) and in Gunton, Bennema, and Munzinger (according to Glaw, *Bockmuehl*, 217–18).

18. Brunner's law of relational closeness comes to use in this context and solves the mistaken juxtapose of reason and faith (Brunner, "Reply to Interpretation," 331).

19. Brunner, *Offenbarung und Vernunft*, 53; ETR 40. Here Brunner measures theology against prayer and concludes that "theology *means* this personal relation, which true faith *is*" (TM).

20. Williams, "Brunner and Barth on Philosophy," 249.

21. Brunner, *Wahrheit als Begegnung*, 40–41; ETR 37; McGrath, *Emil Brunner*, 206.

Here exactly lies one of the main reasons for human offence concerning the gospel: it is not about knowledge, it is not something only to be thought about, and finally it is not something one can own. It is the other way around:[22] God knows me, he thinks of me, and he wants to "own" me. I cannot have this truth, but this truth has me and changes me; it is existential.[23] Consequently, Brunner shows that doubt often is simply an expression of the human emancipation, the "primal act of sin,"[24] an attempt to circumvent the existential decision that comes packaged with true self-despair.[25] Doubt is, according to James 1:8, the split soul, the ἀνὴρ δίψυχος, the human sway between self-determination and God-determination. Hence, the demand for proof misses the mark entirely.[26] Skepticism, according to Brunner, is the means by which humans can remain in their distanced position and avoid the existential crisis and decision.[27] Consequently, a change of mind, conversion, and repentance has to happen. Positively, it is a turning to Jesus; negatively, it is a turning from self-determination and wanting to determine and take hold of an object of faith.[28] "Hence faith is now no longer the simple childlike acceptance of the 'man made in the divine Image,' but it is first of all a painful process, in which I have to say 'No' before I can say 'Yes'";[29] it is dying. Whenever this happens, a true revolution has taken place:[30] the "I, I!" has been reversed to the "You, You!" which is the miracle of love.[31]

---

22. Brunner, *Wahrheit als Begegnung*, 116–17; ETR 116.

23. Brunner, *Wahrheit als Begegnung*, 32; ETR 28; Brunner, *Dogmatik III*, 293–96; ETR 258–61.

24. See section 4b.

25. Brunner, *Offenbarung und Vernunft*, 235–39, 460–62, 467; ETR 212–16, 423–24, 430.

26. Brunner, *Dogmatik III*, 298–99; ETR 263–64.

27. Brunner, *Dogmatik III*, 394; ETR 352.

28. Brunner, *Dogmatik III*, 314, 316, 318–20, 326; ETR 278, 279, 281–83, 289.

29. Brunner, *Man in Revolt*, 481. Brunner does not say that it is another *kind* of faith (trust) but that it is another *point of departure*. He rightly focuses on the painful process and the necessity of *turning*, yet it is a matter of discussion whether or not he put too much weight on remorse and a sense of guilt (see, e.g., Lütz, *Weg zum Glauben*, 263–64, 267).

30. Brunner, *Das Ewige*, 69.

31. Brunner, *Our Faith*, 100–101. Brunner explicates also the opposite, what love is *not*, in Brunner, *Werk des heiligen Geistes*, 48.

b) Happy Asymmetry: God First, Humans Second

This miracle of love, through dying, is not something that can be learned, accomplished, or even be taught; it is God's gift.[32] As human beings, we are not primarily responsible (for a task or duty), but responsive, which points to the fact that there first has to be a call, a person to respond to. This, God's call, comes not as a "You shall!" but as a "You may be!" The indicative of divine love has to come before the imperative.[33] Consequently, "true faith does not originate from the commandment, but from the gift, which is the event of revelation."[34] In this quote, Brunner first reminds us of the centrality of revelation, of God's self-disclosure. Faith cannot be "filled" with random content. It has only one "content": God, as he has revealed himself through Jesus Christ.[35] Thus, faith is asymmetric since it originates only from God's initiative, call, and gift of self-disclosure. Therefore, secondly, faith is an indirect gift, originated from the true gift, which is Jesus Christ himself, "immediated" by the Holy Spirit. In a sense faith is an effect following a cause without simply being a result of cause and effect; there is no automatism with faith but only true reciprocity, which will be explored in the next section. However, the only thing that can overcome humanity's self-determination, mistrust, and contradiction is God's unconditionally self-giving love. Only this self-giving love enables humans to give up their distanced, self-protecting, and fearful position and give themselves wholly to this loving God.[36] Faith has its origin in the love of God; it is out of love, reminding us of the ontic basis of personal correspondence.[37] Only because of God's loving self-disclosure are humans able to disclose themselves to God. Only because of God's loving responsiveness humans are positively response-able. Or, as 1 John 4:19 puts it, "we love because he loved us first" (NET). God's love overcomes us. By loving, he overcomes our emancipation and becomes our Lord.[38] As such, this is a happy asymmetry:

32. Brunner, *Revelation and Reason*, 420.

33. Brunner, *Man in Revolt*, 98–99; Schrotenboer, *New Apologetics*, 63, 69; Volk, *Lehre von dem Sünder*, 35.

34. Brunner, *Offenbarung und Vernunft*, 230; ETR 207.

35. Brunner, *Dogmatik III*, 200; ETR 171. See the revelation-chapter 5.

36. Brunner, *Offenbarung und Vernunft*, 46–48, 54; ETR 34–36, 41. See also Rabens, "Sein und Werden," 121–22.

37. See section 4a.

38. Brunner, *Wahrheit als Begegnung*, 98; ETR 97–98; Brunner, *Offenbarung und Vernunft*, 204; ETR 184.

Through the assurance "You belong *to* me" the Lord places me at His side, not only under Him but beside Him. *That* is the new foundation that is laid under my feet and upon which I can securely stand, and for which I gladly exchange the earlier one, because it ennobles [sic] me [TM: because he lifts me up]. . . . It is not the word of demand which annihilates me, but the word of assurance that creates me anew, which makes the change from autonomy to dependence a reality.[39]

The fact that God's "overcoming" does not "annihilate" the human, instead he wishes to have him as true counterpart, points to a decisive element in Brunner's view of the restoration of personal correspondence: reciprocity in freedom.

c) The Importance of Reciprocity in Freedom

God's grace is the stimulus and trigger for faith, yet faith comes by no means automatically. "[God] does not hurl his grace at us, like a bricklayer throwing mortar at a wall."[40] No, since God calls, there is a real and decisive human answer. Reciprocity, according to Brunner, is biblical and to change the Bible's all-potent (*allmächtig*), all-efficient (*allwirksam*) God into a seemingly "higher" sole-efficient (*alleinwirksam*) God is to lose the biblical God once and for all.[41] The biblical Creator-God gives freedom to his human creature, yet as we have seen,[42] this created freedom is also dependent freedom. "Freedom is the possibility of self-determination, but dependence is being destined, being created."[43] Humans do not possess God's absolute freedom[44] but a relative freedom, or as Oord puts it, "limited-but-genuine-freedom."[45] True responsibility is "a dependent

---

39. Brunner, *Dogmatics III*, 144; GR 171. See also Balswick et al., *Reciprocating Self*, 59–63, 67–68.

40. Brunner, *Our Faith*, 24.

41. Brunner, *Wahrheit als Begegnung*, 97; ETR 97. For a (weak) attempt to integrate God's sole-efficiency with the concept of relationship, see Poythress, *Redeeming Sociology*, 49.

42. See section 4a.

43. Altamira, "Offenbarungsgeschehen," 152 (TM). See also Andersen, "Theological Anthropology," 18–20.

44. See chapter 5.

45. Oord, *Uncontrolling Love*, 58.

freedom and free dependence."⁴⁶ True, God is the Lord, yet a lord that wishes to rule through free obedience.⁴⁷ "He wants to be not only Lord 'over' the human, he wants to be Lord 'of' the human" and this is only possible through true reciprocity and freedom in decision.⁴⁸ As has already been shown concerning the ontic basis,⁴⁹ it's not a freedom *of* decision, since the human in his responsory actuality cannot not decide. It is freedom *in* decision, because humans, in their actual corrupted state, cannot freely and independently choose God without him first disclosing himself; this has been shown in the last section. Nonetheless, when God calls, humans have the freedom to say "yes" or "no" to him. In his earlier works, Brunner tried to solve this tension by postulating that the "yes" is alone God's work and the "no" is alone the human's.⁵⁰ While he had already tried to say that the human possibility to say "yes" is an effect of God's word he was not as clear as in *Truth as Encounter* that the "yes" itself is not a passive effect. In *Dogmatics III*, Brunner summarizes: "Faith is indeed a gift of God, but certainly not an action of God in the sense that it is God who believes in us."⁵¹ Yes, there is an action of God in us, since "[he] speaks not only *to* me but also *in* me"⁵² but it is not unilateral: the miracle of the *testimonium spiritus sancti internum*⁵³ brings God's part and the human part together in one and the same existential and actual event.⁵⁴ When faith has emerged the human being can only say that it was God's grace, *sola gratia*. On the other hand, while in the decision the human can only say: "*I* [spaced type] must believe, I need to decide, I myself."⁵⁵

46. Cairns, "Brunner's Conception," 81.
47. Brunner, *Dogmatics II*, 300. See also Holtzen, *God Who Trusts*, 46.
48. Brunner, *Wahrheit als Begegnung*, 95–96 (TM); ETR 94–95.
49. See section 4b.
50. Brunner, "Die andere Aufgabe," 185.
51. Brunner, *Dogmatik III*, 27; ETR 12. For an alternative explanation of the interplay between God and humans, see Eckstein, *Gerechte*, 17–19.
52. Brunner, *Word and World*, 65.
53. See section 5b.
54. Schroetenboer agrees yet critiques Brunner for not speaking about the Spirit's preparing of the human heart (Schrotenboer, *New Apologetics*, 214). However, Brunner appears to perceive God's call, the Spirit's address, already as the means of preparing the human heart in this very act.
55. Brunner, *Werk des heiligen Geistes*, 42–46 (TM). In this sense, Brunner's question regarding whether love can be commanded needs to be understood. His dialectic answer is that love needs to be commanded, although it cannot be commanded (see Brunner, *Dogmatics I*, 196; Brunner, *Dogmatics II*, 224).

Consequently, Brunner views this "co-respondence" and "interdependence," this reciprocity as God's goal for the human.[56] Since God, in the name of love, gives humans such weight, he makes himself in a certain sense dependent on them.[57] Thus, in not only acting but also reacting, in being responsive to human acts, God even "changes."[58] The human decision is truly decisive! This importance of the human answer leads Brunner to focus the existential and actual. Without the human "yes" the work of the mediator and the immediation of the Holy Spirit do not change the human and consequently the kingdom of God, God's will and love, is not spread throughout the world. From an existential and actual perspective, Brunner is right to put the importance of the human answer on the same level as God's call.[59] This does not reduce God, on the contrary, it reflects God's greatness in his primordial plan for humanity. God's goal is only reached and fulfilled in the free human "yes" since only then personal correspondence is restored:[60] "God's self-communication in Jesus Christ reaches its goal only in faith—in that man inwardly repeats what God says to him: 'You are my Son, it is you, because I want it; it is you, if you believe.' Only in the human's faith does the righteousness of God reach its goal."[61] Therefore, we need to turn to the how of this human answer of faith.

d) Faith as Self-Disclosure in Loving Responsiveness

Based on what has been said thus far it becomes obvious why Brunner depicts faith, *pistis*, as trusting obedience (*Vertrauensgehorsam*), a radical

---

56. Brunner, *Word and World*, 121–22. See also Fretheim, *God and World*, 27, 270–72; Grenz and Olson, *20th-Century Theology*, 181 (concerning Moltmann); Sanders, *God Who Risks*, 124–25, 174.

57. See also Holtzen, *God Who Trusts*, 63; Brümmer, *Model of Love*, 161–63, 176–78, 196.

58. Brunner, *Dogmatics I*, 269–70; Brown, *Believing Thinking*, 41. See also Oord, *Uncontrolling Love*, 126; Peckham, *Love of God*, 265, 269–70.

59. See the comprehensive discussion in section 3c.

60. Exactly this point of view clarifies Brunner's sometimes puzzling statements like "restoring grace . . . is given only to the believer." Brunner, "New Barth," 134. He clearly does not mean any precondition for God's grace but refers to the restoring power of grace that can only unfold its effect when accepted.

61. Brunner, *Dogmatik III*, 237 (TM); ETR 204. Others have called this the *risk* of God: Brümmer, *Model of Love*, 225–27; Sanders, *God Who Risks*, 219–20; Boyd, *Cross Vision*, 230.

trust that can only grow out of the soil of God's radical love. Hence, this trust is different than any other trust one can put in a human being because only in God one encounters the subject per se, the love in person, and the ultimate trustworthy.[62] Consequently, this trusting obedience is the human self-disclosure as correlate to God's self-disclosure: I do not give something of myself but I give myself, my whole person, and in this sense, it is an act of utter subjectivity.[63] Faith is giving oneself without restrictions, no ifs, no buts.[64] Self-disclosure is what Brunner calls a totality-act or even *the* totality-act.[65]

Therefore, biblical faith is clearly much more than right thinking; it is right acting. Faith means an existential coming to God, a self-disclosure that is first and foremost expressed in prayer.[66] Prayer is faith in action, not simply talking; it is the restoration of personal correspondence.[67] Prayer starts and fuels the loving relationship between humans and God and as such is the basic expression of responsiveness.[68] What has been birthed out of love answers out of love. Brunner even goes as far as to postulate that faith is only the vessel for love and that faith by itself is nothing: "faith is about love; love is not about faith."[69] What might appear as a separation of faith and love is not Brunner's intention—in the same passage he says that they are one—he rather tries to highlight the responsive character, the orientation towards the You of God. One has to read a "parallel" section to truly get this important nuance: "God is not faith, but God is love."[70] Hence, it is about being in this love of God, which is identical with the restoration of personal correspondence. Love, namely God, can only be received by loving back (*Wiederlieben*).[71] Consequently,

---

62. Brunner, *Wahrheit als Begegnung*, 106–8; ETR 105–8; Brunner, *Faith, Hope, and Love*, 28–29; Brunner, *Offenbarung und Vernunft*, 19; ETR 9.

63. Brunner, *Wahrheit als Begegnung*, 104–5; ETR 104–5; Brunner, *Offenbarung und Vernunft*, 403; ETR 371; Schrotenboer, *New Apologetics*, 169–70.

64. Brunner, *Wahrheit als Begegnung*, 108; ETR 108; Brunner, *Word and World*, 25, 32.

65. Brunner, *Word and World*, 72; Schmid, *Lehre von Gott*, 104–5.

66. Brunner, *Our Faith*, 113, 116.

67. Brunner, *Dogmatik III*, 364–76; ETR 324–26.

68. For the centrality of human-divine dialogue in the Johannine gospel, see Anderson, *Living Waters*, 6, 18.

69. Brunner, *Faith, Hope, and Love*, 75, 77.

70. Brunner, *Dogmatics I*, 199.

71. Brunner, *Werk des heiligen Geistes*, 39.

faith is responsiveness and as such an ongoing total-act, an ongoing love-encounter, an ongoing self-disclosure. As a result, for Brunner, there is no value in splitting the life of faith into different phases (*ordo salutis*)—justification, union, sanctification—since in the New Testament they all are meaning one and the same relationship from different perspectives. Coming to Christ already grounds my whole being in the love of God, which already *is* the new life.[72] "The existence of the believer is not only new from God's *perspective*, it truly *is* new now." Hence, love, according to Brunner, is the better term to describe this ongoing relationship than faith, yet faith appears to mark its starting point more adequately.[73]

This new existence in self-disclosure out of responsive love is not something that is hidden; it is not a life that needs to be "believed," but rather faith (love) itself is the new life. Since the love of God is poured into our hearts through the Holy Spirit (Rom 5:5), the fruit of the Spirit starts to show.[74] "There is no faith apart from acting";[75] this is not a moral statement but simply pointing to the existential and responsive nature of faith and love. This is how a true relationship works: through closeness,[76] interaction, and communication (prayer) one gets changed.[77] Indeed, the main focus is on the being and not on the doing,[78] yet the life of faith involves and affects all of life.[79] This new life (faith, love) is not a property, it is an acting disposition, an ongoing encounter, a relationship with the living God. It is "being in becoming" (*ein Sein im Werden*).[80]

72. Brunner, *Wahrheit als Begegnung*, 165–66; ETR 165–66. See also Tanner, *Christ the Key*, vii.

73. Brunner, *Werk des heiligen Geistes*, 40–41 (TM). Sometimes Brunner wants to differentiate between love and faith in order to emphasize the human responsibility (see, e.g., Brunner, *Wahrheit als Begegnung*, 105; ETR 104–5). He believes this to be the reason for Paul choosing *pistis* over *agape*. While Brunner might make a valid point in this specific passage, his argumentation for a separation and "succession" seems abstract and contrary to his overall focus of faith being contained in love, yet not the other way around. Thomas Merton makes a similar point in stressing that the commandment to love comes *after* the commandment to believe since first one has to trust in the love of God (Merton, *New Seeds*, 76).

74. Brunner, *Wahrheit als Begegnung*, 167; ETR 167. See also section 1a.

75. Brunner, *Gebot und die Ordnungen*, 103 (TM).

76. For Brunner's thoughts on the closeness of God, see Brunner, *Dogmatics I*, 258–60.

77. See also Brown, "Personal Imperative of Revelation," 427.

78. Brunner, *Dogmatik III*, 342; ETR 303–4.

79. Brunner, "Reply to Interpretation," 339.

80. Brunner, *Dogmatik III*, 300–302; ETR 264–66. See also Rabens, *Holy Spirit and Ethics*, 123, 126, 245–46.

As such, this new life is lived in the tension between the "not yet" and the "already" and remains a struggle.[81] The restoration of personal correspondence is also a process on the battlefield of this current world[82] moving toward its final goal: "faith must become sight."[83] This goal is not any kind of mystical union but remains communion, a responsive relationship between two distinct subjects.[84] Indeed, in this sense, there is no "over-identification, too-closeness, or over-involvement with the other" but only the process and the goal of close community through an ongoing self-disclosure.[85] As such, the "already" is the same as the "not yet" differing only by the quality of the relationship (faith not sight) and the corresponding current "travail."[86] Consequently, salvation is not a distant, individual "going to heaven" but has to be understood as community that has already started, as the complete restoration of personal correspondence.[87] Life in and for the love of God, "life in the Holy Spirit[, then,] is truly 'eschatological existence.'"[88] Hence, God's call and the human answer are inextricably interwoven.[89]

In conclusion, Part II has shown that God-human interaction indeed is reciprocal yet fundamentally asymmetric, marked by an indissoluble difference between the Creator and his human creature, and by God taking the initiative to bridge this gap from beginning to end. As such, God acts and calls in absolute freedom, yet binds himself to humans by giving them relative freedom so that they can freely answer. Moreover, God's ongoing self-disclosure and responsiveness (from creation to the incarnation until the eschaton; through Jesus, the Spirit, the Bible, and the church) is intended to elicit an equally self-disclosing and responsive

---

81. Brunner, *Wahrheit als Begegnung*, 171–72; ETR 171–72; Brunner, *Our Faith*, 102.

82. Brunner, *Man in Revolt*, 483, 487, 488–89, 491, 495. See also McFarlane, *Evangelical Theology*, 57.

83. Brunner, *Dogmatik III*, 381–83; ETR 341–42.

84. Brunner, *Wahrheit als Begegnung*, 163; ETR 163; Brunner, *Dogmatics II*, 215; Brunner, *Dogmatik III*, 421; ETR 376; Gill, "Teacher and Preacher," 311–12. See also Rehfeld, "Seinskonstitutive Christusbezogenheit," 82–85; Shults, *Theological Anthropology*, 78–79; Gunton, *The One*, 169.

85. Andersen, "Theological Anthropology," 275. See also Brunner, *Our Faith*, 120.

86. Brunner, *Dogmatik III*, 445; ETR 398.

87. Brunner, *Dogmatics II*, 298; Brunner, *Das Ewige*, 41.

88. Brunner, *Dogmatik III*, 405–8, 424–25, 442, 445, 460; ETR 362–65, 379, 395, 398, 412.

89. See section 3c.

human reaction, leading to an ongoing intimate relationship. To this relationship analogy we turn now.

III

The Analogy of Relationship
Personal Correspondence in Light of Relationship Science

EMIL BRUNNER CLEARLY BELIEVED that the only appropriate analogy for God-human interaction is the "person-to-person encounter between humans" and that no abstractions will do.[1] Wittgenstein would have approved of such an approach since he proposed that philosophical, and as such also theological understanding is not a result of universal theories, but emerges through simple and clear examples that can be used as a comparison.[2] Consequently, Part III aims to show that and how the relationship between God and humans is analogous to human relationships since only then would it be adequate and intelligent to speak of a God-human relationship, let alone declaring this relationship to be the monistic theological leitmotif. Indeed, this question of analogy is one area where Brunner's leitmotif of relationship needs extension and development. Brunner, in his time, did not yet have the tools necessary to answer the analogy-question sufficiently. We believe that the rise of relationship science offers a stimulating and illuminating "reference science" to compare the nature and taxonomy of Brunner's personal correspondence with current findings within the study of close human relationships. Hence, since we have already defined the intended "vertical" interaction as reciprocal yet asymmetric characterized by freedom, self-disclosure,

---

1. Brunner, *Wahrheit als Begegnung*, 114 (TM); ETR 114. See also McGrath, *Emil Brunner*, 170. He is not alone with this assessment: Fretheim, *God Enters*, 23.

2. Schulte, *Wittgenstein*, 162–66.

and responsiveness, we now turn to the definition of "horizontal" relationships. The preliminary chapter explores the difficulties concerning the term *relationship* and why relationship science is an adequate point of reference to inform what the basic structures and processes of human relationships are. Furthermore, a working theory of analogy is proposed to then compare Brunner's personal correspondence with the findings from relationship science in the main chapter 8. As a result, in Part IV an analogical argument will be constructed as the basis towards a theology of relationship.

7

Analogy of Relationship

Preliminary Considerations

a) What Is a Relationship?

ONE OF THE DECLARED goals of Part III is to answer the question: What is a relationship?[1] The term *relationship* has become a commonplace buzzword in recent decades as well as in academic and scientific discourse[2] and, perceived from a more critical perspective, its definition is far from ubiquitous.[3] While this lack of definitional clarity spans diverse academic disciplines, it has already been shown that it is especially crucial in theology.[4] Whereas *relationship, relation,* or *relationality* are often treated as equivalents,[5] we propose a differentiation. Generally, *relation/relationality* is treated as a broader concept depicting, besides human relations, also the connection of "objects, data, ideas and events," whereas *relationship* is primarily used for relationships between humans or personal beings.[6] Härle makes an additional helpful differentiation *of relationship*

---

1. Fretheim has posed a set of very good questions concerning this issue (Fretheim, *God Enters*, 3).
2. See the introduction.
3. See, e.g., Welker, "Beziehung," 541.
4. See the introduction and section 2b.
5. See, e.g., Welker, "Beziehung," 541.
6. Rabens, "Sein und Werden," 113; Wan, "Relational Realism," 1. For a definition of *relationality* as pointing to the ontological dimension of *being related*, see Krautz, "Relationalität," 16–17. Concerning *relationality* as *relational ontology*, see also section 2b.

and relation (*Bezogenheit*) in that the former includes the relation *and* the parties involved,[7] whereas the latter points only to the relation, the connection itself.[8] In applying these broad differentiations and definitions, it is clear that taking the context into account in each definition is crucial and therefore restricts the considerations necessary.[9] Hence, our focus in this chapter is on human, social relationships.[10] Interestingly, the terminology of *relationship/relation*, meaning the different kinds of human interaction and especially romantic relationships, might have only evolved during the twentieth century.[11] Indeed, these terms cannot be found in the Bible[12] and they are absent in texts from the classical world.[13] According to Catherine LaCugna, the term *relation* was first used in the West by Tertullian (150–220) and in the East by Gregory of Nazianzus (329–390).[14] Having said that, most of what is comprised by the modern term *relationship* has clearly been present throughout all those time periods, only with different wording.[15] As a result, we are facing two challenges: On the one hand, it appears that a simple definition of the term *relationship* is not sufficient and we are reminded by Wittgenstein that "the meaning of a word is its use in the language"[16] or in other words, the important question is how the term is actually filled.[17] Consequently, we

---

7. The technical, neutral term used in German is *Relate*, which appears to be more adequate and precise than *parties* but has no English equivalent.

8. See Meyer zu Hörste-Bührer, *Gott und Menschen*, 17–18.

9. See also Meyer zu Hörste-Bührer, *Gott und Menschen*, 298.

10. For a discussion of the difference of sociality and relationality, see Gunton, *The One*, 229.

11. The English *relation* goes back to the Anglo-French *relacioun* in the late fourteenth century meaning *connection* and correspondence, derived from the Latin *relatio* meaning *report*. *Relationship* in the romantic sense occurs only by 1944 (Online Etymology Dictionary, s.v. "Relation," https://www.etymonline.com/word/relation#etymonline_v_10364; see also the entries "Relate" and "Relationship"). For a scholarly consideration of the similar German etymology of *Beziehung*, see Boschki, *Religionspädagogik*, 96; Brozio, *Vom pädagogischen Bezug*, 77–96.

12. Rabens, *Holy Spirit and Ethics*, 124, 133.

13. Rabens, *Holy Spirit and Ethics*, 133.

14. LaCugna, "The Relational God," 647.

15. For a discussion of the nature and interconnection of some of those relations in antiquity compared with a more modern understanding, see Rabens, *Holy Spirit and Ethics*, 124, 133; Konstan, *Friendship*.

16. Wittgenstein, *Philosophical Investigations*, §43.

17. See also the discussion about Brunner's changing terminology in section 3a.

need to investigate what everyday language[18] refers to by *relationship* and therefore the "breath-taking inner complexity"[19] of the actual structures and processes of human relationships cannot be avoided. On the other hand, since *relationship* is a collective term, a more precise definition and typology of the actual interactions under its umbrella appears to be useful to differentiate the relationship concept as a whole. This is also what Welker calls for: "It would be an important task to develop a typology of interpersonal relationships with different levels of complexity."[20] Indeed, the pressing question is where such a typology and investigation of the processes and structures of interpersonal relationships is to be found since only then can we attempt to answer the question whether and in which way God-human interaction is similar.

b) Relationship Science as Point of Reference

Reflection on relationships has traditionally been the domain of poets, writers, musicians and possibly also philosophers and theologians but not part of scientific investigation.[21] While these domains shed some light on how people experience relationships and what people believe relationships to be, they lack the informativity about the actual processes and structures of human interaction. For instance, there is often a discrepancy between what people say, believe, and feel and how they actually function and live. Hence, among other reasons, it is this discrepancy that makes the study and definition of relationships so complex. This lack of clarity concerning the actual processes and structures of relationships is also the reason why we believe that most definitions of relationships in former works of theology are deficient since they are based almost exclusively on considerations of philosophers and theologians.[22] While those studies are very valuable,[23] by mainly considering philosophers

---

18. Concerning the relevance of everyday language, see Schulte, *Wittgenstein*, 135; Aron and Mashek, "Conclusion," 416.

19. Welker, "Beziehung," 542 (TM).

20. Welker, "Beziehung," 547 (TM).

21. Campbell and Surra, "Research on Close Relationships," 4–5.

22. See, e.g., Brümmer, *Model of Love*, 39–141; Vacek, *Love, Human and Divine*; Glaw, *Bockmuehl*, 200–238.

23. Amongst other things, the mentioned works above *do* at least provide some definitions and reflections on human relationships while most theological endeavors simply utilize the relationship-terminology for the God-human dimension without

and theologians the danger of a pick-and-choose approach, circular reasoning and, thus, of a distorted picture of the nature of relationships arises.[24] In essence, we argue for a more "neutral" description of the processes and structures of human relationships that is based on concrete observation[25] and only then is brought into conversation with theology. Hence, we propose that empirical relationship science provides such an approach and offers an ideal and novel[26] point of reference for theology for three reasons: First, the theories of relationship science are based on empirical research and therefore yield a detailed analysis of the observed relational processes and structures.[27] A good definition of relationship science is that it "includes the theory, methods, observations, and conclusions of relationship-related research";[28] more specifically, the majority of research is concerned with close, dyadic relationships between lovers,

---

any or only a rudimentary consideration of the human processes behind the term (for some of the more positive examples see, e.g., "give-and-take relations" in Sanders, *God Who Risks*, 162; "reciprocity" in Oord et al., *Relational Theology*, 2; "responsible interaction" in McFague, *Metaphorical Theology*, 139).

24. Annette Glaw might be used as an example. While offering a stimulating book on the German theologian Klaus Bockmühl, she appears to have stepped into this trap in her last chapter (Glaw, *Bockmuehl*, 200–238). By depicting the God-human relationship in terms heavily informed by theologians like Brümmer and Vacek, which themselves draw from other theologians and philosophers, she uncritically adapts in certain parts a view of relationships (e.g., the centrality of emotions) that appears to be rather a projection than an investigation.

25. Boschki has a similar argumentation and proposes a phenomenological approach concerning the study of relationships, yet that seemingly "objectivistic neutrality" is a deception. Boschki, *Religionspädagogik*, 38–39 (TM). He advocates an interplay between phenomenology and empirical research and points out that in the *qualitative social sciences* both are united (91–92). See also Sattler, *Beziehungsdenken*, 328.

26. To the best of our knowledge, relationship science has not yet been comprehensively employed for theology. Rudimentarily it can be seen in Rabens, *Holy Spirit and Ethics*, 123; Rabens, "Sein und Werden." Others simply point to certain aspects of relationship science as potentially fruitful for further research (e.g., Glaw, *Bockmuehl*, 238). Usually the rare places to find relationship science within theological endeavors is to explain human behavior (e.g., Boschki, *Religionspädagogik*, 91–174) without making the additional step of analogical reasoning concerning God-human interaction. One exception is Sattler, *Beziehungsdenken*. She confirms that psychological observations so far have not been made fruitful for systematic theology and considers her own attempt to do so (using psychotherapy as reference for soteriology, 179–247) merely "motivational work" for further research (247 [TM]).

27. The appendix offers a brief introduction to and evaluation of the major theories of relationship science for the interested non-psychologist.

28. Gillath et al., "Theoretical Integration and Interdisciplinarity," 4.

Analogy of Relationship

mates, family members or friends.[29] In essence, relationship science has "the potential not only to advance knowledge regarding complex social behavior but also to provide an empirically informed framework."[30] Second, to study those relationship processes more comprehensively, the field of relationship science is becoming increasingly interdisciplinary by bringing together scientists from psychology, sociology, anthropology, communication science, as well as economists, marital and family therapists, health- and neuroscientists.[31] As a result, relationship science, on the one hand, breaks through the individualistic focus and tradition that social psychology usually takes[32] and on the other hand, avoids taking a broad, cultural, group-oriented approach found in anthropology and cultural studies.[33] Indeed, relationship scientists argue that close, dyadic relationships are a, if not the core domain influencing both the individual person and wider culture and therefore need to receive priority attention.[34] Hence, Reis et al. anticipate that "psychological science will be fundamentally altered for the better by recognition of the often central role of relationship processes."[35] In summary, relationship science has been chosen as our point of reference because it answers the "what is a relationship?" question based on reliable empirical and

---

29. Regan, *Close Relationships*, 10.

30. Gillath et al., "Theoretical Integration and Interdisciplinarity," 3.

31. Campbell and Surra, "Research on Close Relationships," 5; Fletcher et al., *Intimate Relationships*, 7–8. Some even count philosophy, history and theology amongst the contributing fields of research (Regan, *Close Relationships*, 18). One of the momentous discussions concerns the question of interdisciplinarity and multidisciplinarity, claiming that currently relationship science is rather multidisciplinary (no real integration between the contributing fields) than interdisciplinary ("integration of knowledge and practice") and that it should be evolving toward the latter (see, e.g., Gillath et al., "Theoretical Integration and Interdisciplinarity," 6; Regan, *Close Relationships*, 18; Reis, "Organizing Theme," 45). However, the majority of contributions at this stage come from social psychology and communication science and instead of major changes only "a gradual evolution" of the field is anticipated in the near future (Perlman and Duck, "Seven Seas," 12–13, 25).

32. Clark and Aragón, "Communal Relationships," 274; Campbell and Simpson, "Blossoming of Relationship Science," 4.

33. Fletcher et al., *Intimate Relationships*, 7. As such, relationship science can also be considered a bridge-builder between the individualism and collectivism dichotomy often pointed out concerning modernity and the biblical testimony (see, e.g., Richards and James, *Misreading Scripture with Individualist Eyes*).

34. Reis et al., "Emergence of Relationship Science," 567–68.

35. Reis et al., "Emergence of Relationship Science," 558–59.

increasingly interdisciplinary research with a non-individualistic yet also a non-collectivistic focus. In other words, relationship science focusses on the structures and processes of dyadic relationships.

Notwithstanding, two critical considerations need our attention, the first coming from outside the field of relationship science and the second coming from within. The first concerns whether psychology (relationship science) is an appropriate reference for theology and if so in what way? Whilst this is a very important question, its proper place for consideration is in the respective sections about transdisciplinary reasoning in Part IV where it will receive a more extensive treatment.[36] At this stage, it is sufficient to clarify that relationship science is appropriate since for now it is exclusively employed to depict the structures and processes of *human relationships* in order to compare them with God-human interaction so as to determine whether *relationship* is an accurate term and concept for this vertical dimension. As such, this book is not yet a truly transdisciplinary work, rather it aims to clarify its foundation in light of the relationship-concept. The second critical query, coming from within the field of relationship science, refers to a major body of work of relationship science that appears to have a "hedonic tone" by focusing on attraction-based relationships and "good feelings."[37] The critics point to the fact that much research is conducted from a modern, Western point of view and within a specific Western context.[38] Admittedly, these observations rightfully cast a shadow upon relationship science and could even question the value it has for our purposes. Hence, reliable research that evaluates the processes and structures of relationships has to be conducted across a vast variety of cultures and the corresponding theories have to approximate panhuman conceptions.[39] Consequently, the less basic and

---

36. See sections 9e and 10a.

37. Loving and Huston, "Back to the Future," 275–76.

38. Adams et al., "Cultural Grounding," 333–36. Major attention has been drawn to important differences between *independent*, individualist cultures (Western) and *interdependent*, collectivist cultures (Non-Western) that construe the self in more relational terms (see, e.g., Goodwin and Pillay, "Relationships, Culture, and Social Change," 698; Adams et al., "Cultural Grounding," 322–24; Cross and Gore, "Relational Self-Construal," 242). Consequently, in collectivist cultures kinship and "romantic" connections are also evaluated differently (Adams et al., "Cultural Grounding," 326–30; Goodwin and Pillay, "Relationships, Culture, and Social Change," 698–99), which leads to the question whether intimacy is a culturally universal concept (Adams et al., "Cultural Grounding," 331–33).

39. A term used by Sanders, *Theology in the Flesh*, 113.

more culturally specific areas of relationship science[40] are ignored in our investigation and we draw mainly from the two "universal" theories that are widely considered to be the grand theories of relationship science and "perhaps the two most influential conceptual frameworks" in this field:[41] *interdependence theory* and *attachment theory*. In essence, the two theories answer the two basic questions most relevant for our investigation: what are relationships (the focus of interdependence theory) and who are the parties involved (the focus of attachment theory)? Furthermore, the two theories overlap, often answer the same questions from two different perspectives and gather other important conceptions of relationship science, from which we will draw, under their "umbrella." For the reader who is not yet familiar with such concepts of relationship science, this would be the point to consider a brief introduction to interdependence theory and attachment theory within the larger context of other frameworks of relationship science, which can be found in the appendix.

Having justified and established our use of relationship science, we return to the proposed requirement of a more precise and nuanced typology of relationships. Relationship science has made many attempts to define the different types of relationships: A widespread typology differs between friendships, romantic-, family- (or kin-) and social relationships (acquaintances),[42] which appears to be too narrow and specific for our purposes. Others are too broad by simply distinguishing between attachments and affiliations.[43] Another differentiation of relationships is made with a complex matrix along the dimensions of voluntary/involuntary and personal/social,[44] or low-power/high-power and low-intimacy/high-intimacy.[45] Yet, the most widespread terminology found in relationship science and everyday life alike adds the relationship descriptors

---

40. Within relationship science the call for core principles is increasingly heard among scholars since unconnected "attention to conceptual and operational nuance may obscure" the results (Reis et al., "Perceived Partner Responsiveness," 202), but the field will benefit from "a better understanding of the core principles" that bring ideas and findings together (Reis, "Organizing Theme," 32).

41. Aron et al., "Self-Expansion Model," 92. See also Simpson, "Foundations of Interpersonal Trust," 597; Clark and Aragón, "Communal Relationships," 275–77; Campbell and Simpson, "Blossoming of Relationship Science," 7.

42. Regan, *Close Relationships*, 10.

43. Weiss's typology depicted by VanLear et al., "Relationship Typologies," 97–98.

44. VanLear et al., "Relationship Typologies," 95.

45. VanLear et al., "Relationship Typologies," 105.

personal, *close* or *intimate*.[46] Admittedly, agreement on the definition and differentiation of those terms is a challenge,[47] for there is no "right" or "wrong,"[48] yet a general consensus does exist among scholars. That said, this rather simple typology offers an ideal combination of precision and broadness as its categories are like levels of a pyramid, each being based on and further defining the former level/type.[49]

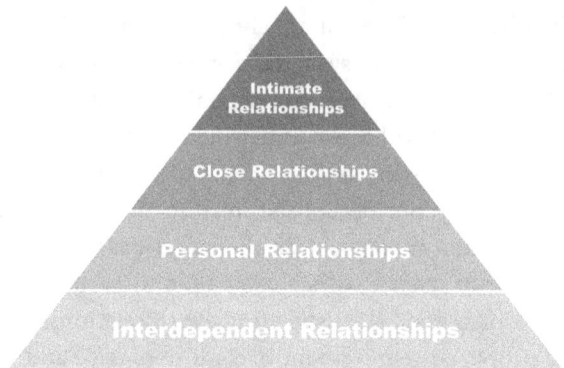

Figure 1: A pyramidal typology of relationships

Therefore, the categorization of personal, close, and intimate relationships has been chosen as the basis for our inquiry and the next chapter will be structured accordingly.[50]

---

46. See, e.g., Bradbury and Karney, *Intimate Relationships*, 8–11. For commonalities and differences between researchers' and laypersons' understandings of these terms, see Aron and Mashek, "Conclusion," 417.

47. Perlman and Duck, "Seven Seas," 27.

48. Berscheid et al., "Measuring Closeness," 83.

49. The pyramid-illustration is inspired and adapted from the funnel in Bradbury and Karney, *Intimate Relationships*, 8–11 (while our definitions of closeness and intimacy are slightly different). This progressing typology also mirrors the development of interdependence theory and can be perceived in Harold Kelley's works and book titles: Kelley and Thibaut, *Interpersonal Relations*; Kelley, *Personal Relationships*; Kelley et al., *Close Relationships*; Kelley et al., *Atlas*.

50. At this point a disclaimer seems mandatory: Chapter 8 does *not* further psychological research, but rather depicts the current findings of relationship science to then *further theology* by sharpening the understanding of the concept and terminology of relationships. Accordingly, the suitable level of depth in our investigation requires only occasionally consulting primary sources and original studies and draws mainly from handbooks and summarizing articles, which are the main hubs in this discipline's theory-building.

c) A Working Theory of Analogy

Part III aims to investigate and analyze the analogy between God-human and human relationships. Analogy, the Greek ἀναλογία, simply means the right relation or accordance[51] and it is this basic meaning that we refer to when using the term analogy in this work. However, it is not this simple since the term has a long and rich tradition in both philosophy and theology—starting from Plato and Aristotle and reaching its high point within the Scholastic theology of Thomas Aquinas[52]—and a diversity of different meanings attached to it.[53] Hence, when contemporary "pop-theological" books implicitly cite Aquinas with the distinction of *univocal, equivocal* and the "solution" of *analogical,* this does not reflect the complexity of the issue.[54] For example, it has been said that Aquinas did not develop a coherent doctrine of analogy and that "students of Thomas' work have come up with different interpretations of his 'theory of analogy,' if such it can be called."[55] Whilst with the Reformation analogy discussions outside of Catholicism had largely dried up,[56] they have at least received renewed attention concerning metaphors in the late twentieth century[57] and especially at the beginning of the twenty-first century due to questions of differences between analogy and metaphors often included in debates about open theism.[58] Accordingly, James F. Ross is correct in averring that "it seems that analogy theory both as linguistic theory and as metaphysical account of being has more innings to play in the history of theology."[59] Furthermore, different theories of analogy are an important part in a

---

51. Balz, "Ἀναλογία," 201. For a brief history of the term, see Ashworth, "Medieval Theories."

52. Aquinas, *Summa*, 1.13.5.

53. For a good, relatively comprehensive yet concise overview of the history of analogy approximately up to the year 2005, see Ross, "Analogy in Theology." For a brief overview of the medieval period, see Ashworth, "Medieval Theories."

54. See, e.g., Sproul, *What Can we Know About God?*, 9–11.

55. Stienstra, *YHWH Is the Husband of His People*, 45. Ashworth even goes as far that Aquinas "has very little to say about analogy as such." Ashworth, "Medieval Theories."

56. Ross, "Analogy in Theology," 141–42.

57. For a good overview, see Brümmer, *Model of Love*, 4.

58. See, e.g., White, "Metaphorical God"; Sanders, *God Who Risks*; Sanders, *Theology in the Flesh*; McFague, *Metaphorical Theology*; Schmid, *Gott ist ein Abenteurer*; DesCamp and Sweetser, "Metaphors for God," 207–38.

59. Ross, "Analogy in Theology," 143.

wide variety of scientific fields like mathematics, the natural sciences, law, psychology, and the arts,[60] which complicates the matter of analogy even more. Nonetheless, we will by and large bypass those current discussions and the overall theological history of analogy due to the lack of space and the focus of this book. Indeed, our desideratum is merely a working theory of analogy[61] for our current task of comparison. To this end, we build predominantly on Paul Bartha's evaluation of analogical theories and "common sense guidelines" and employ his surprisingly simple criteria put forward in *By Parallel Reasoning*.[62] Additionally, we will be critically informed by Dedre Gentner's *structure-mapping theory*,[63] one of the most influential theories of analogy, due to its relational and structural focus that makes it especially fitting for our comparison of relationships.[64]

To create clarity right from the beginning, it is helpful to differentiate between *analogy*, *analogical reasoning*, and an *analogical argument*. Bartha defines them as follows:

> An *analogy* is a comparison between two objects, or systems of objects, that highlights respects in which they are thought to be similar. *Analogical reasoning* is any type of thinking that relies upon an analogy. An *analogical argument* is an explicit representation of analogical reasoning that cites accepted similarities between two systems in support of the conclusion that some further similarity exists.[65]

---

60. For a brief introduction to the different theories, see Bartha, "Analogy and Analogical Reasoning." For a compendium of resources concerning analogy, see Guarini et al., "Resources for Research."

61. This terminology is inspired by the chapter *A Working Theory of Metaphor* in Heim, *Adoption*, 24–75.

62. We focus on the general aspects of his so-called *argumentation model* and not its detailed explication for different scientific disciplines. For an evaluation and appraisal of Bartha's work, see Earley, "By Parallel Reasoning."

63. See, e.g., Gentner, "Structure-Mapping"; Gentner et al., *The Analogical Mind*.

64. The two approaches are complementary (see Bartha, *Parallel Reasoning*, 326): Gentner's research wants to be *descriptive* and focuses on the psychology of the cognitive processes involved in analogical reasoning (59–72, 88). Bartha evaluates and critiques different theories of analogy (also structure-mapping theory) and aims to propose a philosophically plausible *normative* theory for analogical arguments (viii; 3). Both theories belong to the category of *general* or *wide ranging* models (Guarini et al., "Resources for Research," 96).

65. Bartha, *Parallel Reasoning*, 1.

Hence, in this book *analogy* is simply understood as a comparison between God-human interaction (as depicted by Emil Brunner) and human relationships (as depicted by relationship science) with the goal of evaluating their similarity.[66] However, what are the criteria for a good analogy? Not only is this a crucial question, but it is also the foundation for good analogical reasoning and a good analogical argument. Surprisingly, the qualitative evaluation of analogical reasoning has received very little attention.[67] Both common sense and many models of analogical reasoning propose that an analogy is better as more overall similarity two domains possess and becomes weaker as the differences accumulate. Admittedly, this reasoning initially makes sense but by not weighting the similarities and differences, it tends to circularly confirm itself, rendering vulnerable analogies that are built on individual preference.[68] Hence, some similarities and differences are more important than others and the critical question is how this should be evaluated. The surprisingly simple solution consists of a meticulous analysis of each domain separately, their defining properties, objects, and especially their "internal" relations, prior to the actual comparison between the domains.[69] The crucial factors *of* each domain will be the crucial factors of similarity *between* the domains. Furthermore, the comparison of the domains has to be a *structurally consistent* alignment, defined by *parallel connectivity* ("matching relations must have matching arguments") and *one-to-one correspondence*

---

66. Structure-mapping theory claims that "similarity is like analogy," meaning that the process of comparison is the same, namely "a structural alignment and mapping between mental representations" (Gentner and Markman, "Analogy and Similarity," 45). While structure-mapping theory differentiates other comparisons like *metaphor* and *literal similarity*, it treats them as congeneric with *analogy* (see, e.g., Gentner, "Structure-Mapping," 159–61; Gentner and Markman, "Analogy and Similarity," 48).

67. Bartha, *Parallel Reasoning*, vii–viii, 3.

68. Bartha, *Parallel Reasoning*, 12; 19–27. See also Schmid, *Gott ist ein Abenteurer*, 133; Brümmer, *Model of Love*, 6, 15; Gentner and Markman, "Analogy and Similarity," 46.

69. Bartha calls this, based on Mary Hesse, the *vertical relation* (Bartha, *Parallel Reasoning*, 14, 91–93). See also Miner, "Relational and Contextual Reasoning." Structure-mapping theory proposes with its *systematicy claim* that the relevant factors are always the "relations between objects, rather than attributes of objects" and within those relations the *higher-order relations*, which are more systematic, are to be preferred over *lower-order relations* (Gentner, "Structure-Mapping," 162, 164, 168). Whereas this principle clearly makes sense for our analogy of *relationships*, Bartha points out that *systematicy* should not be determining for every type of analogy. Structure-mapping theory's philosophical weakness is that it is too technical, not evaluating the domain on its own terms (Bartha, *Parallel Reasoning*, 59–72, 88).

of elements to avoid generalization.[70] Bartha calls those crucial factors within each domain the *prior association* and its comparison leads to either a positive (some crucial factors are similar) or a negative analogy (some crucial factors are not similar)[71] and it is the responsibility of the advocate of an argument to honestly make the relevant factors explicit, whether they support the argument or not. Hence, this will be the aim of the next chapter. The greater the similarity between the two domains, the more it makes sense to then reason analogically,[72] but without a positive analogy of the prior association, any analogical reasoning is redundant.[73]

Analogical reasoning, as already mentioned, is best expressed as an analogical argument since it requires to make the analogical process, the premises, and the conclusion explicit and therefore does not only aim at satisfying potential critics but also helps the advocate to honestly face the difficulties and weaknesses of a hypothesis. Nonetheless, an analogical argument need not be a complete explication of analogical reasoning but usually focusses on a certain aspect or conclusion.[74] That said, the foundation of every analogical argument is the comprehensive symmetric comparison of two domains.[75] This comparison, however, is in itself not yet analogical reasoning since it is based on theoretical knowledge of both domains one already has. Genuine analogical reasoning starts when treating one domain as the source (or base) for making novel or predictive statements about the target domain.[76] Analogies thus "are employed . . . to demonstrate the plausibility of hypotheses."[77] Hence, the relation be-

---

70. Gentner and Markman, "Analogy and Similarity," 47.

71. Bartha, *Parallel Reasoning*, 14, 25, 58, 94.

72. Again, it is not simply overall similarity but a similarity of the *relevant* factors. Some *positive* similarities are even *negatively* correlated with the argument and vice versa. For example, by treating the marriage of a very old couple as example for successful relationships, this might be *despite* the fact of the husband's power-abuse (for other examples, see Bartha, *Parallel Reasoning*, 71). This is one of the reasons why structure-mapping theory's systematicy claim falls short for an analogical argument since it does not consider the *meaning* of the higher-order relations. In order to reason analogically it is decisive to know *how* the features relate to the analogical conclusion (326–30).

73. Bartha, *Parallel Reasoning*, 103–4.

74. Bartha, *Parallel Reasoning*, 4–6.

75. For symmetry as psychologically natural starting point, see Bowdle and Gentner, "Informativity and Asymmetry," 244–45, 278–79.

76. Bartha, *Parallel Reasoning*, 42–43.

77. Bartha, *Parallel Reasoning*, 2.

tween the domains moves from symmetry to asymmetry[78] as something (XY) that is only known in the *source* is mapped unto the *target* in order to make a hypothesis (XY*) about the target *per facie* plausible.[79] An analogical argument thus takes the form: it is plausible that XY* holds in the target because of some crucial known (or accepted) similarities with the source domain, despite certain known (or accepted) secondary differences.[80] Therefore, the argument can be attacked primarily by criticizing the prior association and/or its comparison and not by questioning the hypothetical analogy.[81] However, flawed analogical reasoning does not always reveal a bad analogy. As Bartha points out, an "analogy has a life distinct from its application to a particular argument" and therefore it is often better "to try to make it work by finding a reformulation rather than to abandon" the analogy and the paradigm behind it.[82]

Consequently, it is our hope that the often flawed and insufficient analogical reasoning of *a personal relationship with God* might be reformulated and expanded rather than dismissed.[83] Our proposed working theory of analogy then has already been employed in chapter 5–7, where our main emphasis was to establish the prior association of God-human interaction through an in-depth study of Brunner's personal

---

78. Bartha calls this the *hypothetical analogy* (Bartha, *Parallel Reasoning*, 13–15). See also Gentner, "Structure-Mapping," 157; Gentner and Markman, "Analogy and Similarity," 47; Wolff and Gentner, "Metaphor Comprehension," 1459; Gentner et al., "Metaphor Is Like Analogy," 221–27.

79. Bartha calls this *generalization* (Bartha, *Parallel Reasoning*, 19–27; 105). In structure-mapping theory XY* are termed *candidate inferences* (Gentner and Markman, "Analogy and Similarity," 47). Usually the domain that is more *informative* is chosen as source (Bowdle and Gentner, "Informativity and Asymmetry," 247, 249, 276, 281) and structure-mapping theory also adds *systematicy* as a factor (Bowdle and Gentner, "Informativity and Asymmetry," 249, 274–75, 279, 281; Gentner and Markman, "Analogy and Similarity," 52).

80. Based on Bartha, *Reasoning*, 15.

81. Bartha, *Parallel Reasoning*, 27. Bartha exemplifies this with the objection of historical bias.

82. Bartha, *Parallel Reasoning*, 71, 330–31.

83. Gentner et al. have found that analogies and metaphors tend to *progressive abstraction*, meaning, initially novel analogies become increasingly conventional, ending up as mere idioms. In essence, this so called *career of metaphor* shows that what has started as comparison or simile (A is *like* B) has lost its novel explanatory power and literal meaning by being abstracted and coming out as polysemy. Gentner et al., "Metaphor Is Like Analogy," 210, 228, 231, 233–35, 238, 240. By implication, this might explain the demise of meaning for the Christian idiom or shibboleth of "a personal relationship with God."

correspondence based on the biblical testimony. For the second domain, the next chapter will establish the prior association of human relationships through a compilation of the main insights of relationship science. Furthermore, the comparison between the two domains will be made alongside every section of relationship science through an evaluation of the relevant similarities and differences. However, whereas the findings of relationship science will be shown in detail, the depiction of the God-human relationship will only be summarizing, implicitly referring to the detailed evaluation already made in Part Two. As a result, after meeting Bartha's requirement of an argumentative approach, the findings of the comparison will be summarized in a tabular representation and final conclusions will be made.

8

Comparing Human and God-Human Relationships

a) A Personal Relationship with God?

THERE IS A WIDE consensus among scholars on what defines any relationship: *interdependence*.[1] Interdependence is defined as "the process by which interacting people influence one another's experiences (i.e., the effects individuals have on other people's thoughts, emotions, motives, behaviour, and outcomes)."[2] Whereas the concept of interdependence is very broad,[3] it nonetheless limits what a relationship is and is not. First, a relationship is between two or more persons and each person's outcomes are not determined individually or independently.[4] Second, in a relationship each person influences the other, meaning that the individual is not

---

1. See, e.g., Arriaga, "Interdependence Theory Analysis," 39; Berscheid et al., "Measuring," 81; Rusbult et al., "Interdependence, Closeness, and Relationships," 144; Bradbury and Karney, *Intimate Relationships*, 7–8; Adams et al., "Cultural Grounding," 324.

2. Van Lange and Balliet, "Interdependence Theory," 65. For similar definitions, see Johnson and Johnson, "Social Interdependence Theory," 288; Cook and Kenny, "The Actor–Partner Interdependence Model," 101; Gaines and Hardin, "Interdependence Revisited," 554.

3. In a sense, "everyone in the world is interdependent . . . with everyone else" (Kelley et al., *Atlas*, 26).

4. However, there are situations within a relationship where two people can withdraw entirely and *appear* independent (see Kelley et al., *Atlas*, 44).

unilaterally dependent.[5] Consequently, every relationship is characterized by mutuality, bi-directionality[6] or reciprocity,[7] which distinguishes it from mere *relation* that can be one-directional.[8] As such, interdependence is the most basic structural characteristic that builds the foundation for the more specific types of relationships.

Reciprocity, the term we have chosen for God-human interaction, clearly reflects this basic feature of relationships and is also inherent in Brunner's terminology of personal correspondence; both terms refer to give-and-take communication and interaction, mutually affecting the persons involved. *Interdependence*, on the other hand, appears to make an even stronger, more pointed statement: both partners depend on each other. Can this be said of God? Is the Creator dependent on the creature? Indeed, this is a very fundamental question and could "choke" our analogy of relationship from the very beginning. However, while *interdependence* could be regarded as meaning symmetric dependence, it is not since it only excludes unilateral but not asymmetric dependence. Hence, we speak of a very clear asymmetric reciprocity or interdependence since God's dependence on humans is very different from the human's dependence on God. Humans are ontologically dependent on God, their very being dependent on him, whereas God's dependence is out of love and choice; God is absolutely free but the human only relatively so. Nonetheless, out of this absolute freedom God creates humans as actual counterparts to himself, with the freedom to say "yes" or "no" to him, and with this love-act God makes himself, in this specific way, dependent on his human creatures and is affected by their answer and by their actions

---

5. Johnson and Johnson, "Social Interdependence Theory," 287. However, there are extreme situations of relationships where one person *appears* to be unilaterally dependent on the other (see Kelley et al., *Atlas*, 47).

6. Bradbury and Karney, *Intimate Relationships*, 7.

7. Defined as "going both ways" and not as "returning the same way." These terms, as well as *interdependence*, are solely structural relationship descriptors and express in no way a qualitative distinction as in other theological works, where they are often used for the theological concept of *perichoresis* as a relational ontology rather than a relationship descriptor (e.g., Balswick et al., *Reciprocating Self*, 37, 72, 340). Whilst the point of bi-directionality instead of one-directionality is the same, these authors often use this terminology for what we have termed *intimacy* in this work. For a similar "neutral" definition of *reciprocal*, see Meyer zu Hörste-Bührer and Bührer, "Schlüssel zu Pluralität und Einheit," 191.

8. See sections 2b and 7a for the differentiation of *relationship* and *relation* pointing to one-directionality. In addition, to *be related to* or to *relate to* does not have to include any action of another agent.

throughout salvation history.[9] Brunner is very clear that the biblical testimony has no room for a sole-efficiency (*Alleinwirksamkeit*) of God but describes true inter-dependence.[10]

The relationship descriptor *personal* characterizes a setting when each person in the interdependent relationship cannot simply be replaced by another person. For example, whereas every role-based relationship between teacher and student is interdependent, it only qualifies as personal when the outcome depends on a specific teacher and/or student.[11] Hence, personal relationships are fundamentally *interpersonal* and *interactional*;[12] *interaction* is defined as a function of two specific people in a specific interdependent situation involving their respective needs, thoughts, motives and wished-for outcomes.[13] Accordingly, the descriptor *personal* more precisely refers to *intrapersonal* (the unique disposition of each person) and *interpersonal* (their unique interaction) and to both being inextricably and uniquely interwoven with each other.[14] Consequently, in personal relationships "*between*-person relations are as meaningful as the individuals themselves"[15] and therefore both statements are true: the relation is formed by the individuals and the individuals are affected and even formed by the relation.[16] In summary, a personal relationship refers to the characteristic of a relationship as unique, interdependent and ongoing interaction of unique individuals.[17]

---

9. For dependence-language see, e.g., Fretheim, *God Enters*, 16, 80.

10. See section 6c. The questions of *freedom* and *asymmetry* will further be evaluated in section 8b about power.

11. See Regan, *Close Relationships*, 6–7.

12. See, e.g., Fehr, "Prototype Model of Intimacy," 20.

13. This renders the formula also referred to as *SABI*: Interaction = f(S, A, B). See the appendix for more context to these kinds of formulas. See also Rusbult and van Lange, "Why Interdependence Theory," 2050.

14. See Rusbult et al., "Interdependence, Closeness, and Relationships," 152; Arriaga, "Interdependence Theory Analysis," 40–42, 45, 48, 52, 54, 59.

15. Rusbult and van Lange, "Why Interdependence Theory," 2050.

16. See Rusbult et al., "Interdependence, Closeness, and Relationships," 156; Aron and Mashek, "Conclusion," 416; Arriaga, "Interdependence Theory Analysis," 51. This circular aspect of relationships forming and being formed by individuals is particularly studied and depicted by attachment theory (see the appendix).

17. What is the difference between *interaction* and *relationship*? While an "interaction episode" technically might be called relationship, the term is usually reserved for *ongoing* or *repeated interactions* and not for "isolated exchanges" (Regan, *Close Relationships*, 4–5). As such, an interaction episode is very similar to what Brunner has termed *encounter*.

Indeed, this indissoluble unity of the intrapersonal and the interpersonal, this interpenetration of the relationship partners and the relationship, is exactly what Brunner's theological anthropology proposes. On the one hand, the person is defined by relationality (relational ontology): First, God, as Trinity, is relational from eternity. Second, humans, as *imago Dei*, mirror God's relationality and thus are relational, interconnected from creation with God, from birth with other humans and, in a third, different sense, also with the rest of creation. On the other hand, the relationship is also formed by the persons and their interaction. Hence, due to the human's revolt against God, the original positive relationship is lost and as a result, the human's very nature, his personal disposition, is in contradiction within himself, which also leads to the brokenness of relationships. This circular process and reasoning is confirmed especially by attachment theory and its effects will be further evaluated below. For now, we hold that God-human relationships are clearly always personal since it is *this* God and *this* human that come together. Brunner's central term *encounter* thus reflects this unique interaction between the unique divine and human persons, leading to a specific kind of relationship that is not primarily role-based or abstracted or even generally "religious" but essentially personal.

b) A Close Relationship with God?

Based on our definition of personal relationships the descriptor *close* further qualifies this type of relationship with "strong, frequent, and diverse interdependence that lasts over a considerable period of time."[18] While many scholars mirror this definition[19] they also point to the term's blurry distinction in relationship science from *intimacy*.[20] However, we use the term *closeness* only for the intensity of interdependent interaction (also

---

18. Kelley et al., *Close Relationships*, 38.

19. See, e.g., Rusbult et al., "Interdependence, Closeness, and Relationships," 157–58; Campbell and Surra, "Research on Close Relationships," 3; Berscheid et al., "Measuring Closeness," 82.

20. See Rusbult et al., "Interdependence, Closeness, and Relationships," 137; Campbell and Surra, "Research on Close Relationships," 3; Gillath et al., "Theoretical Integration and Interdisciplinarity," 4; Berscheid et al., "Measuring Closeness," 82; Loving and Huston, "Back to the Future," 275, 277.

defined as its degree[21] or its variation of strength[22]), hereby temporarily excluding the partner's sentiment for each other and the relationship.[23] Therefore, it is the influence of one or both partners that is measured, its frequency, diversity, strength and duration.[24] This influence can be "good" or "bad," healthy or harmful[25] and can lead, in proportion to the partner's degree of closeness, to either a relational "heaven" or "hell." In other words, one's greatest enemy and one's dearest friend both appear to be very close.[26] Hence, closeness is not identical with relationship satisfaction, since emotionally close (intimate) and behaviorally close relationships are differentiated.[27]

However, the descriptor *close* does not merely refer to a structural property of relationships, but a conscious cognition and a subjective perception of closeness.[28] For example, whereas a relationship between a father and his child is structurally very interdependent, it is only called close by the person being aware of this interdependence. Furthermore, the underlying interdependent structures and processes of closeness are perceived only by their effects;[29] the more intense the closeness the more obvious are its effects. In the father-child example, for instance, the child might only realize the closeness of the father by the "effect" of him being responsive to its needs. This view of closeness as *cognitive interdependence*[30] is also conceptualized as *including other in the self* (IOS), which points to the fact that in close relationships one treats the resources, perspectives and even identities of another person as one's own.[31] IOS, as a conception of closeness, is especially helpful since it offers also a tool to

21. Collins and Feeney, "Attachment Theory Perspective," 164.
22. Reis et al., "Perceived Partner Responsiveness," 217.
23. Berscheid et al., "Measuring Closeness," 82–83; Loving and Huston, "Back to the Future," 277; Aron and Mashek, "Conclusion," 421.
24. Regan, *Close Relationships*, 11–13; Berscheid et al., "Measuring Closeness," 82.
25. Adams et al., "Cultural Grounding," 328.
26. See Rusbult et al., "Interdependence, Closeness, and Relationships," 144.
27. Regan, *Close Relationships*, 100.
28. Rusbult et al., "Interdependence, Closeness, and Relationships," 157–58; Collins and Feeney, "Attachment Theory Perspective," 164; Ickes et al., "Closeness as Intersubjectivity," 357–58.
29. Campbell and Surra, "Research on Close Relationships," 3.
30. Agnew et al., "Cognitive Interdependence," 941, 953.
31. Aron et al., "Self-Expansion Model," 102; Aron et al., "Including Other in the Self," 27. For the connection of IOS with interdependence theory and attachment theory, see Gaines and Hardin, "Interdependence Revisited," 563–64.

measure perceived closeness: the *IOS scale* takes the complex processes of closeness into account and molds them into a simple illustration of two (overlapping) circles as shown in figure 2.³²

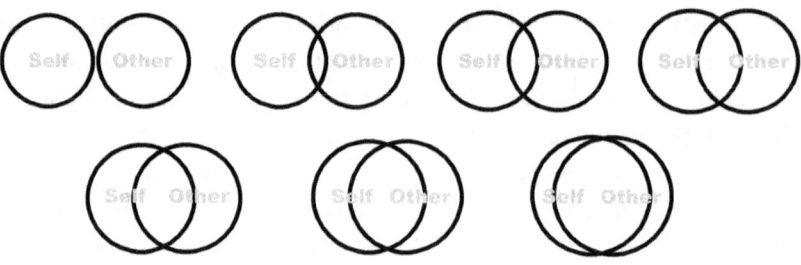

Figure 2: Including other in the self (IOS) scale

Participants in studies are asked to circle the picture which best describes their relationship to help them "access" what they otherwise could not articulate as precisely. Aron et al. suppose that "this measure has been so successful because the metaphor of overlapping circles representing self and other corresponds to how people actually process information about self and others in relationships."³³ Again, whilst one could circle a close connection due to one's relationship satisfaction (wishing for more closeness), one could also circle the same picture due to feelings of "too-closeness" (wishing for less closeness).³⁴ Indeed, the IOS scale simplifies, summarizes, and illustrates our definition of closeness as the intensity of interdependence and we will come back to it in different contexts throughout this chapter.

That said, it has been shown³⁵ that the God-human relation is objectively very close since the very being of humans is dependent on God and God, through creating, has a close love-bond to his creature. However, this structural closeness can be perceived very differently. Indeed, the human perspective can be entirely ignorant of this ontic closeness while this does not the least reduce the actual interdependence. Furthermore, by

---

32. See, e.g., Agnew et al., "Thinking Close," 104.
33. Aron et al., "Including Other in the Self," 33.
34. See, e.g., Aron et al., "Self-Expansion Model," 107.
35. See chapter 4.

perceiving this actual close interdependence, humans can become very hostile, or in Brunner's words revolting, trying to get rid of God due to an illusion of independence. Hence, by perceiving God as enemy, humans become foes, which effects and can be observed in corresponding acts; reminding us of the passage in Colossians 1:21: "And you were at one time strangers and enemies in your minds as expressed through your evil deeds" (NET).[36] However, God is wishing for more closeness and therefore intimacy[37] and does not stop showing his grace in persuading his creature, which might eventually lead humans to perceive these actions as God's love or God's wrath.[38] Therefore, while the structural aspects of closeness are universal, the personal aspects can vary very much according to the parties involved, as is the case in the God-human relationship. Consequently, having defined *closeness*, the actual dynamic of interaction behind this concept requires further investigation, leading us first to the question of motivation for closeness and then to the power-question.

Motivation: Exchange vs. Communal Closeness

There are basically two motivations for or modes of close relationships: *exchange*[39] and *communal* orientations. Simply put, exchange motivation focusses on individual outcomes with the relationship as a means to this end, whereas communal motivation focusses on relationship outcomes as an end in itself. Having said that, this does not necessarily mean that an exchange orientation is more focused on the self (egoistic, selfish) and a

---

36. Concerning the *effects*, see also Brunner's reading of the fruit of the Spirit and the fruit of the flesh in Galatians 5:16–25 (Brunner, *Wahrheit als Begegnung*, 167; ETR 167).

37. See section 8c.

38. While this is not the place to discuss God's wrath it would be an interesting study to analyze Brunner's development in this matter and whether his understanding of wrath has moved from *objective* to *subjective* (or better *relational*). See, e.g., Brunner, *The Mediator*, 495–96, 516–19; Brunner, *Man in Revolt*, 134, 163, 169–70, 187; Brunner, *Werk des heiligen Geistes*, 20; Brunner, *Wahrheit als Begegnung*, 100–101; ETR 101; Brunner, *Dogmatics I*, 161–74, 230; Brunner, *Dogmatics II*, 286–97; Brunner, *Dogmatik III*, 470–73; ETR 420–23; Swarat, "Gesetz und Evangelium," 185–204; Williams, "Brunner and Barth on Philosophy," 246.

39. The term *exchange* in this context is defined in a narrower sense than in the usual context of *exchange theory* (see Clark and Aragón, "Communal Relationships," 257).

communal orientation on the other (altruistic, unselfish).[40] Nonetheless, the "rules" in these two modes of close relationships are entirely different.

Exchange relationships are concerned with equity norms, meaning that benefits are provided "with the expectation of receiving a comparable benefit in return."[41] For example, while in close business relationships actual goods are exchanged and actual books are kept, in social exchange relationships the "goods" might be support, love, or affection and the "books" of obligations and expectations are invisible but nevertheless very real. Caryl Rusbult's *investment model* is a very influential and sophisticated model of this exchange norm.[42] As such, *investment* refers to the model's basic formula:

$$\text{OUTCOME} = \text{REWARDS} - \text{COSTS}$$

Consequently, this model might go beyond an equity norm in relationships, proposing that humans want to maximize their "profit" even in social relationships.[43] According to the investment model, this relationship-profit (satisfaction) is measured by comparing what one gets out of a relationship with what one believes to deserve.[44] However, one only remains in a less-than-perfectly satisfying relationship if one believes that there are no better alternatives available (dependence).[45] Consequently, this model of exchange relationships comes to the rather sober conclusion that humans only commit to a relationship either because the satisfaction is high (they want to) or the dependency is high (they have to).[46] Thus, this explains, at least in part, why people might desire more closeness (satisfaction) or less closeness (dependency). Yet another perspective on exchange relationships is based on the IOS

---

40. Clark and Aragón, "Communal Relationships," 257–58.

41. Clark and Aragón, "Communal Relationships," 257; Reis et al., "Perceived Partner Responsiveness," 205.

42. Regan, *Close Relationships*, 105. For the following depiction of the investment model, see Bradbury and Karney, *Intimate Relationships*, 120–23.

43. For a discussion concerning the normativity of equity and its mixed evidence, see Regan, *Close Relationships*, 100.

44. This is the *comparison level* (CL) leading to the formula: SATISFACTION = OUTCOME - CL.

45. This is the *comparison level for alternatives* (CL_{alt}) leading to the formula: DEPENDENCY = OUTCOME - CL_{alt}. See also Miller, *Intimate Relationships*, 165–66; Finkel et al., "Psychology of Close Relationships," 399.

46. Leading to the formula: COMMITMENT = SATISFACTION + DEPENDENCY. See also Rusbult et al., "Commitment," 618.

concept, perceiving the motivation to include the other in the self as *self-expansion*.[47] Self-expansion refers to the promise of acquiring what another person has and oneself is lacking to expand toward one's ideal self.[48] In other words, one does aspire after a close relationship with the other as means to the end of self-expansion, which has also been called *egological intersubjectivity*.[49] As such, the self-expansion model is congruent with the investment model since the driving question is "what's in it for me" and, consequently, better alternatives lead to relationship dissolution.[50] In summary, an exchange-relationship is stable and "good" when both parties are satisfied due to the more or less equal personal gain they get out of the relationship. Consequently, within exchange-relationships, satisfaction and relational intimacy are not isomorphic.[51]

Communal relationships, in contrast, do not keep track records; a quid-pro-quo approach would even be considered an insult.[52] Communal norms lead to giving benefits in response to other's needs noncontingently, yet with the hope of being reciprocated.[53] Clark and Aragón mention that "they are the relationships that are most difficult to establish and to maintain. They are also the relationships people value most."[54] While most communal relationships are considered to be mutual and symmetric (e.g., friendships), the clearest examples of communal strength are asymmetric parent-child relationships, exemplifying the level of one's care for another's welfare.[55] Yet, as already mentioned, the defining feature of communal relationships is not a radical "you"-orientation (selfless altruism) but a "we"-orientation characterized by a "relatively weak

---

47. Aron et al., "Self-Expansion Model," 90–91, 109.

48. Aron et al., "Self-Expansion Model," 94.

49. Ickes et al., "Closeness as Intersubjectivity," 359–60. Rusbult, referring to the so-called *Michelangelo Phenomenon*, argues that this process is not a "straightforward self-expansion" but an "ideal-self-expansion." Rusbult et al., "Self Processes," 385.

50. Aron et al., "Self-Expansion Model," 100.

51. Prager and Roberts, "Deep Intimate Connection," 47.

52. Clark and Aragón, "Communal Relationships," 261–62, 266. For a slightly more pessimistic view, see Miller, *Intimate Relationships*, 163, 196–200, 204.

53. Clark and Aragón, "Communal Relationships," 257–58, 266; Reis et al., "Organizing Construct," 205.

54. Clark and Aragón, "Communal Relationships," 255.

55. See, e.g., Clark and Aragón, "Communal Relationships," 255–57, 263–64, 266, 273–74; Rusbult and van Lange, "Interdependence, Interaction, and Relationships," 369.

distinction between self and other,"[56] which is illustrated by the IOS scale. According to IOS, in communal relationships, the single pronoun use (I, you) makes way for the first-person plural pronoun (we, us, our, ours) signifying a stronger merging and a closer relationship.[57] In contrast to the self-expansion model, this aspect of IOS refers to a more intimate connection between the partners so that they treat "whatever happens to the other as happening to the self."[58] This intimacy that is even willing to sacrifice one's own benefit for the wellbeing of the relationship or the other will be treated in more detail below.[59] For now, we summarize that within communal relationships, in contrast to exchange norms, relational satisfaction and intimacy are indeed isomorphic. While it has been shown that these two modes of relationship are in theory diametrically opposed to each other, it is not always clear or obvious to distinguish the two in practice.[60] As such, it is possible that one person in a close relationship functions within an exchange framework whereas the other lives according to communal norms, leading to misunderstandings and conflict.

Indeed, this is exactly the dilemma between God and humans. God is not in "exchange-mode" since he does not need anything from humans, yet wants them as whole persons being in community with him.[61] Brunner's interpretation of the biblical testimony renders God's motivation as clearly communal, as an I-You orientation, as love. What Brunner calls *I-You* is identical with what relationship science terms *communal relationships*. Humans on the other hand, due to their *status corruptus*, function by and large in "exchange-mode," which is identical with Brunner's I-it orientation and sin. Interestingly in relationship science, there is an ongoing discussion about whether an exchange framework is too pessimistic or a communal framework is too optimistic.[62] The Bible, how-

---

56. Ickes et al., "Closeness as Intersubjectivity," 361.

57. Agnew et al., "Cognitive Interdependence," 942; Ickes et al., "Closeness as Intersubjectivity," 365.

58. Aron et al., "Self-Expansion Model," 105–6. They also point to the mounting evidence that even the corresponding brain regions for self and other "overlap quite literally."

59. See section 8c.

60. See, e.g., Clark and Aragón, "Communal Relationships," 258–59.

61. In this Brunner appears to be more nuanced then Brümmer's depiction of God's "need"-love (see, e.g., Brümmer, *Model of Love*, 237–42).

62. See Bradbury and Karney, *Intimate Relationships*, 123; Noller, "Bringing It All Together," 772; Miller, *Intimate Relationships*, 163, 196–200, 204.

ever, according to Brunner, depicts human relationality as both, linking the communal orientation to the primal *status integratis* (true human), which is broken but not "lost," and the exchange orientation to the *status corruptus* (real human) that needs redemption and restoration. One of Brunner's examples of this relational confusion is the law. From God's communal perspective he communicates *himself* in the law, yet from a human exchange perspective, the law only communicates *something* that needs to be achieved in order to get *something* from God, resulting in the human dilemma of not being able to "bring" what is needed to "get" what is wanted.[63] In essence, this depiction corresponds perfectly with Rusbult's investment model. Furthermore, since God is all-powerful and does not need anything from humans, the human feels powerless and perceives God in a distorted picture as a harsh Cosmic Ruler and Lord and therefore wishes for less closeness and searches for independence. That said, the investigation of the power-question in relationships will shed further light on this dynamic.

Power: Voluntary vs. Involuntary Closeness

As has already been shown, closeness is a "neutral" concept referring to the intensity of interdependence that can either be desired or despised. However, whether a close relationship is perceived as positive or negative depends on multiple factors and their combinations.[64] One of those factors has been recognized in the preceding section as the question of the relationship motivation or mode as an exchange or communal orientation.[65] Other intertwined factors are structural like the question of whether a relationship is voluntary or involuntary. Voluntary relationships are chosen, like friendships or romantic relationships, whereas involuntary relationships are exogenously established, like family or kin relations.[66] However, since voluntariness does not automatically determine the perception of a relationship as positive or negative, another

---

63. This is not the place to reflect Brunner's understanding of the law in detail. For further investigations see, e.g., Brunner, *Wahrheit als Begegnung*, 122–23; ETR 122; Brunner, *Faith*, 59–62; Brunner, *Dogmatics I*, 282; Brunner, *Dogmatics II*, 223, 229–30; Brunner, *Dogmatik III*, 484–85; ETR 433–34.

64. Mashek and Sherman, "Desiring Less Closeness," 348.

65. That this orientation also reflects one's personality is supported by attachment theory (see section 8c and the appendix).

66. Regan, *Close Relationships*, 10.

decisive structural factor, even the tipping point in the perception of closeness, is power.

Power in relationships is a structural dimension concerning the question of asymmetry vs. symmetry of dependence.[67] Asymmetric dependence means that "one person's actions play a greater role in determining the outcomes of both individuals."[68] In other words, power is defined as "relative control over another's valued outcomes" and as such power is always power over somebody.[69] In essence, power renders two forms of asymmetric dependence: First, dependence as *partner-controlled*, meaning that the power holder unilaterally determines the dependent's outcomes. In its pure and constant form, this dependence appears to be rather extreme and absolute and since there is no interdependence[70] one could question to speak of a relationship at all. The second form is dependence as *jointly-controlled* and means that the power holder has very real power that is used to influence the dependent's actions toward desired outcomes.[71] Indeed, this is the most common form of power within relationships and one of its foremost examples are parent-child dyads,[72] which will soon be further analyzed. This asymmetric influence is commonly based on six resources that make a power holder superior (*bases of power*): rewards, coercion, legitimacy, expertise, reference, and information.[73] Relevant for us is that all of those bases of power involve a certain amount of volition and cooperation on the side of the dependent, who weighs up costs and benefits. Only brute force and manipulation would bypass this freedom of decision and render a completely partner-controlled situation.[74] In summary, power, namely various degrees of asymmetry, is an issue in almost all relationships, even if only situationally or

---

67. VanLear et al., "Relationship Typologies," 104.

68. Kelley et al., *Atlas*, 249.

69. Fiske and Berdahl, "Social Power," 680, 684, 688. As such, "power is not a consequence (influence) or an individual attribute (personality), it is outcome control" (684). See also Miller, *Intimate Relationships*, 362–63.

70. See our definition in section 8a.

71. Kelley et al., *Atlas*, 250–51. Others call this *fate control* and *behavior control* (Miller, *Intimate Relationships*, 364).

72. Kelley et al., *Atlas*, 251–53.

73. Fiske and Berdahl, "Social Power," 680; Miller, *Intimate Relationships*, 365–66.

74. Fiske and Berdahl, "Social Power," 681. Another differentiation of power is *soft* and *harsh power*. Soft power uses social outcomes and harsh power uses economic and physical ones (Fiske and Berdahl, "Social Power," 682). A similar categorization is made with *particularistic* and *universalistic power* (Miller, *Intimate Relationships*, 367).

transitorily.[75] However, the extent of asymmetric dependence determines the intensity of its impact on a relationship. Hence, power and its effects are most clearly perceived and experienced in situations of conflicting interests since the power holder would be able to get his or her way over and against the dependent. Consequently, this lack of control of the less powerful person makes him or her vulnerable[76] and can be one of the reasons for wanting to be less close to the other person.[77] Yet, this relative independence of the powerful vs. the relative dependence of the powerless is not as unambiguous as it generally appears. First, the literature on power widely neglects the aspect of the power holder's responsibility and the potential dilemma that comes along with the decision to use power for the wellbeing of the other.[78] Indeed, a conflicting situation is always costly either for the dependent or the person in power who chooses to be benevolent, yet, since the power holder is responsible for the outcome she or he additionally bears the "burden of decision" to be either self- or other-oriented. Accordingly, the stereotype of the self-absorbed power holder and the generally negative depiction of power does fall short.[79] Furthermore, there is, secondly, an equally ambivalent perception of the power differential for dependents, even when benefitting from a power holder's benevolence. For instance, personal relationships are expected to be mutual, therefore, having to accept the "grace of a benefactor" might lower one's self-esteem, lead to feelings of inferiority, and finally end in a desire for less closeness.[80] The relational dilemma for the less powerful person according to the investment model is, however, the lack of alternatives to receive equally good outcomes.

This power dilemma, for the power holder as well as for the dependent, is fundamentally affected and altered by the two modes of relationship already explored. By understanding and framing a relationship based on exchange norms, the dilemma cannot be solved since the exchange asymmetry always leads to either an abuse of power or to

---

75. Noller, "Bringing It All Together," 784.

76. Rusbult et al., "Interdependence, Closeness, and Relationships," 155.

77. Mashek and Sherman, "Desiring Less Closeness," 344; Laurenceau and Kleinman, "Intimacy in Personal Relationships," 648. See also Kouneski and Olson, "ENRICH," 123–24.

78. Fiske and Berdahl, "Social Power," 686.

79. Kelley et al., *Atlas*, 254–58.

80. Kelley et al., *Atlas*, 259–60; Cavallo et al., "Interpersonal Risk," 124.

feelings of inferiority and, therefore, to a depiction of power as negative.[81] Communal orientation, by contrast, enables a positive perception of a power differential due to the premise that the relationship is an end in itself.[82] The power holder, then, does not merely act beneficially towards the dependent, hereby emphasizing the asymmetry, but empowers. As such, empowerment can be defined as stressing joint-control even when the more powerful person could exercise partner-control.[83] As a result, "perceptions of equality contribute a great deal to feelings of love and acceptance."[84] Consequently, being responsive and "benevolent" in asymmetric communal relationships means that the power holder gives the dependent control and power to also affect him or her.[85] In other words, the dependent is given the power (freedom) to act voluntarily in an involuntary setting. Indeed, in a communal relationship, since the relationship itself is the goal, the less powerful person always has the ability or "power" to affect the more powerful person due to the reciprocal nature of the relationship. Hence, parent-child relationships are a very clear example of this asymmetric communal dynamic: On the one hand, parents are always affected by their children due to their communal bond. On the other hand, it is generally viewed necessary for the healthy development of children that parents also gradually empower them from a young age,[86] which leads to asymmetric reciprocity. Having said that, the relationship still remains asymmetric, yet the social power differential changes gradually and also naturally with the children coming of age. Put differently, from the children's perspective the relationship starts and remains involuntarily (children are always their parent's children), yet it has the potential to become increasingly voluntary, even a friendship[87]

81. Fiske and Berdahl, "Social Power," 685–87.

82. See Miller, *Intimate Relationships*, 376.

83. See Johnson and Johnson, "Social Interdependence Theory," 297, 334.

84. Cavallo et al., "Interpersonal Risk," 124; see also Cross and Gore, "Relational Self-Construal," 239.

85. See Clark and Aragón, "Communal Relationships," 271.

86. Noller, "Bringing It All Together," 783; Dix and Buck, "Emergence of Social Approach," 60–62; Kelley et al., *Atlas*, 263–66. Indeed, Fiske and Berdahl suggest that without parents actively leading their children into "freedom," "Communal orientations could theoretically . . . create paternalistic exploitation in the name of caring." Fiske and Berdahl, "Social Power," 687. For a cultural perspective on this topic see, e.g., Adams et al., "Cultural Grounding," 331. For the general benefits of a developmental perspective on social psychology, see Loving and Huston, "Back to the Future," 279.

87. For characteristics of different types of friendships, see VanLear et al.,

since adult children are able to choose to be intimately connected with their parents.

The power-question lies at the heart of whether one can justifiably speak of a relationship with God and if so, what kind of relationship it is. Humans, as has been shown, often perceive God as the absolute Ruler and Lord—and rightly so. God, as the all-powerful and all-free, could have chosen unilaterally to determine the human's life and outcome, but he did not. Instead, he chose to create an actual counterpart to himself with the freedom to say "yes" or "no" (jointly controlled power). Yet again, the power differential remains, and the relationship is clearly asymmetric: God's freedom is absolute, the human's freedom only relatively so. We have shown that the God-human relationship truly is interdependent but God's dependence on humans is of a different sort than humankind's dependence on God since their very existence depends on him. Hence, as with all relationships, it is not easy to decide whether the God-human relationship is voluntary or involuntary, be it from God's point of view or the human's. The human's fundamental ontic relation to God is involuntary, yet the actual relationship can become voluntary by choice. In turn, from God's point of view, after the voluntary decision to create humankind, the relation becomes voluntarily-involuntary. In other words, this relational structure matches the familial setting of parent-child relationships. Parents do not have to have children, yet from the moment they decide to have them, they cannot "unhave" them. On the other hand, children have no say in being born, yet they have a developing say in the type of relationship they will have with their parents. As such, based on the last section, it is clear that the power-question in God-human interaction has to be answered on a communal background.[88] God might influence (joint-control) humans by using his superiority (bases of power) in legitimacy, expertise, reference, information as well as through rewards and maybe even in some form of coercion,[89] yet he does so with a communal motivation and in order to empower

---

"Relationship Typologies," 103.

88. For examples of implicit and unconscious exchange frameworks influencing the biblical interpretation, see Robinson, *Metaphor*, 137; McIlroy, "Theology of Atonement," 31–32.

89. God's coercion is a matter of discussion and definition. In this context it is not understood as being *unilateral* but rather as putting on pressure. For a discussion see, e.g., Sanders, *God Who Risks*, 222; Oord, *Uncontrolling Love*, 190.

them.[90] Furthermore, God uses his power in a benevolent manner, while, as explicated above, humans perceive this grace based on an exchange framework and therefore wish for less closeness. As a consequence, God "proves" his love and communal orientation by empowering humans *in extremis*, even to the point of letting them kill him on the cross. Indeed, God's love is truly kenotic[91] since it creates room for his creature to affect him in this way with the goal to achieve a positive close relationship. As such, God creates the basis for an asymmetric close relationship that can become intimate. Indeed, as has been shown through relationship science, a power differential in communal relationships does not necessarily reduce the perceived quality of and satisfaction with a relationship if the relationship is experienced as intimate. Therefore, the final relationship descriptor, *intimate*, will receive extensive attention.

c) An Intimate Relationship with God?

Intimate relationships are not defined as physical, sexual or even romantic[92] within this work and are also not equated with close relationships, instead, we define intimacy as a quality of relationships, a qualification of close, communal relationships through ongoing positive, intimate interactions.[93] However, these interactions, as already pointed out, consist of behaviors and experiences leading to the individual perception of a relationship as intimate.[94] In other words, intimacy is a subjective quality of a specific (personal) relationship determined by the interpersonal interaction *and* by the intrapersonal disposition of each individual. That

---

90. See also Holtzen, *God Who Trusts*, 80.

91. Brunner, *Dogmatics II*, 361, 364. For a more extreme vision of kenotic love, see Oord, *Uncontrolling Love*.

92. See Cross and Gore, "Relational Self-Construal," 232; Laurenceau and Kleinman, "Intimacy in Personal Relationships," 637–38; Firestone and Firestone, "Fear of Intimacy," 375; Prager and Roberts, "Deep Intimate Connection," 45; Miller, *Intimate Relationships*, 2–4. For studies pointing to the subordinate role of physical "intimacy," see Fletcher et al., *Intimate Relationships*, 105; Fehr, "Prototype Model of Intimacy," 21; Reis et al., "Emergence of Relationship Science," 562–63. For studies pointing to nonsexual intimacy as prototypical, see Fletcher et al., *Intimate Relationships*, 160, 172–75; Fehr, "Social Psychology of Love," 205–6, 217, 224.

93. See, e.g., Laurenceau and Kleinman, "Intimacy in Personal Relationships," 639.

94. Laurenceau and Kleinman, "Intimacy in Personal Relationships," 640; Laurenceau et al., "Intimacy as an Interpersonal Process," 71.

said, since intimacy is "inherently interactional,"[95] the crucial question is which interactions lead to intimate relationships? In essence, there is a broad agreement among scholars that two factors are decisive to increase intimacy: self-disclosure and responsiveness.[96] As such, it is important to understand that it is self-disclosure *and* responsiveness that lead to intimacy.[97] Hence, self-disclosure alone is not enough since it would only be one side in the transactional process towards intimacy. Self-disclosure needs to be met with a responsive response.[98] In other words, a relationship is perceived as intimate if one discloses oneself and is truly "seen" by the other, thus mirroring the meaning of the Latin *intimus*.[99] Consequently, we will first delve into the acts of self-disclosure and responsiveness to subsequently analyze the summarizing interplay of commitment and trust to be able to finally evaluate God-human intimacy "en bloc" in the last section.

Self-Disclosure and Responsiveness

Self-disclosure has been the prime focus of intimacy-related research for a long time.[100] Self-disclosure is defined as "an interaction between at least two individuals where one intends to deliberately divulge something personal to another."[101] Three aspects of this definition need attention: First, *deliberately* is an important specification since one can also reveal personal information involuntarily or unintentionally. Second, self-disclosure, which is considered "the typical opening step of the intimacy

---

95. Fehr, "Prototype Model of Intimacy," 20.

96. Miller, *Intimate Relationships*, 158; Laurenceau and Kleinman, "Intimacy in Personal Relationships," 642–43; Aron and Mashek, "Conclusion," 416; Collins and Feeney, "Attachment Theory Perspective," 171; Laurenceau et al., "Intimacy as an Interpersonal Process," 62.

97. This is reflected in Reis and Shavers's *intimacy process model* (see, e.g., Reis and Clark, "Responsiveness," 402; Miller, *Intimate Relationships*, 158).

98. Laurenceau and Kleinman, "Intimacy in Personal Relationships," 641–42; Fletcher et al., *Intimate Relationships*, 173–74; Regan, *Close Relationships*, 95–96; Greene et al., "Self-Disclosure," 417, 422; Prager and Roberts, "Deep Intimate Connection," 45–46; Laurenceau et al., "Intimacy as an Interpersonal Process," 63.

99. Firestone and Firestone, "Fear of Intimacy," 375.

100. For a short history of self-disclosure research, see Greene et al., "Self-Disclosure," 410–11. For a critical evaluation of this research, see Perlman and Duck, "Seven Seas," 26; Gillath et al., "Understanding of Attachment," 231.

101. Greene et al., "Self-Disclosure," 411–12.

process," can be verbal and non-verbal.[102] Finally, the "information" that is shared contributes more to intimacy when it is truly personal, even emotional, than mere disclosure of facts.[103] Consequently, this self-presentation is a deeply self-revealing behavior and as such is risky for three reasons: First, while revealing the true self, one risks not being liked for who one is, which in turn is a fundamental condition for intimacy.[104] Second, one risks not being understood accurately and therefore the partner might misinterpret one's personality, dispositions, or motives.[105] Third, one risks not finding the right measure of self-disclosure. For instance, it is possible to disclose too little so that the other might interpret it as a lack of motivation for intimacy or simply responds by also sharing superficially.[106] On the other hand, it is possible to disclose too much too early so that the other's desired level of closeness is exceeded, thus hindering intimacy.[107] Indeed, these risks remain whether the self-disclosure is made directly (face-to-face) or indirectly via a medium or a third-party.[108] As a result, whether self-disclosure leads to intimacy or drives apart depends essentially on the response of the partner, which leads us to the second component in the intimacy process: responsiveness.

"Responsiveness refers to the processes through which relationship partners attend to and respond supportively to each other's needs, wishes, concerns, and goals, thereby promoting each other's welfare."[109] Basically, being responsive is defined as caring for, understanding, and

102. Reis and Clark, "Responsiveness," 402. See also Greene et al., "Self-Disclosure," 420; Laurenceau and Kleinman, "Intimacy in Personal Relationships," 645–47; Laurenceau et al., "Intimacy as an Interpersonal Process," 62. The majority of research has focused on verbal disclosure and has hereby promoted a stinted view of self-disclosure (see Laurenceau et al., "Intimacy as an Interpersonal Process," 72).

103. Laurenceau et al., "Intimacy," 1238; Prager and Roberts, "Deep Intimate Connection," 45; Laurenceau et al., "Intimacy as an Interpersonal Process," 63.

104. Reis et al., "Perceived Partner Responsiveness," 207; Greene et al., "Self-Disclosure," 412.

105. Rusbult and van Lange, "Why Interdependence Theory," 2057; Rusbult and van Lange, "Interdependence, Interaction, and Relationships," 361–62.

106. See Greene et al., "Self-Disclosure," 413.

107. Miller, *Intimate Relationships*, 156–58, 160; Greene et al., "Self-Disclosure," 413; Reis et al., "Perceived Partner Responsiveness," 218; Sprecher and Hendrick, "Self-Disclosure," 858–59. For a perspective on the involved attachment styles, see Mikulincer and Shaver, "Attachment Security," 70–71.

108. Greene et al., "Self-Disclosure," 418–19.

109. Reis and Clark, "Responsiveness," 400. See also Laurenceau et al., "Intimacy as an Interpersonal Process," 64.

validating another individual.[110] As such, all three elements can be understood as a response to self-disclosure, although the latter two in a narrower sense. *Understanding* is a wished-for response to the second risk mentioned above that the partner accurately and appropriately interprets what one has revealed about the true self. *Validating*, on the other hand, meets the first fear of not being liked for who one actually is. However, an important differentiation is made between understanding/validating and agreement; while being understanding and validating one does not have to agree with how a person perceives herself or himself.[111] By extension, the third element of *caring for* another mitigates the third risk of self-disclosure since a caring person meets inappropriate behavior with forgiveness and tolerance.[112] Obviously, caring has a much more encompassing meaning than a mere reaction to self-disclosure; it is simply meeting another's needs. According to interdependence theory, caring acts especially contribute to intimacy when a partner prioritizes one's needs or wishes over and against his or her own wants; this is referred to as *diagnostic situations*.[113] Furthermore, responsiveness, although generally considered reciprocal in an intimate relationship,[114] needs to be differentiated from an exchange process of giving and taking.[115] As already shown,[116] in communal relationships reciprocity is not based on equity norms and therefore responsiveness often has an asymmetric reciprocal structure, which is most clearly observable in parent-child relationships.[117] Indeed, providing care, understanding, and validation, at least in communal relationships, can contribute to an experience of intimacy as much as receiving it.[118] Having said that, a specific need is not always a pre-

---

110. Reis and Clark, "Responsiveness," 403. Summarized by these three terms, they also give a helpful overview of the diverse interpretations of responsiveness in different scientific disciplines.

111. Reis and Clark, "Responsiveness," 403–4; Reis et al., "Perceived Partner Responsiveness," 208.

112. Reis and Clark, "Responsiveness," 406.

113. Reis and Clark, "Responsiveness," 408–9, 411.

114. Clark and Aragón, "Communal Relationships," 271.

115. Reis and Clark, "Responsiveness," 413–14; Reis et al., "Perceived Partner Responsiveness," 205.

116. See section 8b.

117. Reis et al., "Perceived Partner Responsiveness," 205; Dix and Buck, "Emergence of Social Approach," 60–62, 65–67.

118. Laurenceau and Kleinman, "Intimacy in Personal Relationships," 644–45.

condition for this kind of responsive behavior; it can also be the initiative of a person simply having the goal of a more intimate relationship.[119]

Finally, self-disclosure and responsiveness illustrate well why intimacy is fundamentally an interactional process that is not only *inter*personal but also influenced and even guided by an *intra*personal dimension. Therefore, the question needs to be asked whether self-disclosure and even more so responsiveness is an objective or a subjective matter.[120] Harry Reis et al. argue convincingly that not only responsiveness but *perceived responsiveness* is a fundamental factor in the intimacy process.[121] Put differently, it is not only a matter of whether a partner acts in an "objectively" responsive manner, but rather that this is perceived "subjectively" as such, although, there is a very real connection between the two.[122] Hence, two factors within the perceiver are decisive for the intimacy process: his or her *interpersonal expectations* and *intrapersonal disposition*. Firstly, a partner's interpersonal expectations are largely based on the conceived type of relationship since the more exclusive and intimate a relationship is believed to be, the greater the responsiveness that is expected.[123] Consequently, whether or not an identical action is appreciated as responsive depends on the relationship view of the recipient. In other words, "relationships are experienced as satisfying when the other's responsiveness is perceived to meet or exceed one's expectations."[124] Hence, the second factor is even more fundamental

---

119. Reis and Clark, "Responsiveness," 403; Reis et al., "Perceived Partner Responsiveness," 216; Laurenceau et al., "Intimacy as an Interpersonal Process," 69.

120. Reis et al., "Perceived Partner Responsiveness," 210–11.

121. Reis even proposes *perceived responsiveness* as an organizing theme for the study of close relationships in general (see, e.g., Reis, "Organizing Theme," 28). While his framework has its advantages within *communal* relationships, we still argue that interdependence theory and attachment theory is better suited as "grand theories" for the study of personal relationships as a whole and that *perceived responsiveness* fits very well as sub-concept within these larger frameworks (see the appendix). For an integration with interdependence theory, see Reis and Clark, "Responsiveness," 408–9, 411. For an integration with attachment theory, see Reis and Clark, "Responsiveness," 407–8.

122. Reis, "Organizing Theme," 33–34; Reis et al., "Perceived Partner Responsiveness," 203–4, 206, 213–14, 221. See also Laurenceau et al., "Intimacy as an Interpersonal Process," 64, 71.

123. Reis et al., "Perceived Partner Responsiveness," 215–16, 219. This view of exclusiveness is related to *communal strength* and can be hierarchically organized (see Clark and Aragón, "Communal Relationships," 263–64).

124. Reis et al., "Perceived Partner Responsiveness," 217. Interestingly, this type of

than the first and can be treated as its source: *intrapersonal disposition*. Individual personality differences mould perceptions and expectations[125] and attachment theory informs that those differences were formed by and large through prior relationships, especially during childhood.[126] Put differently, past relational experiences are projected on to present partners and situations.[127] Thus, through past and present adaptations to relationship situations *attachment styles* have formed,[128] acting like "glasses" through which one perceives and "filters" a relationship and a partner's actions. Whereas *secure* individuals have a rather realistic perception of the partner's responsiveness and the relationship as a whole,[129] *preoccupied, fearful* or *dismissing* dispositions lead to much more biased so-called *working models*.[130] As such, these working models can become self-fulfilling prophecies and sabotage an intimate relationship.[131]

In conclusion, perceived responsiveness, as a crucial factor towards intimacy, is strongly influenced and biased by given personal dispositions and attachment styles. Hence, since generally some form and degree of insecure attachment is prevalent,[132] this results in a quite pessimistic prospect for intimate relationships[133] unless there is the possibility that

---

expectation is primarily observable in communal and not in exchange relationships (220).

125. Aron and Mashek, "Conclusion," 422; Firestone and Firestone, "Fear of Intimacy," 392.

126. Collins and Feeney, "Attachment Theory Perspective," 173; Miller, *Intimate Relationships*, 18–19; Reis and Clark, "Responsiveness," 416; Reis et al., "Perceived Partner Responsiveness," 205, 208–9.

127. Collins and Feeney, "Attachment Theory Perspective," 171, 182; Cavallo et al., "Interpersonal Risk," 129–30. Interdependence theory calls these "habitual responses" *adaptions* (see, e.g., van Lange and Balliet, "Interdependence Theory," 75; Rusbult et al., "Interdependence, Closeness, and Relationships," 150).

128. Collins and Feeney, "Attachment Theory Perspective," 182. For a brief introduction to attachment styles for non-psychologists, see the appendix.

129. Collins and Feeney, "Attachment Theory Perspective," 174–75. See also Mikulincer and Shaver, "Attachment Security," 75. Concerning positive projections and idealizations, see Cross and Gore, "Relational Self-Construal," 237–38; Clark and Aragón, "Communal Relationships," 270.

130. Collins and Feeney, "Attachment Theory Perspective," 167–68, 175–77; Firestone and Firestone, "Methods," 376. A different yet similar perspective of the *self-system* is found in Prager and Roberts, "Connection," 48–52.

131. Sanderson, "Pursuit of Intimacy Goals," 261.

132. Fletcher et al., *Intimate Relationships*, 122.

133. For a discussion of the question of "good enough," see Collins and Feeney, "Attachment Theory Perspective," 182–83.

these dispositions can change. Indeed, there is evidence that, almost ironically, perceived partner responsiveness has the potential to affect one's working models,[134] and since actual, "objective" support indeed does contribute first and foremost to its positive perception,[135] there is a reason for hope. In other words, this evidence indicates that the specific interpersonal action even plays a larger role in the intimacy process than the individual intrapersonal disposition.[136] Therefore, we will take a closer look at the correlated and specific responsiveness processes of commitment and trust.

Commitment and Trust

Intimate relationships, as has been shown throughout the preceding sections, are highly interdependent and therefore always include the risk that a partner will not be responsive to one's needs. Consequently, at the heart of every intimate connection lies a dilemma: the desire for close connection and the fear of being rejected or disappointed.[137] As a result, trust is one of the most central and decisive relational components[138] and closely connected to the issues of perceived responsiveness and personal dispositions discussed in the last section. Interestingly, most theory and research has focused on trust as an intrapersonal disposition and neglected its specific interpersonal dimension.[139] In contrast, we propose that "in a complementary manner, trust reflects an individual's confidence in the partner's prosocial motives."[140] In other words, trust is initiated by the perception of a partner's commitment to be responsive and not merely because one is a rather trusting individual.[141] While from an interdependence theory perspective there are three bases for commitment—"have to" (*constraint commitment*), "ought to" (*moral commitment*), and "want

134. Reis and Clark, "Responsiveness," 412.
135. Reis et al., "Perceived Partner Responsiveness," 212.
136. Wieselquist et al., "Commitment," 963.
137. Cavallo et al., "Interpersonal Risk," 116–17, 132.
138. Simpson, "Foundations of Interpersonal Trust," 587, 604; Fletcher et al., *Intimate Relationships*, 179–80.
139. Wieselquist et al., "Commitment," 944; Simpson, "Foundations of Interpersonal Trust," 588–90, 599; Fletcher et al., *Intimate Relationships*, 179–80; Rusbult and van Lange, "Why Interdependence Theory," 2064.
140. Rusbult and van Lange, "Interdependence, Interaction, and Relationships," 368.
141. Arriaga, "Interdependence Theory Analysis," 49–50.

to" (*personal commitment*)[142]—within our current emphasis on intimate relationships the "want to" commitment is especially relevant and thus will be focused on.[143] This type of positive personal commitment, as has already been investigated,[144] can be conceptualized as IOS and one of its markers is a greater use of plural pronouns (we, us, our).[145] As a result, one central aspect of commitment is the "willingness to make sacrifices for the relationship" and the partner.[146] Precisely the perception of this pro-relationship and pro-partner motivation is crucial to elicit trust,[147] which leads to two refining observations. First, this motivation is most unambiguous, obvious and perceivable in diagnostic situations.[148] Put differently, in extreme or novel situations one has the chance to present and disclose oneself "objectively" as truly responsive so that the partner "subjectively" perceives it as such[149] and his or her expectations are met or even surpassed. Hence, in asymmetric relationships, where a power holder acts responsively for the benefit of the dependent, trust is forged especially strongly.[150] Second, for trust to form someone has to take the initiative and must be willing to take the risk to give before receiving,[151] which can be considered another form of asymmetry. In summary, the

---

142. Miller, *Intimate Relationships*, 207–8; Harvey and Wenzel, "Theoretical Perspectives," 39–40; Wieselquist et al., "Commitment," 944. See also section 8b.

143. For the difference between commitment and dependence, see Agnew et al., "Cognitive Interdependence," 940–41.

144. See section 8b.

145. Agnew et al., "Cognitive Interdependence," 941–42, 953; Miller, *Intimate Relationships*, 208.

146. Mikulincer and Shaver, "Attachment Security," 74. For an exemplary study of forgiveness as such a sacrifice, see Karremans and van Lange, "Role of Forgiveness."

147. Simpson, "Foundations of Interpersonal Trust," 599; Wieselquist et al., "Commitment," 963.

148. Wieselquist et al., "Commitment," 944–45; Simpson, "Foundations of Interpersonal Trust," 594–95, 603; Rusbult and van Lange, "Interdependence, Interaction, and Relationships," 362.

149. Van Lange and Balliet, "Interdependence Theory," 72–73. In interdependence theory, the *principle of transformation* and *information availability* refers to this process. See the appendix for a brief introduction to interdependence theory for non-psychologists.

150. Simpson, "Foundations of Interpersonal Trust," 594, 596, 604; Johnson and Johnson, "Social Interdependence Theory," 297; See also section 8b.

151. Wieselquist et al., "Commitment," 944, 964; Simpson, "Foundations of Interpersonal Trust," 599. See also Mikulincer and Shaver, "Attachment Security," 77, 82. This appears also to be true for the risk of self-disclosure (Simpson, "Foundations of Interpersonal Trust," 600; Wheeless and Grotz, "Measurement of Trust," 256).

"intimacy process is cyclical,"[152] meaning that partner A's initiative of commitment (responsiveness and self-disclosure) causes trust to form in partner B (through perceived responsiveness), which leads to partner B's greater commitment and in turn elicits greater trust within partner A and so forth.[153] Indeed, research has shown that this cyclical interaction and interdependence can change personal dispositions and attachment styles.[154] However, it becomes clear that much depends on the secure disposition of the person taking the initiative and the unambiguity of the situation so that his or her commitment and responsiveness is also perceived as such.

Summary: Intimate Relationship with God

Commitment and *trust* summarize well the dynamic and goal of God-human relationships and correspond with Brunner's structure of *call* and *answer*. *Intimacy*, as a quality of close, communal relationships that are characterized by ongoing positive, intimate interactions, matches precisely what Brunner terms *personal correspondence* or an *I-You relationship*.[155] Furthermore, these positive interactions correspond with Brunner's focus on encounter, as an actual reciprocal action and not an abstract conception. As such, intimacy is a relationship quality that cannot be accomplished individually; it demands commitment *and* trust hereby reflecting the structure of revelation *and* faith in Part Two. Hence, based on this structure the God-human relationship is not only asymmetric due to the power differential but also clearly asymmetric in God taking the initiative of commitment. God's commitment is a "want to"-commitment by his free choice and out of his perfect security. In turn, from the human point of view God "must" take the initiative since humans are trapped in their contradiction or what attachment theory calls insecurity: a preoccupied, dismissing, or fearful disposition. Thus, since

---

152. Cross and Gore, "Relational Self-Construal," 235.

153. This is illustrated by the *model of mutual cyclical growth* (see, e.g., Wieselquist et al., "Commitment," 942, 945). For the negative counterpart, see Rusbult et al., "Commitment," 628. In interdependence theory this ongoing process refers to the *temporal structure* of a relationship (see the appendix).

154. Bradbury and Karney, *Intimate Relationships*, 115; Reis et al., "Perceived Partner Responsiveness," 210; Fletcher et al., *Intimate Relationships*, 112; Cavallo et al., "Interpersonal Risk," 130.

155. See also Anderson, *Living Waters*, 4, 18; Kovacs, *James E. Loder*, 82.

the corrupted but actual God-human relationship is either merely "being related" or even hostile, God taking the initiative is a true saving act in order to restore what long has been lost. Indeed, the two central terms of intimacy, *self-disclosure* and *responsiveness*, take on the uttermost meaning in God's commitment to humanity and are biblically summarized by the term love, *agape*, as the very heart of God's being. These two terms are also the central terms that Brunner uses for the divine restoration project. As such, self-disclosure is God's "opening step," by revealing not only something of himself (information) but himself, hereby meeting the intimacy-criteria of self-disclosure. Furthermore, God's deliberate self-disclosure is a responsive self-disclosure as he always has the addressee, the human, in focus and not himself, which corresponds with relationship science's requirement of an interconnection of the two terms. In summary, the analogy of parent-child relationships matches precisely, not merely on an ontic level but very concrete since God acts like a loving parent of a rebelling teenager by keeping up "unilateral intimacy" despite the negative reaction, always wishing to empower the child towards a friendship (e.g., John 15:15).[156] In all of this, God does not overpower since his self-disclosure is "hidden" and not overwhelming, responsively coming close as the man Jesus of Nazareth. Indeed, Jesus Christ is the incarnation of God's commitment, fulfilling the three hallmarks of responsiveness: *understanding*, *validating*, and *caring*. First, by becoming human God comes to our level and understands our human condition (e.g., Heb 4:15).[157] Second, Jesus, throughout his life, validated people without having to agree with them (e.g., John 8:3–11) exemplifying Isaiah 42:3: "A crushed reed he will not break, a dim wick he will not extinguish; he will faithfully make just decrees" (NET), which leads to the third hallmark *caring*.[158] Jesus cared deeply for the people, not only healing the sick but also the sickness of the spirit by forgiving, showing hereby who God is (e.g., John 14:9). God's commitment, responsiveness, and self-disclosure climaxes by making a radical sacrifice on the cross, by giving himself away (John 15:13: "greater love has no one"),[159] which in terms of relationship science is clearly a diagnostic situation: the ultimate power holder makes the ultimate sacrifice.

156. See, e.g., Barclay, *Paul and the Gift*, 28–29; Vacek, *Love*, xv–xvi, 106, 285–86, 295; Sanders, *Theology in the Flesh*, 247.

157. See, e.g., Brunner, *Dogmatics II*, 323; Boyd, *Cross Vision*, 219.

158. See, e.g., Twelftree, *Miracle Worker*, 126.

159. See, e.g., Boyd, *Crucifixion of the Warrior God*, 252.

Having said that, God's commitment through self-disclosure and responsiveness is the initiative and foundation but not yet the consummation of intimacy. The divine call needs the human answer to reach its intended goal. However, the human answer depends on this divine call since trust depends on commitment. That said, since the human perception of God's factual responsiveness is critical,[160] God's commitment is extreme, shown on the cross in the most diagnostic situation possible to make his loving intention as unambiguous as possible.[161] As a result, humans are empowered to make themselves vulnerable by abandoning their preoccupied, dismissive, or fearful coping mechanisms and enabled to risk trusting God.[162] In this sense faith *is* a divine gift without ignoring the human action involved; it is a freedom *in* decision and not *of* decision. Due to God's commitment, what we have called *happy asymmetry*, humans are able to trust, to risk self-disclosure, and to start being responsive to God, other people, and creation as a whole.[163]

This cyclical intimacy process *is* God's project of restoration since through it humans are changed in a way that otherwise is humanly impossible. God is, informed by attachment theory, the perfect partner, mother, father, and friend. That said, while through this cycle of commitment and trust God is affected, it is only the broken human person who is deeply changed and restored.[164] Indeed, through this intimate relationship, humans are made "whole" and freed to be truly human, true humans, which, according to Brunner, will be seen by the fruit of the Spirit (Gal 5:22–23). Consequently, divine-human intimacy is not a one-time event but an interaction process, an ongoing encounter that happens amid brokenness, imperfection, and insecurity with God himself as the only security.[165]

Hence, congruent with IOS, the more intimate the relationship that is perceived, the more the partner is included in the self, and the more the circles overlap voluntarily.[166] Importantly and objectively, even the

---

160. See also Boyd, *Cross Vision*, 18–19, 106, 246; Glaw, Bockmuehl, 203, 230–31.

161. In this section the role of the Holy Spirit in immediating these historical events is implied but not explicated (for details, see section 5b).

162. It becomes obvious how crucial an accurate and how destructive a distorted "re-presentation" of Jesus is for the human perception and the "ability" to trust him.

163. See also Kovacs, *James E. Loder*, 85–86, 92–93.

164. See also Tanner, *Christ the Key*, vii, 16, 105.

165. See also Cavey, *End of Religion*, 219–20.

166. See figure 2.

highest degree of intimacy does not lead to total oneness, a fusion with the loss of the individual self (total overlap in the IOS scale), but to a voluntarily increasing interdependence of "both partner's distinct, individual selves."[167] Sometimes "the illusion of fusion" is even considered psychopathological.[168] Nonetheless, in the intimacy process, the individual will be fundamentally affected and changed.[169] In the same way, Brunner stresses that this process of intimacy does not lead to a mystical union, but rather to a "comm-unity" in the Holy Spirit, preserving and emphasizing the individuals yet uniting them in a new "we."[170] Therefore the biblical language of Χριστὸς ἐν ὑμῖν, Christ in you (Col 1:27) or "he who abides in me, and I in him" (John 15:5 NKJV) and the "being transformed into the same image" (2 Cor 3:18 NKJV) correspond well with the concept of including other in the self (IOS) and Brunner's emphasis of an I-You relationship.[171]

d) Conclusion: The Analogy of Relationship

In this chapter, we have met the requirement of our working theory of analogy by critically depicting and comparing a detailed representation of the prior associations of each domain. Additionally, we believe it to be helpful to summarize our findings in a tabular form:[172]

---

167. Prager and Roberts, "Deep Intimate Connection," 56. See also Cross and Gore, "Relational Self-Construal," 242; Ickes et al., "Closeness as Intersubjectivity," 360–63; Collins and Feeney, "Attachment Theory Perspective," 173; Aron et al., "Including Other in the Self," 29.

168. Firestone and Firestone, "Fear of Intimacy," 375–78.

169. Aron et al., "Including Other in the Self," 31; Arriaga, "Interdependence Theory Analysis," 51; Aron and Mashek, "Conclusion," 416. For the aspect of perceiving the other as similar to the self, see Agnew et al., "Thinking Close," 113–14; Lösel and Bender, "Modelle der Paarbeziehung," 55; Cross and Gore, "Relational Self-Construal," 239.

170. See also Balswick et al., *Reciprocating Self*, 24. Conversely, many ancient Jewish concepts were merging self and other (Putthoff, *Ontological Aspects of Early Jewish Anthropology*, 215–23).

171. See, e.g., Brunner, *Dogmatics I*, 215–16.

172. Concerning advantages and perils of tabular representations, see Bartha, *Parallel Reasoning*, 13–15.

RELATIONSHIP PARTIES personal God ≠/≈ humans		
secure ≈ true human		insecure ≈ real human
RELATIONSHIP		
intimate ≈ **personal correspondence**	**close** ≈ **responsory actuality**	**hostile** ≈ **responsory actuality in revolt**
interdependence perceived as positive	interdependence ≈ reciprocity	interdependence perceived as negative
power differential as empowering	symmetric or asymmetric ≠/≈ asymmetric	power differential as threatening
relatively voluntary ≈ freedom in the "yes" to God	voluntary or involuntary (relatively voluntary) ≈ freedom to say "yes" or "no" (relative freedom)	relatively involuntary ≈ unfreedom in the "no" to God
communal norms ≈ I-You relationship with God ≈ self-disclosure ≈ responsiveness	norms	exchange norms ≈ I-it relationship with God
"want to" commitment ≈ fellowship with God	commitment ≈ responsibility	"have to/ought to" commitment ≈ under the law and wrath of God

Table 2: Overview and comparison of human relationships (relationship science) and God-human interaction (Emil Brunner). The dotted line at the top illustrates the interpenetration of personal dispositions and actual relationships. The dotted lines in between the columns illustrate that *close* is primarily a structural descriptor that is either explicated towards intimacy or hostility. The symbol ≈ stands for "almost equal to" rendering a positive comparison between human and God-human relationships, the symbol ≉ stands for "not almost equal to" rendering a negative comparison (grey highlight).

Part III explored Brunner's personal correspondence in light of relationship science to conclude whether there is a positive analogy between God-human and human relationships. After the critical comparison, we hold that *personal correspondence* and *intimate relationships* are substantially similar since both are characterized by *reciprocity/interdependence*, *freedom/voluntariness*, *self-disclosure*, and *responsiveness* (see table 2). Consequently, it was and is God's intention to have an *intimate* relationship with humanity. This statement can be made without reserve but with one constraint: *asymmetry*. The God-human relationship is always asymmetric, whereas human relationships are not. This important difference, however, does not lead to a negative analogy but constricts the relationship analogy to asymmetric relationships. In other words, within the broad concept of relationship, asymmetry must always be kept in mind.[173] Furthermore, "it is when a pair . . . is similar that their differences are likely to be important."[174] As such, the parent-child relationship is the Bible's prime metaphor for God-human relation and the most comprehensive depiction of the relational dynamic between God and humans.[175]

This asymmetry leads to another limitation of the analogy due to the nature of the parties, the persons involved. While the *relationship* is analogous, the *relationship parties* are not or only relatively so. God is not a human; he is perfectly secure, loving, committed, self-giving, and responsive and as such the perfect partner. Human relationships, and

---

173. For examples where *asymmetry* is not sufficiently preserved, see McFague, *Metaphorical Theology*, 167; Vacek, *Love*, 285–86; and maybe the late Moltmann (Grenz and Olson, *20th-Century Theology*, 183–84).

174. Gentner and Markman, "Analogy and Similarity," 50–51. Interestingly, the authors draw attention to the fact that it is easier to list differences when the compared domains are similar and harder when dissimilar.

175. See DesCamp and Sweetser, "Metaphors for God," 234–37; Sanders, *Theology in the Flesh*, 219–25; Rabens, "Sein und Werden," 140; Balswick et al., *Reciprocating Self*, 345; Robinson, *Metaphor*, 125.

therefore also relationship science, can only theoretically point to this kind of ideal partner. As such, this explains why Jesus, for example, while constantly referring to God as Father, corrected the common image and perception of human fathers by explaining that God is a different, better Father.[176] Furthermore, even the analogy of the human is relative. Whereas Brunner's *real human* is identical with the range of human relationship parties that relationship science studies and depicts, this cannot be said in the same way of the *true human* since the God-dimension is not part of relationship science. Theologically spoken, humans move towards being the "perfect" partner in as much as they move towards being true humans, being the *imago Dei*, in an intimate relationship with God. As such, an intimate relationship with God both is very similar to but also transcends the intimate relationships that relationship science studies due to the nature of the parties involved.[177]

By proposing a positive analogy of *intimate relationships* and *personal correspondence*, we also propose a positive analogy of the other relationship types since intimacy is only the tip of the pyramid (see figure 1). Hence, the tabular representation (see table 2) shows a structurally consistent alignment between the two domains,[178] which is one of the requirements in our working theory of analogy. The descriptor *close* has its "formal" or structural correlate in Brunner's *responsory actuality* and *intimate*, as qualitative or "material" classification, has its equivalent in *personal correspondence*. Furthermore, also the negative qualitative classification of the relationship, termed *hostility*, although only explored as non-intimacy, is a precise match with Brunner's *revolt*. Whereas these relationship types refer primarily to the interpersonal, the relationship itself, the descriptor *personal* emphasizes the intrapersonal dispositions of the parties involved, the persons, thus correlating with Brunner's differentiation between God, the real, and the true human. Therefore, we always speak of a personal relationship between this God and this human, meaning that there is no "general relationship" but only a specific interaction between the perfect God and a specific imperfect human moving towards a specific relational expression be it intimate or hostile. However, whilst the analogy of relationship always must be specified, it

---

176. See, e.g., Matt 7:9–11; Luke 11:11–13; 15:11–32; John 6:46; 8:19.41–47; 12:45; 14:7–11.

177. See also Bracken, "Toward a New Philosophical Theology," 709.

178. Compare with table 1 in section 4c.

is nonetheless a very useful, if not the only, meta-analogy for the whole biblical range of God-human interactions.

In summary, Brunner's assertion of the analogy of relationship, albeit in less detail, matches well what has been proposed in this chapter and therefore will be cited at length:

> The only analogy to this [God-human encounter] is the encounter between humans, from person to person. From this analogy are also taken the conceptual means of expression by which we render what happens between God and the human in faith in the word. And yet it is only an analogy, . . . the encounter between two humans is usually not a personal one, but a more or less impersonal [*sächliche*] one. . . . That is why this personal encounter and this community is also only an analogy to what happens between God and me in the relationship of revelation and faith. But this relative analogy can still direct us to what is non-relatively, unconditionally meant in faith.[179]

---

179. Brunner, *Wahrheit als Begegnung*, 114–15 (TM); ETR 114–15.

IV

Towards a Theology of Relationship

WE BEGAN OUR ENDEAVOR with the notion that while the concept and the expression of *a personal relationship with God* could be current and relevant within both popular culture and the academia, it is in danger of being abandoned due to the lack of definitional clarity and adequate theological conceptions. Therefore, Part I has shown that Brunner's dynamic leitmotif of relationship, termed personal correspondence in his basal work *Truth as Encounter*, offers a rich starting point for every theological endeavor with relationship at its core; it has also been argued why Brunner should be preferred in this respect over so-called relational theologies, trinitarian theologies and Karl Barth. While Brunner is widely forgotten and has been misinterpreted or even ignored by many, this specific relational contribution is crucial to be reconsidered. It might even be postulated that his relational work better fits in our current time than in his own and therefore inheres an almost prophetic dimension; McGrath calls it "madness not to make better use of it."[1] After the reconsideration of the manifold critique brought forward against this core-conception of Brunner, it must be concluded that he has not been persuasively refuted so far. Relationship then, as explicated by Brunner, appears not only to be an appropriate but a central and even a monistic leitmotif for the whole of the biblical message.[2] Through the detailed analysis of Brunner's concept of personal correspondence in Part II evolved a valuable taxonomy

---

1. McGrath, *Emil Brunner*, 237–38.
2. Against Rössler, *Person und Glaube*, 143.

to better grasp the nature of what Brunner terms I-You relationship or the center, "basic category," and "cause of the Bible":[3] *reciprocity, asymmetry, freedom, self-disclosure,* and *responsiveness*. This terminology has not only proven to be intrinsic to Brunner and consistent with his overall thought and theology, but it has also shown to reflect accurately the biblical depiction of the God-intended interaction with humans. Hence, the broad conclusion of the two Brunner-focused parts is that he offers a very good starting point and gives the possibility of expansion of his central leitmotif of relationship. Consequently, the proposed goal of this book is to move towards a theology of relationship not by moving past Brunner, but by building upon his legacy. As such, the first area that needed expansion was Brunner's central analogy of relationship. By the appropriation of relationship science, Part III has shown without reserve that the relation between God and humans is indeed analogous to asymmetric human relationships. However, it has been reasoned analogically that this relationship analogy can only be extended relatively to the relationship parties since God is not a human and the human, as *imago Dei*, is broken and/or in the process of restoration.

In this final part, after having investigated the specific questions of analogy, the scope will be widened again and the analogical considerations will, first, be condensed and formulated as an analogical argument in respect of a theology of relationship, followed by a treatment of three potential objections (structural, material, and formal). Secondly, based on this rather abstract and dense culmination, we will propose and briefly offer ten theses for further research towards a comprehensive theology of relationship, building on Brunner's accomplishments and developing his shortcomings. Hereby, we attempt answering Fretheim's question posed at the beginning: "What if we took the word relationship seriously? What if we spoke of the Godhuman [*sic*] relationship as real and genuine? . . . If we did this, what are the implications of such an understanding?"[4] Furthermore, we are beginning to flesh out how the Christian Faith could be considered an intimate relationship rather than a religion[5] and as such

---

3. Brunner, *Wahrheit als Begegnung*, 102 (TM); ETR, 102.

4. Fretheim, *God and World*, 16.

5. We are aware that this differentiation is a stretch. However, by *religion* we refer to some kind of exchange relation with the divine (see 8b), as this term is usually understood in everyday language. *Religion* as scientific term is very hard to differentiate (see, e.g., Yong, *Beyond the Impasse*, 15; Paloutzian and Park, "Recent Progress," 8). The word itself could have originated from the Latin *religare*, meaning re-connecting

IV: Towards a Theology of Relationship

take seriously Cavey's provocative statement from the introduction: "For too long, people have assumed that religion is how we connect with God, whereas relationship is how we connect with people."[6]

(Burkhardt, *Gott in allen Religionen*, 16–18), which, taken as such, would fit very well with our description of relationship.

6. Cavey, *End of Religion*, 196. For a similar statement, see McFarlane, *Evangelical Theology*, 8.

9

The Analogical Argument

a) The Categorical Argument

Premise: The structures and processes of the God-human relationship are like the structures and processes of human relationships and as such ordinary and not *sui generis*.[1]

Premise: The divine partner in the God-human relationship is transcendent and perfect and as such extraordinary and *sui generis*.[2]

Premise: The intrapersonal (person) affects the interpersonal (relationship) and vice-versa.[3]

Conclusion: The God-human relationship is not categorically but actually and existentially *sui generis*.

b) The Existential Argument

Premise: Human existence is first and foremost existence in relation and interaction with God.[4]

---

1. See section 8d.
2. See section 8d.
3. See section 8a.
4. See chapter 4.

Premise: God-human interaction is free, reciprocal, yet asymmetric, and intended to be characterized by self-disclosure and responsiveness.[5]

Premise: Human close relationships are free, reciprocal, sometimes asymmetric, and, if intimate, characterized by self-disclosure and responsiveness.[6]

Conclusion: Humans exist in a close relationship with God, which is intended to be intimate but can also be hostile or ignorant.

c) The Epistemological (Theological) Argument

Premise: The center of the biblical testimony is the God-human relationship. The Bible is primarily the narrative of its intimate beginning, its break-up (with its consequences), and its restoration.[7]

Premise: Systematic theology is reasonable and ordered thinking about what is (God, humans, world, and their interactions) based on God's self-revelation as witnessed and reflected in the Bible.

Premise: The systematicy of theology must be aligned with and adequate to the center of the Bible. Hence, for its dynamic content, the term *leitmotif* is most fitting.[8]

Conclusion: The God-human relationship must be the leitmotif of systematic theology.

d) The Argument towards a Theology of Relationship

Premise: The existential is primal and has priority over the epistemological.[9]

Premise: Relationship is existential.

Premise: Systematic Theology is epistemological.

---

5. See chapters 5–6.
6. See chapter 8.
7. See chapter 1 and Part Two.
8. See section 3b. Others have proposed different terms that try to avoid the static *framework* or *system*: *coordinates* (Gunton, *The One*, 166), *through-line* (Boyd, *Cross Vision*, 33), *key conceptual model* (Brümmer, *Model of Love*, 21–29).
9. See chapter 1.

Conclusion: All systematic theology revolves around an actual relationship and as such is a theology *of* relationship and not merely *relational* theology.

e) Objections

While this analogical reasoning proposed as an analogical argument is based on a solid theological, biblical, and logical foundation and several possible objections have already been discussed implicitly throughout this work, we nevertheless want to address one structural, one material, and one formal concern explicitly.

Structural Objection: Circular Reasoning

Since Brunner was influenced by personalism/I-You philosophy and employed its corresponding personalistic terminology, it is reasonable to expect that a comparison with relationship science confirms his depiction of God-human interaction. Hence, this analogy is nothing but circular reasoning and only confirms Brunner's personalism but not relationship as a solid theological leitmotif.

This is a serious objection concerning the methodology of this book. Since we are arguing for a theology of relationship informed by Brunner's encompassing proposal this would mean that our wider ramifications in Part IV are obsolete since we would only make an "inner-brunnerian" and not a general analogical statement. However, we have already argued that Brunner claims that his leitmotif of encounter is not based on personalism but rather employs it as conveying a fundamentally biblical conception and that his claim is justified.[10] Furthermore, we have amplified the validity of this relational assertion of the Bible throughout Part II not only by depicting Brunner's personal correspondence but also, if only rudimentarily, with reference to a wide range of systematic and biblical theologians who all highlight the Old Testament and the New Testament as deeply and fundamentally relational as Emil Brunner does. Therefore, while Brunner leans heavily towards a systematic approach, he shows nevertheless superb implicit exegetical involvement with the biblical texts. Admittedly, it is a matter for regret that Brunner's "biblical" leitmotif has not been presented with more explicit and perceivable exegetical

---

10. See section 1b.

engagement and that he chose rather to paraphrase. Notwithstanding, the biblical testimony is not only full of God-human interaction, as the grand story of God and humanity, it might even be considered nothing but its depiction with the incarnation of Christ as God's central, unambiguous, and ultimate relationship affirmation within history.[11] In other words, one cannot lose relationship as leitmotif without losing the very essence of Christianity: Jesus of Nazareth, the Christ, who is God's relationship statement in the flesh. Thus, broadly supported, it can be predicated that Brunner's contribution takes this biblical relationality particularly seriously by elaborating it theologically in a uniquely comprehensive way.

Material Objection: Anthropomorphism

The analogy of relationship projects human concepts and depictions on God and recasts him (and the human's relation with him) in anthropomorphic terms thus remodeling God in our own likeness which is idolatry.

This objection of *anthropomorphism* is not to be taken lightly as the extensive history of its discussion shows.[12] Whilst this is not the place for a comprehensive treatment, it will be briefly shown how Brunner has countered his critics in this respect since Brunner was well aware that with his personalist approach he was in the thick of this debate. As has already been shown, Brunner did himself fight fiercely against any projection on to God[13] and any form of subjectivism, be it in the form of Schleiermacher or within the emergence of the psychology of religion. Yet, he neither settled for a *via negativa*, nor retreated to any form of abstract, philosophical God-talk.[14] Rather, as a theologian of revelation, he proposed a twofold defense of his leitmotif and his analogy of relationship against this accusation of anthropomorphism.

First, as humans, we have no other way than to speak humanly about God. Brunner points out that the Bible is justifiably full of such anthropomorphisms since it is the only way for humans to treat God as a real "You," a subject and person. Hence, any other talk about God will become abstract and consequently, God would be treated like an "it," an

---

11. See section 5a.
12. For a brief overview, see Lim, "Anthropomorphism and Anthropopathism."
13. See, e.g., Brunner, *Dogmatics I*, 246.
14. See section 1b.

object. Brunner concedes that this personal way of speaking about God is in a sense symbolic and as such inadequate, but the only adequately inadequate way for humans. Furthermore, this kind of anthropomorphism is justified through God's revelation, his "coming down" to our level of comprehension in showing himself "primitively" as father, king, lord, or through other personal expressions.[15] Indeed, with his ultimate self-revelation in Jesus Christ God sealed this anthropomorphism by becoming human.[16] Thus, we can only know about God what God has revealed of himself; everything else is speculation.[17] As such, Brunner argues for a top-down approach, also called condescension,[18] to embrace the only possible, that is anthropomorphic, way God could have shown himself to humans. Brunner even goes as far as to call any other approach "sin," since it wants to understand God on its own terms, thereby rejecting God's revelation leading to mere projection.[19] Consequently, Brunner counters his critics: "If anyone wants to be critical let him be above all critical in the use of his criteria!"[20] Brunner is not alone with this way of reasoning, as both conservative theologians before and after him[21] and contemporary open theists[22] show.

Secondly, Brunner defends his anthropomorphic leitmotif of relationship not only with the condescension argument but proposes a second layer of reasoning to solve the ontological dilemma. Brunner explicitly speaks against any form of *analogia entis*, the analogy of being,

---

15. See, e.g., Brunner, *Offenbarung und Vernunft*, 435–36; ETR 400–401; Brunner, *Dogmatics II*, 268–69; Brunner, *Dogmatik III*, 453–54; ETR 405–7. See also Sanders, *Theology in the Flesh*, 249–62; Fretheim, *God and World*, 17.

16. Brunner, *Offenbarung und Vernunft*, 443–44; ETR 408, 411. See also Hartenstein, "Relationalität als Schlüssel," 167–68; Peckham, *Love of God*, 278; Duvall and Hays, *Relational Presence*, 8; Fretheim, *God and World*, 18; Sanders, *Risks*, 28 (he calls Jesus the "consummate anthropomorphism").

17. See section 2b.

18. See, e.g., Brunner, "Anknüpfungspunkt," 248. For this common terminology, see also Oei, "The Impassible God," 238–47, 243–44.

19. Brunner, *Dogmatics I*, 124–26. For a similar secular perspective on projection, see Spaemann, "Wirklichkeit als Anthropomorphismus," 43–45.

20. Brunner, *Dogmatics II*, 270.

21. See, e.g., Keil and Delitzsch, *Moses*, 70; James, "Anthropomorphism," 152–54; Caneday, "Veiled Glory," 192.

22. See, e.g., Sanders, *Theology in the Flesh*, 244, 249–62 (citing Aquinas and Calvin); Schmid, *Gott ist ein Abenteurer*, 130; Holtzen, *God Who Trusts*, 24–26.

understanding it as a principle of incorrect natural theology.[23] Hence, God, as Creator, remains the "Wholly Other" over and against his creation and creature, yet as Creator, he also created humans as subjects, as persons, as *imago Dei*.[24] In essence, as has already been explored,[25] Brunner allows an ontological analogy between God and humans, yet importantly, as relational ontology, not as any form of substance ontology. Consequently, the substantial similarity between God and humans lies in being a true subject, defined by its corresponding relational attributes, while upholding the essential difference between Creator and creature.[26] Brunner even adapts Barth's terminology of an *analogia relationis*,[27] hence uniting God's relational condescension and the ontological analogy.[28] However, since Brunner is a revelation-theologian the direction of this analogy is of utmost importance: it is not bottom-up, which would be the way of projection, but top-down, which is the way of revelation. God is not considered personal because we perceive him anthropomorphically as such; to the contrary, we humans are persons, because we are created in the image of God, the person per se:[29]

> The Perfect is not an "intensification of the imperfect"; for the intensification of the imperfect would be only that which is still more imperfect. It is also no "abstraction," the "elimination of the imperfect" for in order to eliminate the imperfect I must use the idea of Perfection as the rule for elimination. Only complete stupidity can entertain the idea that the Idea can be derived from the perception.[30]

23. See, e.g., Brunner, *Dogmatics I*, 175–78; Brunner, *Dogmatics II*, 43–44; Andersen, "Theological Anthropology," 12.

24. Brunner, *Dogmatics I*, 175–76.

25. See chapter 4.

26. Sanders argues very similarly (Sanders, *God Who Risks*, 29).

27. See, e.g., Meyer zu Hörste-Bührer, *Gott und Menschen*, 145. Brunner gladly accepts Barth's terminology, while pointing out that the underlying concept had already been developed in his own anthropology *Man in Revolt* (Brunner, "New Barth," 125). See also the brief discussion in section 2b and 4b.

28. White proposes a similar solution in "Metaphorical God," 180–81, 188–89.

29. This revelation-approach is according to Wolf also the primary difference between Brunner and the so-called personalists. Wolf identifies three different ways to understand God as person, yet misses that Brunner unites all three with his relational leitmotif. Wolf's overall conclusion then is not very helpful (Wolf, "God as Person," 26–32).

30. Brunner, *Man in Revolt*, 175–76. This goes against Rössler's unfortunate interpretation that Brunner has to potentiate and radicalize God from human experience and perception as "absolute subject" or "true You." Rössler, *Person und Glaube*, 87–88.

As such, Brunner postulates that to talk about God as a person and in personal categories is not an *anthropomorphism*, but a *theomorphism*.[31] Brunner is not alone with this reasoning: Barth,[32] Gunton,[33] and Vanhoozer[34] are some prominent proponents among others,[35] and even the terminology of theomorphism has been deployed by others.[36]

Hence, Brunner stresses the fact that while, for epistemological reasons, we have to employ those anthropomorphic means of expression in a way bottom-up to be able to communicate and to grasp anything, we have to immediately turn the tables to a top-down, revelatory, theomorphic view.[37] In other words, the anthropomorphic has to be taken up in the theomorphic. Thus, in light of our working theory of analogy, this means the following: We have started symmetrically with a simple comparison between the human and the God-human domain and concluded that while the relationship structure and processes are similar, even the same,[38] the human and divine subjects are not (or only relatively so). Consequently, since genuine analogical reasoning starts when treating one domain as the source for making novel or predictive statements about the target domain,[39] while we start by treating human relationships as source to comprehend something about the divine, we then engage them hermeneutically in that we reinterpret these adequately inadequate "projections" in light of God's revelation as the more informative[40] and

---

31. Brunner, *Wahrheit als Begegnung*, 28–30; Brunner, *Dogmatics I*, 139–40.

32. Meyer zu Hörste-Bührer, *Beziehungen*, 114–26.

33. Gunton, *The One*, 165, 167.

34. Vanhoozer, *Remythologizing Theology*, 64, 77–78. Cited also in Peckham, *Love*, 267.

35. See, e.g., Poythress, *Redeeming Sociology*, 24–29, 46–47; Knauer, "Ontología Relacional," 11–12; Hartenstein, "Relationalität als Schlüssel," 162, 170.

36. See, e.g., Heschel, *The Prophets*, 334, 349, 409; Keil and Delitzsch, *Moses*, 70; Vanhoozer, *Remythologizing Theology*, 64, 77–78. Rössler points out that Ebner already used this term and might have influenced Brunner (Rössler, *Person und Glaube*, 87). An interesting side note: *theomorphism* has also been used in a different context within the psychology of religion (Barrett, "Exploring Religion's Basement," 240).

37. Brunner, "Anknüpfungspunkt," 244–45, 259–60.

38. Concerning the difference between *literal similarity* and *analogy*, see Gentner, "Structure-Mapping," 159–61.

39. Bartha, *Parallel Reasoning*, 42–43.

40. For the informativity principle, see Bowdle and Gentner, "Informativity and Asymmetry," 247, 249, 276, 281.

The Analogical Argument

adequate source. While this bidirectional analogical process is not extensively considered in structure-mapping theory[41] and is also an ongoing discussion in theology,[42] it nonetheless is exemplified by Jesus's person and his teaching, as we have already shown.[43]

Formal Objection: Relationship Terminology

While the analogical reasoning makes sense, the term relationship is not appropriate for a theological leitmotif as it is an extrabiblical terminology that brings too much cultural "baggage" along with it.

Indeed, this objection is to be taken seriously and we believe that we have done just that throughout this work. From the very beginning, the unconcerned usage of the term *relationship* has been problematized.[44] We have pointed out that *relationship* is not a biblical term and highlighted the necessity for further definition.[45] Accordingly, the terminology has been analyzed and extensively compared with the biblical depiction of God-human interaction.[46] However, it nonetheless is appropriate to test once again, alongside the final argument, the usage of *relationship* as a theological leitmotif: why introduce a foreign term when many biblical alternatives would be available? Since the Bible is a relationship book,[47] this has become thoroughly clear, it by and large narrates those relationships, treats them existentially, very concretely, and not systematically.

---

41. Wolff and Gentner hint in this direction by showing that metaphor (or analogy) "lives a double life" since it not *only* works directionally, but also bidirectionally, changing the comprehension of the base. Wolff and Gentner, "Metaphor Comprehension," 1456–58, 1483.

42. The discussion revolves primarily around whether a projection on to God is valid or not (DesCamp and Sweetser, "Metaphors for God," 210, 222). Sallie McFague is a proponent for this mutual effect of metaphor, but her approach is fundamentally different from what we propose here. In fact, it is the opposite, since McFague does not think from revelation but only from projection. Consequently, for her, Jesus is only a metaphor for God and not his actual self-revelation (McFague, *Metaphorical Theology*, 19, 51).

43. See, e.g., sections 5a and 8d.

44. See the introduction.

45. See section 7a. Besides, many other terms we take as given and helpful are not "biblical" like *theology, Trinity,* and *person*, to only name a few.

46. See chapter 8.

47. Boschki, *Religionspädagogik*, 224–25, 239–40, 326.

Yet, a theological leitmotif is just that, a systematic through-line. Hence, Brunner argues that the apostle Paul also adapted the existing vocabulary of his time, sometimes redefining it, to communicate and systematize the theological content.[48] Moreover, Brunner even proposes that "the theologian's understanding of the Bible comes out—paradoxically—in the very fact that he does not use the language of the Bible."[49] Indeed, others have attested that while Brunner's language was often not "biblical," it was all the more helpful and accurate.[50] Whereas Brunner points out that one might use biblical terms but miss the biblical content entirely and another utilizes non-biblical language to accurately capture the biblical essence,[51] he nonetheless stresses emphatically, time and again, that doctrinal language needs to reflect accurately the narrative and existential focus of the Bible.[52] Consequently, a "biblical" leitmotif must not be superimposed on but should be extracted from the biblical testimony while adapting a "heuristically valuable terminology."[53] As such, we propose that *relationship* is a very adequately termed leitmotif.[54]

Duvall and Hays offer three helpful criteria for a biblical leitmotif: "First, does this theme drive the plot of the biblical story from beginning to end? . . . Second, how extensively does this theme appear throughout the Bible? . . . Third, does the proposed center best account for other main themes, or is it also a subcategory?"[55] The first two questions have already been unambiguously answered in favor of our proposed leitmotif. The third question highlights the specific value of our chosen terminology of relationship since it is a collective term, a meta-analogy,[56] for the whole biblical range of God-human interactions. Therefore, we propose that while other terminological "candidates" for a relational leitmotif are very

---

48. Brunner, *Offenbarung und Vernunft*, 455–56; ETR 418–19.

49. Brunner, *Dogmatics I*, 83. For the broader discussion of Brunner's use of words, see section 3a.

50. See, e.g., Dowey, "Redeemer and Redeemed," 190.

51. Brown, *Believing Thinking*, 103.

52. Brown, "Personal Imperative of Revelation," 426–27; Williams, "Systematic Theology." See also section 10c.

53. Rehfeld, "Seinskonstitutive Christusbezogenheit," 71 (TM). Concerning Barth's similar view, see Meyer zu Hörste-Bührer, *Gott und Menschen*, 101, and our discussion in section 1b.

54. See also Sattler, *Beziehungsdenken*, 424.

55. Duvall and Hays, *Relational Presence*, 325–27.

56. See section 8d.

valuable and might appear more "biblical," they are not encompassing enough and are rather subcategories or concretizations of the overarching theme of relationship. As such, some examples might illustrate the point just made. Firstly, *covenant* can be considered one of the prime contenders for the position of leitmotif[57] and has been employed by many theologians,[58] not least by Barth.[59] However, while space does not allow an in-depth treatment of this immense topic,[60] and due to the fact that its depiction and interpretation varies widely, e.g., as contractual (exchange) or communal relationship,[61] we simply refer to the many theologians who treat covenant as a subcategory of relationship.[62] That said, we have no intention to minimize the centrality of covenant as a specific expression of the God-human relationship but it would be hard-pressed to serve as a leitmotif for the whole range of biblical texts.[63] Secondly, *community* or *communion* might be considered an adequate leitmotif.[64] While it is certainly a central term, it only comprises the positive (we have called this personal correspondence or intimate relationship) and not the broken aspects of the relationship as well.[65] These other themes of the Bible (e.g., sin) would then have to be defined as absence of community which in turn would commend relationship as the main category. Thirdly, the same point can be made concerning *love* as a leitmotif.[66] Furthermore, whereas one could argue that love is more specific than the generic term relationship the terminology would nonetheless need definitional clarity,[67] which is not an easy undertaking as has been indicated variedly.[68] Again, this is not to diminish the centrality of these terms but rather to mark them

57. See the introduction.

58. E.g., John Calvin, Jonathan Edwards, John Murray, Herman Bavinck, J. I. Packer, Vern Poythress.

59. Meyer zu Hörste-Bührer, *Gott und Menschen*, 289.

60. For some introductions, see Horton, *Introducing Covenant Theology*; Merkle, *Discontinuity to Continuity*; Waters, *Covenant Theology*.

61. See section 8b.

62. See, e.g., Fretheim, *God and World*, 15; Gunton, *The One*, 222; Glaw, *Bockmuehl*, 204–5.

63. Meyer zu Hörste-Bührer and Bührer, "Schlüssel zu Pluralität und Einheit," 200.

64. See, e.g., Gunton, *The One*, 215.

65. See sections 4c and 8d.

66. See, e.g., Oord, *Uncontrolling Love*.

67. See, e.g., Gergen, *Relational Being*, 43.

68. See, e.g., section 4c.

as subcategories of relationship. Fourthly, *faith* could be and has been proposed as a leitmotif—also for Brunner's conception—but emphasizes primarily the human part and as such only one aspect of the God-human relationship.[69] Moreover, it has been pointed out that *faith* is far from being unambiguously understood and needs serious relational reconsideration.[70] Lastly, one could choose some of the Bible's prime metaphora theological leitmotif. However, by stressing a certain metaphor, the kind and nature of the relationship is defined by it and gets changed when the metaphor is changed.[71] Hence, while the relational biblical analogies and metaphors like parent-child, friends, spouses, or king-subject show important and specific aspects, relationship, as an overarching theme, or what McFague calls a *root-metaphor*, is safeguarding that not any of the metaphors will be absolutized.[72] Having said that, while the specific metaphors need the frame of relationship for their unity in diversity,[73] relationship as leitmotif needs the specific metaphors to be animated.[74] As such, we propose, the leitmotif of relationship is a valid and important simplification for the systematic-theological task[75] that transcends and at the same time unites all compartmentalizations.[76] However, these remarks show also, that while the relationship-concept, its meaning and reality, must be conserved, the specific terminology is subject to changes of language in the future and might have to be adapted.

---

69. See section 3b.

70. See sections 3a and 6a.

71. DesCamp and Sweetser, "Metaphors for God," 212.

72. McFague, *Metaphorical Theology*, 108–12, 125–28, 146, 194. While her overall point is very important, her specific critique of certain metaphors is a matter of discussion.

73. Heim, *Adoption*, 325–29.

74. Sattler, *Beziehungsdenken*, 326–28. See also Boschki, *Religionspädagogik*, 106.

75. Sattler, *Beziehungsdenken*, 427.

76. Heim, *Adoption*, 333.

10

Outlook

Ten Propositions Expanding Emil Brunner's Leitmotif of Relationship

IT HAS BEEN ONE of the goals of this book to show that Emil Brunner's theology, permeated by his dynamic leitmotif of relationship, is without equal to this day.[1] However, Brunner himself was always keen to point out that "being finished seems . . . almost identical with being dead" and therefore his theology must always be "theology on the march."[2] Consequently, Brunner would have welcomed, and has explicitly done so,[3] that the leitmotif of his theology is expanded and adapted by the generations to come. We agree with Brunner that his leitmotif leads to a revolution of theology and the church[4] and we believe that this revolution has not taken place yet, at least not in the direction Brunner has pointed to and hoped for.[5] While this is by no means the first attempt to build on Brunner's legacy, we hold that his central leitmotif has thus far not been considered and expanded sufficiently although it should have been the center of Brunner scholarship.[6] As has been pointed out, Brunner was well aware of the unfinished character

---

1. See chapter 2.

2. Brunner, "Reply to Interpretation," 325. See also Brunner, *Dogmatik III*, 257; ETR 225; Altamira, "Offenbarungsgeschehen," 255.

3. Brunner, "Missionary Theology," 817–18.

4. Jehle, *Emil Brunner*, 425. This conviction has lead the author to create a website dedicated to this relationship revolution: www.relavution.net.

5. See, e.g., Wisse, "Truly Relational Theology," 159–60; and section 2b.

6. Alister McGrath has confirmed this observation in a personal meeting in 2018.

of his work, indeed, we believe that Brunner realized that his integration of this leitmotif was insufficient. This might be reflected in Brunner's absorbance with the "how" of the Faith: How do people come to faith? How do people remain in this intimate relationship? Brunner could not yet find satisfactory answers which is reflected in an unpublished chapter for his *Dogmatik III* with the title *Der Weg zum Glauben* (the way to faith).[7] Brunner admitted that its quality was insufficient but that this would be one of the most important areas for further research, leaving this task to future generations.[8] This assessment leads to two observations: First, it reflects Brunner's remark that due to their encompassing nature "the questions that worry the layman are both more interesting and more difficult than those which are the favored subjects of discussion by the theologians."[9] Second, Brunner was on the right path and would have had the "pieces" together to answer this all-encompassing question but could not integrate them: There is his central concern with the leitmotif of relationship and its dogmatic explication; there is his focus on a missionary theology and the corresponding question of communication and grasping; there is his vision of a Christian philosophy; there is Brunner's passion for the church and the increasing attempt to bridge the chasm between laypeople and academic theology; and finally there is his ethics, not only as a theological discipline but as a personal challenge. In essence, all of these areas combined could have led to a comprehensive theology of relationship, but Brunner did not quite live up to this. One can only speculate the reasons: Maybe he was yet lacking the integrative tools necessary, e.g., developments in psychology like relationship science? Maybe he was too absorbed by his quarrels with Barth and others? Maybe he was still too much bound up with classical reformed orthodoxy? However, we agree with McGrath[10] that Brunner's overall theology is like a series of snapshots or film scraps; everything is there but not yet edited and combined into a masterpiece.[11] Consequently, we propose that the effective integration and interconnection of all those

---

7. Brunner, *Weg zum Glauben*. See also Lütz, *Weg zum Glauben*, 251–63.

8. Brunner, "Reply to Interpretation," 331.

9. Brunner, *Faith, Hope, and Love*, 11. For similar statements, see Volf and Croasmun, *Life of the World*, 1, 6–7, 11, 33, 64, 81; Hempelmann, "Editorial"; Hilberath et al., *Communicative Theology*, 29.

10. Pointed out in a conversation in 2018.

11. This is one of the reasons why we consider *Truth as Encounter* Brunner's "masterpiece" since this short book comes closest to this overall integration, if only in a nutshell.

areas by the leitmotif of relationship is Brunner's greatest attempt, but also his main "shortcoming" and the prime expansion area towards a theology of relationship. Hence, starting with the main integration-thesis, we submit ten propositions of a theology of relationship, based on Emil Brunner, as fruitful and important subjects for further research.[12] The remaining nine theses will be grouped under three aspects of the relational leitmotif: its material, existential and formal integration.[13]

Thesis One: Integration

A theology of relationship is a systemic theology, integrating the focal point of relationship with God into all of its aspects and disciplines.

By referring to a *theology of relationship* one considers it part of systematic theology[14] and this is certainly the case. However, the term *systematic* is usually understood as being according to a specific system, plan, or method, hereby highlighting the structure. While this is valuable, we propose that *systemic theology* might be the more fitting term. *Systemic* emphasizes the relatedness to the whole (system), especially as opposed to emphasizing a particular part.[15] Since the center of life and theology is a relationship, this must permeate and affect every aspect of life and

---

12. After finishing this chapter, my doctoral supervisor Graham McFarlane's book *A Model for Evangelical Theology: Integrating Scripture, Tradition, Reason, Experience, and Community* came out. The similarities between many of his propositions and the ones in this chapter are coincidentally but very welcome and confirming (they are referenced subsequently in the footnotes).

13. For similar threefold categorizations, see Meyer zu Hörste-Bührer, *Gott und Menschen*, 9–10; Hilberath et al., *Communicative Theology*, 75, 81, 89; Sattler, *Beziehungsdenken*, 99, 477–78.

14. This is not the place to discuss the term and nature of *theology* (for a brief, specific discussion, see section 2b) and its differentiation from *systematic theology* or *dogmatics*. However, it has been pointed out that for the majority of church history theology as a whole has been identified with dogmatics (Leonhardt, *Grundinformation Dogmatik*, 63). Wayne Grudem defines systematic theology as "any study that answers the question, 'What does the whole Bible teach us today?' about any given topic." Grudem, *Systematic Theology*, 21. Grudem then goes on to differentiate it from other theological disciplines. For a very good more nuanced definition, see Fischer, *Systematische Theologie*, 237. However, some interpret *systematic* as referring to a closed system that as such needs to be overcome (Mühling, "Relationalität, Narrativität und Werte," 67; Mühling, *Post-Systematische Theologie I*).

15. For further considerations of the term *systemic*, see Schlippe and Schweitzer, *Lehrbuch der systemischen Therapie*, 31.

theology. Consequently, a theology of relationship must not only be systematic but is by definition systemic and, due to the existential scope and nature of the subject matter, all-encompassing.[16] Furthermore, a systemic understanding naturally and necessarily connects everything and integrates what materially often remains apart: theory and praxis, church and academia, dogmatics and ethics, theology and philosophy (or the sciences), the kingdom of God and "the world," the individual and the community, etc. Finally, a systemic understanding must also integrate the formal aspects of communication and grasping since epistemologically both are concerned with the perception of reality. Indeed, with a systemic view of theology, relationship becomes a *threshold concept*[17] or the hermeneutical lens for everything[18] and we propose that future research towards a theology of relationship must have a systemic view integrating the following nine theses.

a) Material: Towards a Systemic Theology of Relationship

Thesis Two: Dogmatics

A theology of relationship develops every dogmatic *topos* consistently with relationship as its leitmotif.

Brunner explicitly attempted to develop his relational leitmotif throughout the different dogmatic *topoi* within his three volumed *Dogmatics*.[19] In many respects he has accomplished this proposed goal, to "materialize"

---

16. Benedikt Göcke points out that theology is the *regina scientiae*, queen of the sciences, since it is concerned with God and humans (world) in relation and therefore encompasses the whole of reality. Göcke, "Theologie als Regina Scientiae." At the same convention Ingolf Dalferth has pointed out that theology is "more than a scientific discipline" and has a meta-perspective since "as *theology* it uses every form of reason, experience, and science that helps it to do its business, but as *evangelical theology* it critically and discerningly judges all these means and methods, tasks and results in the light and under the guidance of the gospel" (TM). See also Dalferth, *Crucified and Resurrected*, viii; McFarlane, *Evangelical Theology*, 31, 90. As per this definition, Brunner did not call it *theology* but cast the vision of a *Christian philosophy* and with his *law of relational closeness* he even had a very helpful tool in place.

17. See Abraham, "The Offense of Divine Revelation," 258–59. Also cited in McFarlane, *Evangelical Theology*, 52.

18. For the term *hermeneutic of relationship*, see Boschki, *Religionspädagogik*, 34.

19. Brunner, *Dogmatics II*, v-vi; Brunner, "Intellectual Autobiography," 16; Brunner, "Reply to Interpretation," 329.

his leitmotif, well.[20] Therefore, Gloege's critique that Brunner's personalism remains sheer formal principle, on the one hand, is simply wrong, yet on the other, he is right that there are aspects of Brunner's *Dogmatics* that lack the consequential personalism of his leitmotif.[21] However, the focus and space of this book do not allow to evaluate and dive deeper into these specific *topoi* although their assessment and critique would be an illuminating and important enterprise and worthy of further research. said, we believe that the main effort should be invested into a dogmatics with *relationship* as its consequential and explicit basic concept (*Grundbegriff*).[22] While Brunner is considered the first to have presented such a dogmatics,[23] it is our conviction that this can be done better by exploiting his "deep pass" and that this has not been "scored" thus far. How would the vision of an intimate relationship, defined as reciprocal, asymmetric, free, self-disclosing, and responsive affect theology proper, anthropology, hamartiology, soteriology, Christology, pneumatology, eschatology, ecclesiology, and even angelology, etc.?[24] How could existing attempts,[25] for example from trinitarian theology, other relational theologies, or Karl Barth,[26] be integrated and made fruitful? Hence, while this section is brief, the task itself might well be the most encompassing and daring endeavor of all the propositions since it concerns the theological foundation for everything else.

Thesis Three: Interdisciplinary

A theology of relationship is interdisciplinary and interrelates the different theological disciplines.

20. See also Cairns, "Theology of Emil Brunner," 305; Hauge, "Truth as Encounter," 133, 145–46.

21. Gloege, "Gläubiges Denken," 76. However, *Truth as Encounter* has been called "almost a whole dogmatics in nuce" (Althaus, "Wahrheit Als Begegnung: Rezension," 135–38, 137 [TM]) and we consider it Brunner's foremost example of a consequential explication of his leitmotif.

22. See also Boschki, *Religionspädagogik*, 325, 459; Meyer zu Hörste-Bührer, *Gott und Menschen*, 3, 405.

23. Jewett, *Concept of Revelation*, 68. Concerning Karl Barth's *Church Dogmatics*, see section 2b.

24. For the same proposal, see Duvall and Hays, *Relational Presence*, 326–27.

25. See the introduction.

26. See section 2b.

IV: Towards a Theology of Relationship

Relationship is systemic and therefore not only interrelates the dogmatic *topoi* but also bridges and interconnects the diverse theological disciplines. While the interrelation of dogmatics and exegesis has already been pointed out and appears to be obvious,[27] the leitmotif of relationship transcends all compartmentalizations be it biblical, systematic, practical, philosophical, and even historical theology, as well as apologetics, ethics, and missiology. That said, one might point out that this specialization was not yet highly evolved at Brunner's time and that he himself was more or less involved in all the disciplines. Indeed, while this is one of the strengths of Brunner's work, the call for interdisciplinarity has become stronger in recent years due to an increasing differentiation and lack of integration of the theological disciplines[28] and we propose that the relationship-lens brings them yet again closer together.[29] Hence, what is needed is not merely a multidisciplinary (no real integration) but an interdisciplinary (actual integration of knowledge and praxis) approach to theology[30] without devaluing or obscuring each disciplines specific contribution. Indeed, a relationship-view of the theological disciplines can prevent a mishmash or unification of the disciplines since it values the individual contribution while connecting it into a whole.[31] As such, future research should show how the leitmotif of relationship can positively affect interdisciplinary work materially as well as relationally[32] and communicatively.[33]

---

27. See section 9e. See also Brunner, *Dogmatics I*, 83; Rehfeld, "Seinskonstitutive Christusbezogenheit," 70; Meyer zu Hörste-Bührer and Bührer, "Schlüssel zu Pluralität und Einheit," 190, 195–97, 205, 216–17, 219.

28. See, e.g., Volf and Croasmun, *Life of the World*, 1, 6–7, 11, 33, 64, 81; Hempelmann, "Editorial."

29. See also Meyer zu Hörste-Bührer and Bührer, "Bindeglied zwischen Exegese und systematischer Theologie," 3–4, 7–8.

30. Concerning multidisciplinary and interdisciplinary relationship science, see our brief discussion in section 7b and Gillath et al., "Introduction," 6.

31. See Sandage and Brown, "Relational Integration (Part I)," 169–71. The principle is the same as with IOS in dyadic relationships (see section 8b).

32. See thesis six.

33. See thesis eight.

Thesis Four: Transdisciplinary

A theology of relationship transcends its discipline and is in dialogue with other scientific fields while each has its respective expertise and relevance.

Throughout this work, it has been shown that a theology of relationship has always both humans and God in its focus. Consequentially, what Brunner has called *theanthropocentrism*[34] speaks strongly for a theological approach where the anthropological is as important as the theological and the main question is how the two correlate.[35] Hence, Brunner's missionary theology with its recognition of a point of contact[36] leaves room for engagement with the sciences.[37] He believed that the Christian theologian was well equipped, by the law of relational closeness,[38] to engage in such a critical dialogue. While Brunner also had the natural sciences and philosophy in mind, he clearly placed the human sciences especially close to the actual center of God-human relationship. Indeed, he pointed out that "the way to faith" needs a novel transdisciplinary approach, especially as a dialogue between theology and psychology.[39] Nonetheless, Brunner warned that psychology, for example, can never be the base for theological reasoning or the source to inform a "neutral" anthropology since such a neutral discipline does not exist.[40]

While this remains true, much has changed since Brunner's death in 1966 and for the last fifty years, the conversation between theology and psychology has moved on from being novel.[41] It appears to be common sense that a holistic approach is needed and Shults points out that

---

34. See section 3c.

35. See also section 9e. As a reminder (see section 7b), this book specifically employs relationship science as a reference science in order to clarify the bases for theological analogical reasoning concerning *relationship*. As such, it has only clarified and cleared the ground for subsequent distinctly transdisciplinary research toward which thesis four points.

36. See section 2b.

37. Torrance had a similar view. See Palma, "Reformed Theology," 30.

38. See section 1b.

39. Brunner, "Reply to Interpretation," 331; McGrath, *Emil Brunner*, 73–74; Jehle, *Emil Brunner*, 372. See also Sattler, *Beziehungsdenken*, 247; Boschki, *Religionspädagogik*, 23–26, 61, 223; Balswick et al., *Reciprocating Self*, 31–34; Rabens, *Holy Spirit and Ethics*, 124, 129, 132, 252.

40. See, e.g., Cairns, "Brunner's Conception," 77.

41. Sandage and Brown, "Relational Integration (Part I)," 165.

a transdisciplinary approach discloses "aspects of reality that would have remained concealed if we had hidden behind disciplinary walls."[42] Many have taken up the baton offered by Brunner to fulfil his vision: James E. Loder, directly and indirectly influenced by Brunner, proposed such a transdisciplinary approach to spirituality.[43] LeRon Shults and Steven Sandage, themselves indebted to Loder,[44] have done much work at the intersection of theology and psychology[45] and others have followed their lead.[46] While those examples come from a strong theological background, the reverse, approaches where the psychological is primary, is also common and attachment theory is a very prevalent lens.[47] That said, the question of how the two disciplines correlate remains and is discussed variedly. For example, is psychology descriptive and theology prescriptive or are both, depending on the context?[48] Where lies the primacy, the starting point for integration, if there is any?[49] The answers to these questions are decisive and should not be taken lightly concerning future research. As has already been mentioned in the last thesis, we advocate an approach that weights each field according to its subject matter without fusion of the two. Hence, psychology is only concerned with humans and inner-worldly processes and not with transcendent realities. Theology, on the other hand, offers a transcendent view;[50] first, by being primarily concerned with God's self-disclosure to humans, but also second, by placing human nature within its transcendent reality, thus "completing" a merely psychological anthropology.[51]

Our proposed leitmotif is once again key, also for a transdisciplinary approach, since it postulates that God-human interaction is an actual,

---

42. Shults, *Theological Anthropology*, 47, 175–85.

43. Kovacs, *James E. Loder*, 16–17, 58–60, 63, 86–87; Loder, *The Logic of the Spirit*.

44. Kovacs, *James E. Loder*, 91.

45. See, e.g., Shults and Sandage, *Transforming Spirituality*; Sandage et al., "Relational Spirituality"; Majerus and Sandage, "Differentiation of Self."

46. See, e.g., Balswick et al., *Reciprocating Self*.

47. See, e.g., Granqvist, *Attachment in Religion*; Granqvist et al., "Religion as Attachment"; Kirkpatrick and Shaver, "Attachment Theory and Religion"; Moriarty et al., "Understanding the God Image through Attachment Theory"; Zahl and Gibson, "God Representations."

48. Sandage and Brown, "Relational Integration (Part I)," 172–73.

49. Sandage and Brown, "Relational Integration (Part II)," 180.

50. See also Balswick et al., *Reciprocating Self*, 99.

51. See especially chapter 4.

investigatable relationship but with the ultimate, transcendent "other" that can only be grasped through self-revelation. Whenever the difference of the divine and human subjects is not heeded, one is on dangerous ground; but also, whenever the two are taken apart, one misinterprets reality. When theology ignores empirical data concerning the human side of the relation, it is not grounded on no psychology but on bad or folk psychology.[52] When psychology (or anthropology, sociology, etc.) oversteps and wants to make claims about ultimate reality and the transcendent, it has left its scientific ground.[53] As theology needs psychology for the study of human processes, the human sciences need theology (and philosophy) to be set in the larger context of reality.[54] Future transdisciplinary research would do well to heed Brunner's cautions but also his constructive law of relational closeness to consequentially differentiate the human side in light of God's self-disclosure while constantly perceiving them as interrelated.

b) Existential: Towards an Intimate Relationship with God

Thesis Five: The Theologian

A theology of relationship is undertaken by theologians having an intimate relationship with the triune God.

The most influential component in any theology is doubtless the theologian.[55] This is especially true for a theology of relationship since it revolves around and attempts to fathom an existential reality. This reality of relation to God is a given that no human being can escape.[56] Consequently, it is impossible for the theologian to take a distanced, objective perspective

---

52. Sandage and Brown, "Relational Integration (Part I)," 174.

53. The psychology of religion might be in danger of this and therefore Brunner has considered it the least useful of the psychological disciplines (see section 1b). Another emerging field is neuroscience that should not attempt to naturalistically explain what they cannot (see, e.g., Hempelmann, "Wunder," 211–12; Schweitzer, "Illusion," 7–11; Fuchs, *Das Gehirn*, 17–19). A very good example in anthropology for a positive differentiation by explicitly focussing on the human side is Luhrmann, *God Talks*, xxiv–xxv, 223.

54. See, e.g., Hempelmann, "Wunder," 210; Harris, "Personhood," 222; Oster, *Person-Sein*, 97; Poythress, *Redeeming Sociology*, 24–29, 46–47.

55. See, e.g., Sandage and Brown, "Relational Integration (Part I)," 172–74.

56. See chapter 4.

because existentially she is always already personally involved, be it consciously or unconsciously, be it intimately or distanced. Hence, this is the unique disposition of the theologian and the unique circumstance of her subject matter.[57] One could argue that this is not unique at all since, for example, relationship scientists are also always involved in relationships and yet can take an observant position. While this is certainly true to some degree, allowing for the fact that the "objective" standpoint is questioned in most disciplines,[58] the theologian's position remains different since she is involved with the specific relationship partner she investigates. As such, it would be as if the relationship scientist would study his father's relationships; he cannot not be part of it. However, while this might appear like a disadvantage, for theology it is a given and cannot be escaped and as such Brunner calls the theologian a "wanderer between two worlds."[59] Furthermore, it becomes clear why the nature of the relationship the theologian has with God is crucial. When the heart and goal of the Christian faith is an intimate relationship, then it is of utmost importance that the theologian has first-hand knowledge of the subject matter which revolves not around a thing or a doctrine but the living triune God himself. Without encounter there is no actual knowledge of God, reminding us of Brunner's *Truth as Encounter*.[60] Consequently, this knowledge of God and the corresponding reflection and communication can only be accomplished and sustained through an intimate relationship.

According to Kierkegaard "a person must come to know the truth of the Christian faith by giving his life over to the God who reveals himself in Jesus Christ."[61] Influenced by Kierkegaard, Brunner puts it this way:

> The true theologian does not only think about the Faith and about the revelation given in faith, but in the very act of thinking he continually renews the act of faith; as a believing man he turns his attention to the revelation granted to faith. . . . Only

---

57. This is also one of the main points McFarlane makes throughout his work, be it for the academic or the "ordinary" theologian (McFarlane, *Evangelical Theology*, 7, 27–29, 34, 39–42, 58, 163–68, 215–17).

58. Brooks, *Social Animal*, 247, 250, quoting a Japanese proverb: "Don't study something. Get used to it." See also Luhrmann, *God Talks*, 114.

59. Brunner, *Wahrheit als Begegnung*, 113 (TM).

60. See chapter 1. See also Palma, "Reformed Theology," 8, 23; Hempelmann, "Editorial."

61. Torrance, *Freedom to Become*, 25.

where faith and rationality are rightly interlocked can we have true theology, good dogmatics.[62]

Again, since every theologian is in relation to God, the alternative to an intimate relationship would be a distanced, ignorant, or hostile relationship which would lead to a distorted picture of God and make it impossible to do theology well since it is a theology *of* relationship. Indeed, the only honest alternative to this would be to consider the endeavor a distanced study of religions which would have nothing to do with Christian theology.[63] While the perception of this intrinsic interweaving of theology and theologian is by no means new,[64] it nonetheless requests further research. Volf, for example, gives this interrelation quite extensive consideration in his manifesto and comes to a similar conclusion summarized by a quote from Jürgen Moltmann: "without theological life, there is no proper theological work."[65] Indeed, if theologians would more readily embrace and recognize this interconnection of personal life and theology, it would help bridge the gap between the academy and the church. Hilberath et al. even indicate that "academic theology itself laments the evident lack of connection with Christian practice."[66] Therefore, we propose that the leitmotif of relationship frames this conjointness perfectly, highlights its compelling logic, and offers at the same time the focal point for its accomplishment. To put it in the words of Thomas Merton: "Contemplation, far from being opposed to theology, is in fact the normal perfection of theology."[67]

Thesis Six: The Community

A theology of relationship affects and is affected by relationships.

The focus of this work has explicitly been the vertical God-human relationship as the central and primal relationship dimension;[68] however, the

---

62. Brunner, *Dogmatics I*, 76.

63. See, e.g., McFarlane, *Evangelical Theology*, 8.

64. See, e.g., Brown, "Personal Imperative of Revelation," 433–34; Wan, "Relational Missiology," 1–4; Brümmer, *Model of Love*, 18–19.

65. Volf and Croasmun, *Life of the World*, 115–35.

66. Hilberath et al., *Communicative Theology*, 29.

67. Merton, *New Seeds*, 258–59.

68. See also Boschki, *Religionspädagogik*, 299.

influence of and ramifications for horizontal relationships are of utmost importance and have only been considered rudimentarily.[69] Hence, we propose that the findings of relationship science, only employed for analogical statements in this book, have also shown the potential reciprocal influence of vertical and horizontal relationships and that this is an important area for future research. In other words, it should be investigated how human relationships affect one's theology and relationship with God, and how one's relationship with God affects human relationships. A good example concerning relationships affecting theology is Tanya Luhrmann's anthropological study *When God Talks Back*, where she investigates and documents the American evangelical church community's influence on personal faith and faith praxis.[70] Furthermore, some studies are using attachment theory to shed light on the interconnection of parental relationships and spiritual development.[71] Concerning the theological process, *communicative theology* has focused on the communal dimension of doing theology and how the communication and relationship between scholars influence their theology.[72] However, there is much room left for additional research and the interconnection with relationship science appears to be a promising field. Vice versa, theology affecting the view and praxis of human relationships (ethics) is at least as worthy of further research: God's self-disclosure shows how relationships are meant to be and his relationship with us becomes the prototype for our relationships with each other.[73] Besides Emil Brunner,[74] Karl Barth's *analogia relationis* points in this direction.[75] One recent monograph that treats this question with a

---

69. See sections 1a and 5b. Some might even argue that this vertical focus mirrors Brunner's underexposure of the corporate dimension of faith, which indeed would be an interesting area for Brunner research. However, for now we hold that while Brunner's *reflection* of this subject matter might have been insufficient his *praxis* was certainly not.

70. See, e.g., Luhrmann, *God Talks*, 62, 131, 222, 279.

71. See, e.g., Granqvist et al., "Religion as Attachment," 54.

72. Hilberath et al., *Communicative Theology*, 35, 59. Their very helpful categorizations of dimensions and interaction processes contain also the theologian (thesis five) and the world (thesis seven). Concerning transdisciplinary relations, see Sandage and Brown, "Relational Integration (Part I)," 165–67. For the communal dimension of theology, see McFarlane, *Evangelical Theology*, 25.

73. See, e.g., Hilberath et al., *Communicative Theology*, 57; Poythress, *Redeeming Sociology*, 24–29, 46–47.

74. See section 9e concerning a *theomorphic* understanding.

75. See, e.g., Deddo, *Theology of Relations*, 412–14, 419; Meyer zu Hörste-Bührer, *Gott und Menschen*, 145.

transdisciplinary approach is *The Reciprocating Self: Human Development in Theological Perspective*.[76] However, much more research is needed not only on the cognitive level of influence but also on the existential level, studying how an intimate relationship with God affects the manner we interact with human persons. Again, relationship science appears to be of seminal importance since its empirical approach sheds further light on theological convictions.[77]

A biographical example for this bidirectional influence, as we have seen,[78] is Brunner's collision with the praxis of the Oxford Group that had an important and arguably positive impact on his life and work as a theologian. Thus, what are the disruptive and maybe controversial movements today that might act as existential catalysts and challenge the theologians?[79] Finally, this theme of relationships influencing theology and theology influencing relationships might also be made fruitful considering the ecumenical dialogue, but only with a robust theology of relationship in place.

Thesis Seven: The World

A theology of relationship is persistently in conversation with current culture and challenges, and points to the existential centrality of a relationship with God.

Emil Brunner's commitment to a missionary or missional theology has been emphasized throughout this work and is one of the unique characteristics of his life's work.[80] The leitmotif of relationship intrinsically relates, so to speak, heaven to earth and earth to heaven. Consequently, the existence of points of contact with current culture and experience matters fundamentally and Brunner has brought this time and again to the forefront of the theological task. However, today Brunner is not alone with this mission and well-known theologians like Alister McGrath

---

76. See especially Balswick et al., *Reciprocating Self*, 17, 28, 55, 73, 302.
77. See also thesis four.
78. See section 1a.
79. For a similar point concerning disruptive experiences and movements, see McFarlane, *Evangelical Theology*, 179.
80. See especially section 2b.

concerning apologetics[81] and Miroslav Volf with his public theology[82] emphasize similar points. However, all three do not stress *relationship* as the central point of contact but rather as an outcome.[83] Brunner, as has been shown, does not consequentially integrate his leitmotif with his missional focus; both remain largely separate and therefore relationality is not much reflected missionally. McGrath proposes faith as "inherently relational" and repeatedly points in this direction, yet does not explicitly employ the potential of such a relational approach for postmodernity's challenges.[84] Volf, in his manifesto, has chosen *flourishing life* as the leitmotif and the underlying implicit answer to the question of flourishing as well as the means to accomplish it is an intimate relationship with God,[85] the center from which every other area of life and the world as a whole is affected.[86] As much as we agree, we propose, however, that the relevance of relationship should not be in the background but the foreground:

> True intimacy with others is one of the highest values of human existence; there may be nothing more important for the well-being and optimal functioning of human beings than intimate relationships, . . . relationships give meaning to life; all else is background![87]

This assessment is not merely a point made by relationship science but a deep awareness of humankind, at all times and everywhere on planet earth, indicative of our ontic being related, of our being the *imago Dei*.[88] This "relational ontology" can be detected as a hunch in secular literature[89] and has been proposed as the only relevant path to give an account of the Christian Faith in our time.[90] We speculate that this growing awareness of relationality might be reflected in a decrease of religiosity

---

81. See, e.g., McGrath, *Mere Apologetics*, 37.

82. See, e.g., Volf and Croasmun, *Life of the World*, 1, 6–7, 11, 33, 64, 81.

83. McFarlane's proposal might be considered "in-between" (see McFarlane, *Evangelical Theology*, 231–36).

84. McGrath, *Mere Apologetics*, 31–34.

85. Made explicit here: Volf and Croasmun, *Life of the World*, 150, 163, 165–81.

86. Volf and Croasmun, *Life of the World*, 7, 75, 86.

87. Prager and Roberts, "Deep Intimate Connection," 43. See also Reis et al., "Emergence of Relationship Science," 559.

88. See chapter 4.

89. See, e.g., Brooks, *Social Animal*, xv, 372.

90. Knauer, "Ontología Relacional," 17.

and an increase of spirituality.[91] From a sociological and philosophical perspective, Hartmut Rosa calls this encompassing relational human predisposition *resonance*.[92] His seminal book *Resonanz: Eine Soziologie der Weltbeziehung*[93] offers a penetrating analysis of late modernity's desperation and quest for lost resonance while at the same time clinging to fantasies of feasibility even concerning resonance itself.[94] Consequently, this leads to unrewarding "resonance-simulations" since true resonance cannot be "self-made." Rather, it has to "come to you"[95] and can only be a response to a call.[96] As such, Rosa's proposal of the centrality of resonance sounds very much like Brunner's encounter and is quite controversial since Rosa intends not only to show how it is (descriptive) but how it ought to be (normative).[97] While Rosa's analysis is to be commended in its understanding of society and for even making a space for faith and religion,[98] ultimately his secular solution misses the mark by remaining intra-worldly. Hence, his weakness, limitation, and finally contradiction are as follows: to provide the necessary "vertical" resonance the world itself must be subjectivized and personalized (nature, art, immanent religion) to occupy the place of a genuine transcendent "other."[99] As such, Rosa's resonance is stuck in an "echo chamber" although he tries to avoid it.[100] In other words, spirituality can become a form of pseudo-relationship (pseudo-resonance) where God is substituted with the spirituality (resonance) itself leading to a sense of connection without an actual personal counterpart.[101] We propose that this resonance-failure is the fate of every relational ontology without an actual transcendent You

---

91. Oman, "Religion and Spirituality," 23–24, 40. McFarlane goes further and argues that spirituality is relationship (McFarlane, *Evangelical Theology*, 248).

92. Rosa, *Resonanz*, 295.

93. Translated as *Resonance: a Sociology of Our Relationship to the World*.

94. Rosa, *Resonanz*, 522, 596, 599–600, 621, 623–24, 677, 688, 706–7, 722, 739.

95. Rosa, *Resonanz*, 619, 626, 653.

96. Rosa, *Resonanz*, 305, 447.

97. Rosa, *Resonanz*, 747–48, 756.

98. Laube, "Eine bessere Welt ist möglich," 370; Kläden, "Hartmut Rosa als Gesprächspartner," 395–96.

99. Rosa, *Resonanz*, 289, 325, 331, 339, 435–36, 437–38, 443, 447, 452, 456, 482, 485, 491. For a similar critique, see also Rosenstock, "Konturen einer resonanzsensiblen Theologie," 401–3.

100. Rosa, *Resonanz*, 495, 621.

101. See Guthrie, "Anthropomorphism," 39.

as its foundation¹⁰² and that only a theology of relationship can provide answers for the challenges of the human-world relationship as portrayed by Rosa. Thus, to execute Brunner's vision of a missionary theology, future research should find ways to relate cultural questions, wants, and issues (e.g., the environment) to the opportunity and relevance of an intimate relationship with God. Consequently, this leads to the challenge of communication.

c) Formal: Towards a Communication of Relationship

How do people learn something? Wittgenstein answers threefold: It has to be explained with an analogy. It has to be taught with a story. It has to be shown by example.¹⁰³ Indeed, we propose that this is precisely the path a theology of relationship has to take in order to communicate its existential content well and consequently, the next three theses are structured accordingly.

Thesis Eight: Language

A theology of relationship avoids abstractions and stays close to the language game of relationship.

The central thesis of this work and the central content of Brunner's theology is based on an analogy, the analogy of relationship.¹⁰⁴ However, Brunner's thought appears to have been a "work in progress" concerning matters of grasping and communicating this analogy. While in *Wahrheit als Begegnung* he still clothed the explication of the I-You relationship in sometimes very abstract and technical terms, he later turned increasingly towards laypeople and slightly adapted the mode of communication accordingly.¹⁰⁵ This process makes sense since by opposing abstractions materially he would also have to avoid them formally, hereby doing justice to his own proposal of the interconnection between form and

---

102. See the discussion in section 2b. For more examples from pedagogy, see Krautz, "Relationalität," 23–24; Spaemann, "Wirklichkeit als Anthropomorphismus," 46–50.

103. Schulte, *Wittgenstein*, 207.

104. See chapter 9.

105. See, e.g., Brunner, "Natur und Gnade," 372; Lütz, *Weg zum Glauben*, 31–32; Althaus et al., *Briefwechsel*, 169; Dowey, "Redeemer and Redeemed," 202–3.

content in language.[106] Radically put, language "creates" content and in a specific understanding even constitutes reality.[107] Consequently, a theology of relationship must also find an adequate language. Whilst the call for a relational language[108] or a new language of faith[109] is not new, however, we propose that one need not invent a new *language game*, as Wittgenstein has called it. On the contrary, since the analogy of relationship is not *sui generis*, the "religious" language of the relationship with God should not be likewise.[110] We even propose, rather, that "God-talk" has to become "normal" and vernacular[111] and that its terms and expressions have to be constantly changed and culturally adapted so that the original meaning is preserved.[112] As such, we believe that any fideism must not only be rejected materially but also formally: there must not be a Christian language game![113] Indeed, we state that this "reverse translation" from religious to vernacular language is not only the task and the sign of a good apologist (McGrath),[114] or a good theologian (Holmer),[115] but that it is the only adequate form to speak about a relationship and therefore to enter the language game of relationship fitting the analogy of relationship. What does this mean concerning the scientific language game of academic theologians? According to Wittgenstein, scientific, objective language is inadequate for absolute truth.[116] As did Brunner before him, he perceives scientific language on another level than the first-order language of relationship; speaking about God is different from speaking to him.[117] However, Brunner has made clear that even scientific

106. See, e.g., Brunner, "Anknüpfungspunkt," 241–42. Torrance has made the same point (Palma, "Reformed Theology," 8, 13).

107. Rosa, *Resonanz*, 152–53; Volf and Croasmun, *Life*, 135.

108. Fretheim, *God and World*, 16, 301.

109. Rollefson and Gouwens, *Kierkegaard and Wittgenstein*, 123–24.

110. See, e.g., DesCamp and Sweetser, "Metaphors for God," 215; Barrett, "Basement," 236–37; Guthrie, "Anthropomorphism," 42.

111. Against Suk, "Personal Relationship with Jesus." Wittgenstein has said the same concerning philosophy (Schulte, *Wittgenstein*, 135).

112. See section 3a.

113. Comstock, "Truth or Meaning," 756. See also the discussion in Ross, "Analogy in Theology," 141–42.

114. McGrath, *Mere Apologetics*, 20, 37.

115. Rollefson and Gouwens, *Kierkegaard and Wittgenstein*, 74, 117.

116. Schulte, *Wittgenstein*, 102–3.

117. Brunner, *Dogmatics I*, 38–39, 62–64; Brown, "Personal Imperative of Revelation," 427–29. See also Rollefson and Gouwens, *Kierkegaard and Wittgenstein*, 109.

theological language needs to stay close to the existential reality it talks about. Otherwise, its content gets objectified, distorted, and thus misunderstood.[118] We believe that this relational "vernacularisation" of theological language might be instrumental to bridge the divide between the academy and the church both ways.[119] Not only would theology be better understood by laypeople, but the church's relationship-language would then also become more considered and thus more theological.[120] Future research towards a theology of relationship should focus on the question of how this theology can be done and communicated by staying close to the language game of relationship. We propose that one fruitful marker of this language game is narration and as such to be found in the Bible.[121]

Thesis Nine: Narration

A theology of relationship rediscovers narration to communicate adequately and effectively.

Theology is concerned with narration since "narrative is a central element in the founding document of Christianity. The Bible tells stories."[122] However, the question is whether theology also purposefully employs narration or whether it rather focusses on abstracting and systematizing the biblical content. We have already discussed that Brunner is very critical of the latter and advocates the former.[123] Indeed, Brunner might well be considered a proponent of a *narrative theology*,[124] along with Paul

---

118. Hauge, "Truth as Encounter," 145; Brunner, *Dogmatik III*, 228; ETR 196; McFarlane, *Evangelical Theology*, 44–48. For a similar point of view from sociology, see Rosa, *Resonanz*, 287; and from pedadogy, see Künkler, "Relationalität menschlicher Existenz," 63–64.

119. See also Meyer zu Hörste-Bührer, *Gott und Menschen*, 405.

120. For a similar train of thought, see Mauz, "Theology and Narration," 275.

121. See, e.g., McFague, *Metaphorical Theology*, 20, 43, 48; Anderson, *Living Waters*, 23.

122. Mauz, "Theology and Narration," 261.

123. See section 3b. See, e.g., Brunner, *Our Faith*, 33; Schmid, *Lehre von Gott*, 128–29.

124. *Narrative theology* is no "neutral" terminology but also referring to a certain stream of theological thought whose depiction and differentiation is beyond the scope of this book. For a brief introduction to the English speaking stream, see Comstock, "Truth or Meaning"; Köstenberger, "Aesthetic Theology"; and for the German speaking discussion, see Mauz, "Theology and Narration." For an evaluation of narrative

Ricoeur,[125] Eberhard Jüngel,[126] Kevin Vanhoozer,[127] or Alister McGrath,[128] that emphasizes "the story" and stories not only as an important cognitive instrument but as the adequate form for its material content.[129] As such, we propose that narration exists not for its own sake[130] but "transports" relationships[131] since through narration a person is known, if only indirectly, and it is the primary language for relationships.[132] Furthermore, with stories the accuracy lies in the whole that cannot be reduced to specific or abstract terms. As such, stories are more precise by being less precise.[133] Put differently, while being very comprehensible and adequate to the subject matter, narration, simultaneously, repulses ultimate conceivability by safeguarding mystery.[134] Hence, a theology of relationship is also narrative theology. Future research should explore the variety of narration that communicates the God-human relationship. What is the role of the original biblical story with its diverse stories? What is the role of parables, both biblical and contemporary?[135] How could metaphorical language be understood as personal language, "mini-narrations," without making the personal metaphorical?[136] What is the role of the personal

---

approaches in exegesis, see the monumental work Heilig, *Paulus als Erzähler*. However, what we refer to is not the "theological theory of narration" but a "storytelling theology" (Mauz, "Theology and Narration," 277).

125. See, e.g., Comstock, "Truth or Meaning," 756.

126. See, e.g., Mauz, "Theology and Narration," 275–77.

127. See, e.g., Vanhoozer, *Drama of Doctrine*, 273.

128. See, e.g., McGrath, *Mere Apologetics*, 138–39.

129. Brunner has even been called a forefather of narrative theology (Olson, "Narrative Theology").

130. See also Mauz, "Theology and Narration," 268–71.

131. Rosa, *Resonanz*, 268.

132. Meyer zu Hörste-Bührer, *Gott und Menschen*, 321–39. See also Rollefson and Gouwens, *Kierkegaard and Wittgenstein*, 104; LaCugna, "The Relational God," 662–63.

133. See, e.g., Brunner, *Dogmatik III*, 453–54; ETR 405–7; Härle, "Relationale Erkenntnistheorie," 26–27; Maurer, "Metapher als eigentliche Rede," 44–47; Heim, *Adoption*, 322.

134. The maintenance of mystery is something that is consistently called for in theology (e.g., Seubert, "Kommunizieren in unserer Zeit," 9). However, we propose that a theology of relationship is both graspable and enigmatic. See also Fretheim, *God Enters*, 15.

135. See, e.g., Rollefson and Gouwens, *Kierkegaard and Wittgenstein*, 79.

136. For this differentiation, see Maurer, "Metapher als eigentliche Rede," 39–40. Concerning metaphors, see also White, "Metaphorical God," 197–98; Sanders, *Theology in the Flesh*, 49–52. See also our brief discussion concerning the difference of metaphor and analogy (section 7c).

story of faith, the so-called testimony?[137] Furthermore, how could and should narration in all these forms not only be part of preaching and the church realm but also in academic theology? We believe that through relationship as a material and existential leitmotif, the formal adjustments follow more easily, yet this is not to say that it follows automatically. Emil Brunner himself is a good example, whilst he theoretically emphasized a narrative approach, he did not use much narration in his works.[138] Indeed, he once stated: "As a systematician narration is not in my nature."[139] That said, we hold that this statement is no "easy way out" for the systematic theologian and that Brunner's lack in this respect is challenged by others who actually implemented narration in their systematic endeavors. Karl Barth, for example, gives the biblical narrative room repeatedly in his *Church Dogmatics* and hereby changes the tone of his systematic and more abstract considerations.[140] Klaus von Stosch boldly and innovatively frames each chapter of his introduction to systematic theology with a fictional love story between two students.[141] Others have purposefully, yet tentatively, integrated occasional stories into their works, showing that there is still much room for improvement concerning the stories' content, structure, and integration among systematic theologians.[142]

Thesis Ten: Encounter

A theology of relationship emphasizes encounter with God represented and presented by the church.

Naturally, by considering the formal aspects of a theology of relationship one tends to speak of the communication *about* God; consequentially, thesis eight and nine have focused primarily on third-person language. However, the existential encounter with God is fundamental to the knowledge about and the grasping of God[143] and therefore must

---

137. See, e.g., Luhrmann, *God Talks*, 8, 326.
138. Lüdemann, *Denken*, 295.
139. Brunner, "Oxforder Gruppenbewegung," 268 (TM).
140. Meyer zu Hörste-Bührer, *Gott und Menschen*, 321–39.
141. Stosch, *Einführung Systematische Theologie*.
142. See, e.g., Sattler, *Beziehungsdenken*, 458–60, 464. However, there are many story-tellers that explicitly implement systematic theology in their works (most famously Lewis, *Chronicles of Narnia*; Young, *The Shack*).
143. See also thesis five.

be considered part of the communication process. While Brunner says that true learning only occurs when God himself teaches[144] and Merton agrees by emphasizing that "the only One Who can teach me to find God is God, Himself, Alone,"[145] we have briefly shown that the church (the Christian, the theologian) also has an important role to play in this self-disclosure and "teaching" of God.[146] Indeed, teaching and therefore speaking about God has an important place but in order to lead to encounter, the communication has to be more than words. Cognition of persons and relationships happens as "embodied human experience"[147] where words and praxis merge.[148] Wittgenstein's conviction has already been mentioned, namely, that for a person to learn something it has to be shown by example and the theoretical has to be made practical.[149] Relationship, therefore, has to be exemplified by the communicator and ultimately experienced by the addressee. As such, then, a theology of relationship must address these issues and any future research should focus on developing adequate answers. We propose two fruitful areas for further investigations: the church's communication through re-presentation and presentation.

First, the church represents God and as such is God's embodied self-communication. Brunner puts it thus: "Theology is the science of communication. The self-communication of God is its theme. But this is at the same time the essence of the *ekklesia*."[150] How then does the church not simply *bring* the message but also practically *be* the message by embodying the Holy Spirit?[151] What is the role of the fruit of the Spirit concerning this representation?[152] Furthermore, how can the church as the representative of Jesus re-present, show, and model an intimate relationship

---

144. Brunner, *Dogmatik I*, 24. The German wordplay with *lehren* and *lernen* can only be translated inadequately.

145. Merton, *New Seeds*, 38.

146. Section 5b.

147. Sanders, *Theology in the Flesh*, 19–20. See also Smedes, "Emil Brunner Revisited," 200–201.

148. See, e.g., McGrath, *Mere Apologetics*, 38, 138; Gergen, *Relational Being*, 34.

149. See, e.g., Schulte, *Wittgenstein*, 34–35; Rollefson and Gouwens, *Thinking*, 128–30.

150. Brunner, "Reply to Interpretation," 329. See also Brunner, *Dogmatik III*, 17–18; ETR 4–5.

151. Brunner, *Dogmatik III*, 124–25, 159–60, 162; ETR 102, 134, 137. See also Gunton, *The One*, 217–18.

152. See section 1a for Brunner's emphasis on this topic.

with God and invite others to partake in its first-person language of faith and encounter? What would this communication and teaching through embodied representation mean for the academic discipline of theology? Future research should, led by the motif of relationship, invest in these questions.

Secondly, if encounter is the goal of communication then the church, as a signpost, or more relationally put as a matchmaker, must present God.[153] As Philip said to Nathanael "come and see," the church needs to (metaphorically speaking) take people by the hand and lead them to Jesus himself.[154] This story from John 1:43–51[155] shows well the role of the church in this encounter: it is a pointer, a presenter, but the actual encounter is God's responsibility.[156] However, further research should show how this "arranging" of encounter can happen today with Jesus not being physically present. Brunner, as has been shown,[157] discovered increasingly what he has called the *dynamism* or the power of the church. We believe that this is an important and fruitful avenue that should be rediscovered and investigated within a relational framework: what the New Testament calls signs[158] and wonders leads to encounters with God administered through the church in partnership with the Holy Spirit as matchmakers.[159] Brunner was well aware that the so-called supernatural or miraculous is an affront for the modern person, especially the academic,[160] and this might be the reason why there is not much academic work done in this area.[161] All the more, a theology of relationship could provide the larger context for this specific issue since there

---

153. Others have called this role *broker, middlemen*, or *mediator* (Richards and James, *Misreading Scripture*, 276–85).

154. See also McGrath, *Mere Apologetics*, 44–45, 77, 129.

155. For the corresponding exegesis see, e.g., Schnelle, *Evangelium nach Johannes*, 66.

156. See also McFarlane, *Evangelical Theology*, 54.

157. See sections 1a and 5b.

158. See, e.g., Anderson, *Living Waters*, 12.

159. Concerning the Spirit as divine matchmaker, see Leithart, "Common Spirit," quoting James Jordan.

160. Brunner, *Offenbarung und Vernunft*, 323; ETR 294. The same assessment is made by Hempelmann, "Wunder," 204–5.

161. For a monumental case for miracles, see Keener, *Miracles*. For an argument for the centrality of miracles in the ministry of Jesus, Paul, and the early church, see the works by Graham H. Twelftree. For the role of the supernatural in charismatic church praxis from an anthropologist's perspective, see Luhrmann, *God Talks*.

is a true relationship and interaction between the transcendent and the immanent. Consequently, the miraculous should not only be expected[162] but be part of both relationship praxis and theological reflection.

A relationship can only be partly communicated with words. An intimate relationship must be experienced and lived. It is our calling as church, as individual Christians, as well as theologians to make this encounter with the living God the priority for ourselves as well as to help others toward this goal. Trappist contemplative, Thomas Merton, adds helpfully: "The highest vocation in the Kingdom of God is that of sharing one's contemplation with others and bringing other men to the experimental knowledge of God that is given to those who love Him perfectly."[163] Pastor-author Bill Johnson puts it even more briefly: "I owe the world a Spirit-filled life, for I owe them an encounter with God."[164]

---

162. Hempelmann, "Wunder," 202.
163. Merton, *New Seeds*, 275.
164. Johnson, *When Heaven Invades Earth*, 197.

Epilogue

THE PROJECT OF THIS book was more than a project, it was personal, and it remains personal. It involves me. What I have been proposing in this book has been put to the test personally during its development along all three lines of thought towards a theology of relationship: materially, existentially, and formally.

At the time of writing these lines, the world is in the middle of a crisis. The Coronavirus (COVID-19) epidemic has its grip around our planet as well as the hearts and minds of its human inhabitants. While the initial shock, confusion, and measures (major lockdowns) belong in most places already to the past, the present is marked by a confusion concerning *the truth* in all of this, leading to opposing camps that have become increasingly radical. Social media observance suggests that people are desperate to find footing and stability in the knowledge of how things actually are. Indeed, this desperation for some stability in a world and age of constant change and uncertainty (also called postmodernity) appears to be one of the general markers of our time and shows little evidence of subsiding soon. Therefore, especially in these times, Brunner's take on truth as a relational category is very helpful. While it does not solve everything, it does point to a security that lies in a connection with a very capable "Other." By extension, in these encounters with God, there is the possibility of an indirect solution for many of the worlds pressing problems as they are intrinsically interwoven with us as human beings.

Amid this present crisis, I find this perspective on truth very helpful and a plausible antidote to extremism as well as ignorance.

Secondly, this book has challenged me existentially. To write theoretically about the fact that the main thing is an intimate relationship with God and not theoretical knowledge has proven to be unexpectedly demanding. Whilst this book is the product of four years of focus on thinking about the relationship with God, this thinking did not automatically result in living the relationship. At times, the dichotomy between knowledge and praxis has been experienced more strongly than probably ever before: to better understand something increases the responsibility to live accordingly. However, with a heightened focus on thinking and writing, it became a heightened challenge to write not simply *about* God but *with* God, to continue to grow in intimacy with God, and to stay on task in helping people encounter him.[1] That said, it has been serendipitous to have had only very limited time for the book and the role of being a pastor has grounded me and saved me from getting lost in thinking. Yet, I now better understand Brunner's struggle between theory and praxis.[2] At the same time, the asymmetry of the relationship with God, his grace and his taking the initiative, has become even more comforting a reality. Overall, this research has been a twofold gift in providing a clearer and stronger foundation of a theology of relationship and correspondingly, an even higher expectation of what to aim for in life.

Finally, it has been a constant joy to see the theology of relationship being at work in praxis, besides writing about it. Uncountable encounters with Christians and Not-Yet-Christians, speaking to young people and the older generation, explaining the basics of faith as well as discussing complex theological issues, facing crushing tragic and joyous excitement; and in all of this, the relevance and impact of a theology of relationship has proven to be enormous. Given that this book has pointed towards a communication of relationship,[3] I want to illustrate this with a brief story that stands for many more like it.

One Sunday night after church I was chatting with a young man. Jason[4] visited our service for the first time. Since he was in a relationship with a young woman from our church, he wanted to give it a try.

1. See theses five and ten.
2. See section 1a.
3. See section 10c.
4. For matters of privacy the name is changed and the details of the story are slightly obscured.

Epilogue

However, Jason would not consider himself a Christian and was very critical despite his positive experience that evening. He bombarded me with many good, relevant, and probing questions.

I loved it.
I told him so.
He loved that, too.

I also told him that we might need more time and asked whether he would consider meeting for coffee to engage further. He agreed. We met weekly and tackled questions on heaven and hell, grace and sin, suffering and peace, amongst others, and I helped him to gain a fresh perspective on these issues through a lens of relationship.

He was intrigued.

For the first time in his life, those matters made sense and my relational analogies and my non-religious language helped him grasp otherwise abstract conceptions. Nonetheless, he kept his inner distance and always brought new questions to the table. At one point, he asked about my personal relationship with God and how he would have to imagine this intimacy with the transcendent. I explained and gave him examples of how I believe to hear God's voice.

Once again, Jason was intrigued.

I told him that in our next meeting we would postpone the questions and that I believe he would hear God's voice for himself.

He was nervous.
I was, too.

The following week we started our time together with a simple question he wanted to ask God. It was a very personal question. After a short instruction, he "heard" a very personal and very brief answer from God: "yes!"

I was not impressed at first.
But he was.

He burst into tears.
I did not understand.
But God understood and Jason understood.

Jason had an encounter with God and it changed everything. It changed him. The questions were still there but moved from the forefront to the back. After this encounter and Jason's corresponding trust in this Jesus and this God, I explained, biblically and theologically, what just had happened with him. At home, Jason went on to have such "conversations" with "his" God and those encounters became an intimate relationship with all its ups and downs.

In my experience, this story is almost prototypical for many others, although not every encounter results in an intimate relationship with God. But it might.

An encounter with the living God might change everything.
This is what I live for.
This is what I write and teach for.
This is what I pray for.

Thus, the last words of this book should be a prayer, the concrete expression of a genuine relationship:

Father, let us fathom more of your love.

Jesus, let us live more as you lived.

Holy Spirit, let us take your presence more into account.

God, let us be matchmakers in your love story with the world.

Appendix

A Brief Introduction to the Major Frameworks of Relationship Science

IT IS ONLY WITHIN the last three to four decades that empirical testing concerning an understanding of relationships became acceptable,[1] whereas previously relationships were the domain of poets, writers, musicians, or possibly philosophers. The change began with the interest of social scientists in the 1960s and 1970s and on this soil, the relatively young field of the study of close relationships grew and gained momentum.[2] Indeed, Perl and Duck compare the research on interpersonal relationships from the latter half of the 1990s with a "boomtown during the gold rush days of the American West."[3]

Across the literature, there are five major conceptual frameworks of relationship science that are seen to be complementary: *evolutionary theory, social learning theory, social-ecological models, interdependence theory*, and *attachment theory*.[4] Each one of those theories answers a different question concerning relationships and the purpose of this

---

1. Perlman and Duck, "Seven Seas," 13.

2. Campbell and Surra, "Research on Close Relationships," 4–5.

3. Perlman and Duck, "Seven Seas," 27. For an additional overview of the development and history of relationship science, see Reis et al., "Emergence of Relationship Science."

4. See, e.g., Bradbury and Karney, *Intimate Relationships*, 144–46; Harvey and Wenzel, "Theoretical Perspectives," 45; Schneewind and Wunderer, "Prozessmodelle," 225.

appendix is to give a brief overview and an evaluation in light of the goal of this book.

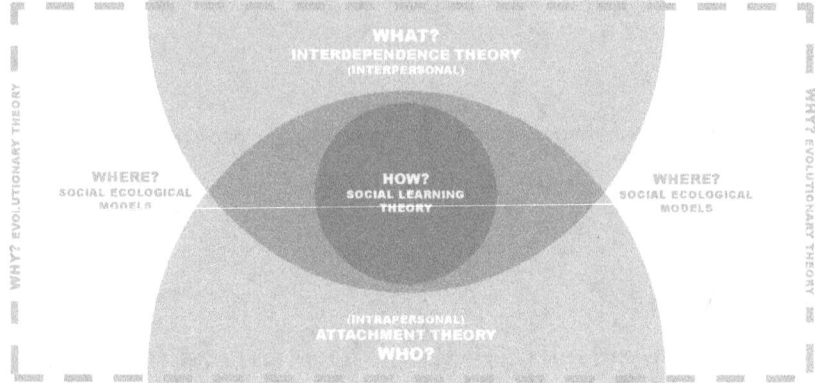

Figure 3: The questions and interconnection of the five major conceptual models of relationship science

However, since our evaluation of relationships is primarily based on interdependence theory and attachment theory, these two conceptions will be displayed in more detail.

a) Interdependence Theory

Interdependence theory (considered part of the social exchange theories)[5] answers *what* relationships are and consequently is the main foundation for our investigation of the structures and processes of interpersonal relationships. Interdependence theory was first proposed by John Thibaut and Harold Kelley in 1959, based on Kurt Lewin's work and influenced by game- and exchange-theory.[6] While Thibaut and Kelley's interdependence theory was not the only theoretical interdependence-framework during that time,[7] it is considered "the most comprehensive theoretical framework for understanding interdependence and social interaction"

---

5. For a differentiation between exchange-, equity- and interdependence theory see Kelley et al., *Atlas*, 15; Clark and Aragón, "Communal Relationships," 276; Noller, "Bringing It All Together," 772; Perlman and Duck, "Seven Seas," 17; Harvey and Wenzel, "Theoretical Perspectives," 38–40, 46.

6. For a short history of interdependence theory see van Lange and Balliet, "Interdependence Theory," 65–92, 65–67, 75–78.

7. See, e.g., Johnson and Johnson, "Social Interdependence Theory."

A Brief Introduction to the Major Frameworks of Relationship Science 219

due to its consistent development in the last sixty years.[8] Three monographs are regarded as milestones in this development: Thibaut and Kelley's *The Social Psychology of Groups* (1959), Kelley and Thibaut's *Interpersonal Relations* (1978), where they referred to their theory as interdependence theory for the first time, and Kelley et al.'s *An Atlas of Interpersonal Situations* (2003), which defined twenty-one specific yet abstracted prototypical interpersonal situations. Today, there are four basic assumptions in interdependence theory: the principles of *interaction, structure, transformation,* and *adaption.*[9]

The principle of interaction stands for the primary subject of interdependence theory. Relationships are fundamentally interpersonal and interactional[10] and as such concrete "interaction is the centerpiece of interdependence theory."[11] What are interactions? Interactions consist of people *and* situations, rendering the formula also referred to as *SABI*:

$$\text{Interaction} = f(S, A, B)^{12}$$

Interaction is a function (f) of two specific people (A, B) in a specific interdependent situation (S) involving their respective needs, thoughts, motives, and wished-for outcomes.[13] As such interdependence theory bridges the intrapersonal and interpersonal since the situation as well as the involved individuals can be profoundly affected and changed by the interaction.[14] Consequently, "*between*-person relations are as meaningful as the individuals themselves."[15] In other words, a relationship is essentially interactional since it does not exist solely in person A or B or the situation but in the combination of all of these.[16] That said, the question arises whether there is a difference between *interaction* and *relationship*? While an "interaction episode" technically might be called relationship, the latter term is usually reserved for ongoing or repeated interactions

---

8. Van Lange and Balliet, "Interdependence Theory," 65.
9. Van Lange and Balliet, "Interdependence Theory," 68.
10. See, e.g., Fehr, "Prototype Model of Intimacy," 20.
11. Arriaga, "Interdependence Theory Analysis," 61.
12. See, e.g., van Lange and Balliet, "Interdependence Theory," 73.
13. Rusbult and van Lange, "Why Interdependence Theory," 2050.
14. Rusbult et al., "Interdependence, Closeness, and Relationships," 156; Aron and Mashek, "Conclusion," 416; Arriaga, "Interdependence Theory Analysis," 51.
15. Rusbult and van Lange, "Why Interdependence Theory," 2050.
16. See Rusbult et al., "Interdependence, Closeness, and Relationships," 152; Arriaga, "Interdependence Theory Analysis," 40–42, 45, 48, 52, 54, 59.

and not for "isolated exchanges." Thus, interdependent interaction is "a necessary condition for a relationship to exist."[17]

The principle of structure is the second principle of interdependence theory that follows logically since it is the specific structure of the interaction that determines the relationship.[18] This principle lies at the heart of interdependence theory, for by analyzing and defining the structure and processes of interpersonal interaction interdependence theory provides a rather simple framework for very complex relationship phenomena.[19] There are six dimensions of interdependence structure.[20] The first three are structural and raise the power question:[21] *Level of dependence* qualifies how strong, *mutuality of dependence* how reciprocal, and *basis of dependence* in what manner (actor control, partner control or joint control) interaction partners influence each other's outcomes. Based on these, the second three dimensions are not only structural but also manifest or affect a person's motivation and decision: *Covariation of interests* "discerns the extent to which outcomes for actor and partner are positively correlated (corresponding interests) versus negatively correlated (conflicting interests)"[22] and *temporal structure* and *information availability* influence this perception of the situation.[23] The time dimension is important since relationships are evolving and changing and considerations of the future influence the actual situation in the now.[24] The dimension of certainty or uncertainty of information is crucial in order to consider the outcome of a situation and the

---

17. Regan, *Close Relationships*, 4–5.

18. Rusbult et al., "Interdependence, Closeness, and Relationships," 146.

19. Rusbult and van Lange, "Interdependence, Interaction, and Relationships," 369–70. It has been proposed that from this framework many other areas of psychology would benefit (Rusbult and van Lange, "Why Interdependence Theory," 2049–50; Laursen et al., "Incorporating Interdependence," 33).

20. Van Lange and Balliet, "Interdependence Theory," 71; Rusbult and van Lange, "Why Interdependence Theory," 2052–54; Rusbult and van Lange, "Interdependence, Interaction, and Relationships," 354–56; Rusbult et al., "Interdependence, Closeness, and Relationships," 139–44.

21. See section 8b.

22. Rusbult and van Lange, "Interdependence, Interaction, and Relationships," 354.

23. Initially the taxonomy consisted only of the first four dimensions, the last two were added in 2003 (van Lange and Balliet, "Interdependence Theory," 76).

24. Rusbult et al., "Interdependence, Closeness, and Relationships," 143.

character, motives, and goals of each interaction partner.[25] Hence, these three dimensions together are closely correlated with the following third principle of interdependence theory.[26]

The principle of transformation[27] is not so much concerned with the structure of interaction but its process. It describes the process of a transformation of motivation from the so-called *given situation* to the *effective situation*. The given situation describes the perception of the situation with "direct, gut level [sic] interests" (like small children) without broader considerations. The effective situation labels the situation after broader considerations have taken place.[28] Some of those broader motivations that can transform conflicting interests into corresponding interests and vice-versa are cooperation, competition, altruism, individualism, as well as communal and exchange norms.[29] Hence, the transformation process reveals the individual's true or unique self[30] and as such happens in *diagnostic situations* that consist of (expected) conflicting interests.[31] By extension, this leads to the last principle of interdependence theory.

The principle of adaption describes another process of interdependence theory whereby "repeated experiences in situations with similar structure give rise to habitual response tendencies," namely interpersonal dispositions, relationship-specific motives, and social norms. Social norms are adapted societal or moral rules about how to respond in particular situations. Relationship-specific motives are tendencies to habitual responses within specific relationships. Interpersonal dispositions are especially relevant since they are adaptions that have formed and become part of the self.[32] This "interpersonal self" can be defined as "the sum of

---

25. Rusbult et al., "Interdependence, Closeness, and Relationships," 143–44.

26. See, e.g., van Lange and Balliet, "Interdependence Theory," 72–73.

27. Introduced in 1978 for the first time in Kelley and Thibaut, *Interpersonal Relations*.

28. Rusbult and van Lange, "Interdependence, Interaction, and Relationships," 358–59.

29. Van Lange and Balliet, "Interdependence Theory," 72–73. For the evaluation of exchange vs. communal norms, see section 8b.

30. Rusbult et al., "Interdependence, Closeness, and Relationships," 147–48.

31. Rusbult and van Lange, "Interdependence, Interaction, and Relationships," 362.

32. Van Lange and Balliet, "Interdependence Theory," 75.

one's adaptions to previous interdependence situations and partners."[33] In other words, it becomes the personal basis for every interaction and relationship. That said, this process of the self is comprehensively treated by attachment theory.

In summary, interdependence theory is an overarching framework for an "inherently *interpersonal* analysis," the foundation to depict the structure and processes of close relationships with interaction at its core.[34] An additional strength of interdependence theory is the initial exclusion and subsequent separate treatment of the partner's sentiment for each other,[35] making it very adaptable and empirically validated cross-culturally[36] and thus it does not fall into the category of biased relationship research mentioned earlier.[37]

b) Attachment Theory

Attachment theory answers *who* the parties in a relationship are and was first developed by John Bowlby (1969, 1973, 1980).[38] Whereas Bowlby's original theory focused on infant-caregiver relationships, its focus today is much more encompassing.[39] Hazan and Shaver's landmark paper on adult attachment (1987) initiated an immense body of work using attachment theory as an organizational framework for close relationships in general.[40] The theory has a normative component (attachment) and, as its outcome, an individual-difference component (attachment styles).[41] The normative aspect of attachment theory can be defined as "the propensity to make intimate emotional bonds to particular individuals as a basic

---

33. Rusbult et al., "Interdependence, Closeness, and Relationships," 150.

34. Rusbult et al., "Interdependence, Closeness, and Relationships," 137–62, 137–38; Rusbult and van Lange, "Why Interdependence Theory," 2049–50; Arriaga, "Interdependence Theory Analysis," 39, 61; Fletcher et al., *Intimate Relationships*, 19; Rusbult and van Lange, "Interdependence, Interaction, and Relationships," 369–70.

35. Berscheid et al., "Measuring Closeness," 82–83.

36. Johnson and Johnson, "Social Interdependence Theory," 301–2.

37. See section 7b.

38. See, e.g., Finkel et al., "Psychology of Close Relationships," 385.

39. Hazan and Shaver, "Organizational Framework," 17; Reis et al., "Emergence of Relationship Science," 563; Collins and Feeney, "Attachment Theory Perspective," 170.

40. Noller, "Bringing It All Together," 777–80.

41. Fletcher et al., *Intimate Relationships*, 102–3; Gillath et al., "Understanding of Attachment," 235.

component of human nature, already present in germinal form in the neonate and continuing through adult life into old age."[42] In other words, all humans develop bonds with significant others to find emotional or physical closeness (*proximity maintenance*) when threatened, challenged, or stressed.[43] Additional features of this bond are that attachment figures are a *safe haven* and a *secure base* for the attached individual and that separation from them results in increased anxiety (*separation distress*).[44] As a result of one's personal history with attachment figures and primarily formed during childhood, *attachment styles* evolve that influence current relationships. While *secure* individuals point to a history of responsive relationships, *insecure* individuals did not perceive their attachment figures as responsive and in turn developed coping mechanisms that are reflected in their personality and thus also in their behavior in relationships.[45] These coping mechanisms are conceptualized today as dynamically progressing along two dimensions, *anxiety* and *avoidance*, rather than being understood in static categories.[46] Nonetheless, in essence, this dynamic leads to four distinct attachment tendencies or styles: *secure, preoccupied, dismissing* and *fearful*.[47]

---

42. Collins and Feeney, "Attachment Theory Perspective," 163.

43. Finkel et al., "Psychology of Close Relationships," 385; Edelstein and Shaver, "Avoidant Attachment," 399; Collins and Feeney, "Attachment Theory Perspective," 165; Fletcher et al., *Intimate Relationships*, 115.

44. Collins and Feeney, "Attachment Theory Perspective," 165, 170.

45. See, e.g., Bradbury and Karney, *Intimate Relationships*, 106; Collins and Feeney, "Attachment Theory Perspective," 182.

46. Bradbury and Karney, *Intimate Relationships*, 114.

47. Bradbury and Karney, *Intimate Relationships*, 113; Miller, *Intimate Relationships*, 17; Collins and Feeney, "Attachment Theory Perspective," 167–68.

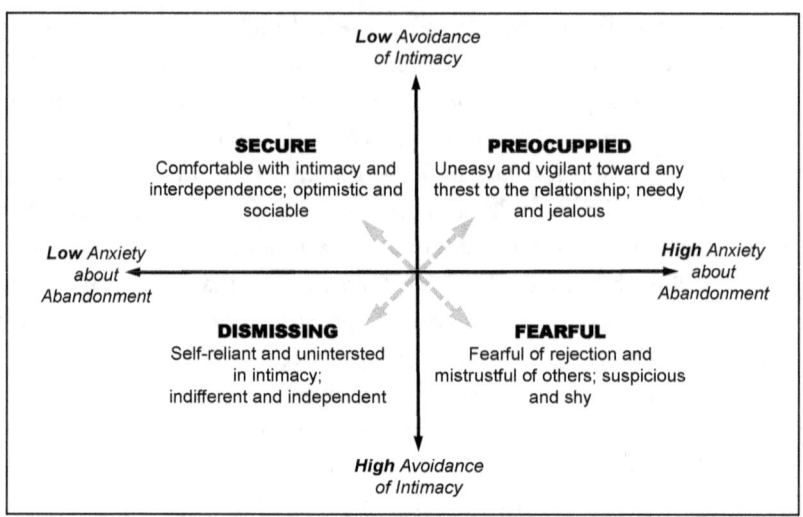

Figure 4: Dimensions and styles of attachment[48]

Clearly, the more secure an individual is the better is the basis for healthy relationships,[49] whereas the insecure attachment styles are even considered "pathological outcomes" that sabotage relationships.[50] Hence, attachment styles largely influence who the people in a relationship are and how they act and react.[51] In conclusion, attachment theory has a very broad scope of understanding human development, yet at the same time also a very narrow focus on the individual.[52] While interdependence theory, like attachment theory, also bridges the gap between interpersonal and intrapersonal psychology,[53] the intrapersonal aspects of attachment theory are more specific and therefore complementary

---

48. Adapted from Miller, *Intimate Relationships*, 17; Bradbury and Karney, *Intimate Relationships*, 113.

49. Mikulincer and Shaver, "Attachment Security," 75; Collins and Feeney, "Attachment Theory Perspective," 174–75.

50. Fletcher et al., *Intimate Relationships*, 122; Mikulincer and Shaver, "Attachment Security," 75; Collins and Feeney, "Attachment Theory Perspective," 174–75.

51. See, e.g., Miller, *Intimate Relationships*, 18–19; Lösel and Bender, "Modelle der Paarbeziehung," 61.

52. Bradbury and Karney, *Intimate Relationships*, 106, 116.

53. Rusbult et al., "Self Processes," 376–77; Rusbult and van Lange, "Interdependence, Interaction, and Relationships," 353, 367; Rusbult and van Lange, "Why Interdependence Theory," 2066.

A Brief Introduction to the Major Frameworks of Relationship Science   225

to interdependence theory.[54] Consequently, this means for our current purposes that attachment theory is well equipped to inform about the individual humans and the general human need in relationships, but not so much about the relationship itself.[55]

c) Evolutionary Theory

Evolutionary theory (aka evolutionary life-history perspective,[56] sociobiological hypothesis)[57] tries to answer *why* human beings are relational from an evolutionary point of view. Obviously, evolutionary theory[58] takes a very broad perspective to find answers. Whilst this perspective might offer some intriguing insights,[59] it is insufficient for our purposes for three reasons. First, it is agreed among many relationship science scholars that it is the most speculative and controversial theory of the "big five" because it "moves *beyond* mere description" and tries to address the "ultimate questions" based on a "common assumption."[60] Second, its scope is too broad and "simplistic"[61] for our utilization of relationship science. Third, since it wants to answer the "big why" based on an explicitly materialistic worldview[62] it introduces a different paradigm than the biblical-theological ontic foundation provided earlier.[63]

---

54. Mikulincer and Shaver, "Attachment Security," 83.
55. See, e.g., Bradbury and Karney, *Intimate Relationships*, 116.
56. Kenrick et al., "Evolutionary Life History Perspective."
57. Lösel and Bender, "Modelle der Paarbeziehung," 49 (TM).
58. It is argued that it is more of a collection of theories than a single theory (Noller, "Bringing It All Together," 780).
59. E.g., that from an evolutionary perspective "the human brain is designed for social relationships" (Kenrick et al., "Evolutionary Life History Perspective," 13).
60. Bradbury and Karney, *Intimate Relationships*, 104–5. See also Harvey and Wenzel, "Theoretical Perspectives," 35; Lösel and Bender, "Modelle der Paarbeziehung," 49; Miller, *Intimate Relationships*, 6, 35; Noller, "Bringing It All Together," 782; Fletcher et al., *Intimate Relationships*, 7. See also section 10a (thesis four).
61. Noller, "Bringing It All Together," 782.
62. Fletcher et al., *Intimate Relationships*, 8.
63. See chapter 4.

d) Social Learning Theory

Social learning theory (aka cognitive-behavioral models,[64] communication theories) answers *how* relationships function well and how partner-communication can be successful. It comes as no surprise that the behavioral focus of this theory[65] has had the most influence on public opinion of intimate relationships (John Gottman being a famous "father" of this approach) and has found its way into many popular self-help books as their basis.[66] However, since this approach has a rather narrow focus on specific relationship behavior, its quality, and conflict resolution,[67] social learning theory appears to be less basic, structurally relevant, and culturally adaptable and therefore less useful for our undertaking concerning the analogy of relationships.

e) Social-Ecological Models

Social-ecological models investigate *where* the relationships occur, what their external circumstances are, and how they are influencing dyadic interaction. As such, these models only form the "backdrop" of our investigation of the actual dyadic relationship. Nonetheless, since this approach is based on anthropology and sociology rather than psychology[68] it widens the scope of relationship science to be aware of important cultural, societal, social, and physical environmental factors[69] already mentioned.[70] In essence, "environments shape our behavior"[71] and "no relationship exists in a vacuum."[72]

---

64. Harvey and Wenzel, "Theoretical Perspectives," 42, 45.

65. It rather is a "group of theories" than one uniform perspective (Noller, "Bringing It All Together," 773).

66. Bradbury and Karney, *Intimate Relationships*, 127–28, 132–33.

67. Lösel and Bender, "Modelle der Paarbeziehung," 57; Schneewind and Wunderer, "Prozessmodelle," 233; Bradbury and Karney, *Intimate Relationships*, 127.

68. Bradbury and Karney, *Intimate Relationships*, 135–41.

69. Regan, *Close Relationships*, 15.

70. See section 7b.

71. Arriaga et al., "Beyond the Individual," 301.

72. Regan, *Close Relationships*, 16.

Bibliography

Abraham, William J. "The Offense of Divine Revelation." *Harvard Theological Review* 95 (2002) 251–64.

Adams, Glenn, et al. "The Cultural Grounding of Closeness and Intimacy." In *Handbook of Closeness and Intimacy*, edited by Debra J. Mashek, 321–42. London: Routledge, 2004.

Agnew, Christopher R., et al. "Cognitive Interdependence: Commitment and the Mental Representation of Close Relationships." *Journal of Personality and Social Psychology* 74 (1998) 939–54.

Agnew, Christopher R., et al. "Thinking Close: Measuring Relational Closeness as Perceived Self-Other Inclusion." In *Handbook of Closeness and Intimacy*, edited by Debra J. Mashek, 103–16. London: Routledge, 2004.

Altamira, Alfredo H. "Das aktuale und personale Offenbarungsgeschehen nach Emil Brunner." Doctoral diss., Universität München, 1971.

Althaus, Paul. "Brunner, Emil, Wahrheit Als Begegnung: Rezension." *Theologische Literaturzeitung* 90 (1965) 135–38.

Althaus, Paul, et al. *Paul Althaus, Karl Barth, Emil Brunner: Briefwechsel, 1922–1966*. Edited by Gotthard Jasper. Göttingen: Vandenhoeck & Ruprecht, 2015.

Andersen, Carlton S. "Theological Anthropology and Christian Social Ethics: The 'Imago Dei' as Relational Ontology in the Political Thought of Emil Brunner and Douglas John Hall." PhD diss., Luther Seminary, 2001.

Anderson, Paul N. *Navigating the Living Waters of the Gospel of John: On Wading with Children and Swimming with Elephants*. Wallingford, PA: Pendle Hill, 2000.

Aquinas, Thomas. *Summa Theologica: Part I (Prima Pars)*. New York: Benzinger Brothers, 1947.

Aron, Arthur P., and Debra J. Mashek. "Conclusion." In *Handbook of Closeness and Intimacy*, edited by Debra J. Mashek, 416–28. London: Routledge, 2004.

Aron, Arthur P., et al. "Closeness as Including Other in the Self." In *Handbook of Closeness and Intimacy*, edited by Debra J. Mashek, 27–42. London: Routledge, 2004.

Aron, Arthur P., et al. "The Self-Expansion Model of Motivation and Cognition in Close Relationships." In *The Oxford Handbook of Close Relationships*, edited by Jeffry A. Simpson and Lorne Campbell, 90–111. Oxford: Oxford University Press, 2013.

Arriaga, Ximena B. "An Interdependence Theory Analysis of Close Relationships." In *The Oxford Handbook of Close Relationships*, edited by Jeffry A. Simpson and Lorne Campbell, 39–61. Oxford: Oxford University Press, 2013.

Arriaga, Ximena B., et al. "Beyond the Individual: Concomitants of Closeness in the Social and Physical Environment." In *Handbook of Closeness and Intimacy*, edited by Debra J. Mashek, 287–304. London: Routledge, 2004.

Ashworth, E. Jennifer. "Medieval Theories of Analogy." In *The Stanford Encyclopedia of Philosophy*, edited by Edward N. Zalta. https://plato.stanford.edu/archives/fall2017/entries/analogy-medieval/.

Balswick, Jack O., et al. *The Reciprocating Self: Human Development in Theological Perspective*. Downers Grove, IL: InterVarsity, 2016.

Balz, Horst. "Ἀναλογία." In *Exegetisches Wörterbuch zum Neuen Testament*, edited by Horst Balz and Gerhard Schneider, 201. 3rd ed. Stuttgart: Kohlhammer, 2011.

Barber, Katherine. "When Adjectives Become Verbs." http://18.134.44.140/2013/11/14/whats-wrong-with-this-verb/.

Barclay, John M. G. "Paul and the Faithfulness of God." *Scottish Journal of Theology* 68 (2015) 235–43.

———. *Paul and the Gift*. Grand Rapids: Eerdmans, 2015.

Barrett, Justin L. "Exploring Religion's Basement: The Cognitive Science of Religion." In *Handbook of the Psychology of Religion and Spirituality*, edited by Raymond F. Paloutzian and Crystal L. Park, 234–55. 2nd ed. New York: Guilford, 2015.

Barth, Karl. *The Epistle to the Romans*. London: Oxford University Press, 1980.

———. *On Religion: The Revelation of God as the Sublimation of Religion*. London: T. & T. Clark, 2006.

Barth, Karl, and Emil Brunner. *Karl Barth—Emil Brunner: Briefwechsel, 1916–1966*. Edited by Eberhard Busch. Zürich: TVZ, 2000.

———. *Nein! Antwort an Emil Brunner*. München: Kaiser, 1934.

Barth, Karl, and Amy Marga. *The Word of God and Theology*. London: T. & T. Clark, 2011.

Barth, Karl, et al. *Friedrich Gogartens Briefwechsel mit Karl Barth, Eduard Thurneysen und Emil Brunner*. Edited by Hermann G. Göckeritz. Tübingen: Mohr Siebeck, 2009.

Bartha, Paul F. A. "Analogy and Analogical Reasoning." In *The Stanford Encyclopedia of Philosophy*, edited by Edward N. Zalta. https://plato.stanford.edu/archives/spr2019/entries/reasoning-analogy/.

———. *By Parallel Reasoning: The Construction and Evaluation of Analogical Arguments*. New York: Oxford University Press, 2010.

Bebbington, David. *Evangelicalism in Modern Britain: A History from the 1730s to the 1980s*. London: Routledge, 1993.

Beckes, Lane, and James A. Coan. "Toward an Integrative Neuroscience of Relationships." In *The Oxford Handbook of Close Relationships*, edited by Jeffry A. Simpson and Lorne Campbell, 685–703. Oxford: Oxford University Press, 2013.

Berra, Michael. *R3—Radical Relationship: Die drei Dimenisonen eines krassen Christen*. Basel: Brunnen, 2007.

Berscheid, Ellen, et al. "Measuring Closeness: The Relationship Closeness Inventory (RCI) Revisited." In *Handbook of Closeness and Intimacy*, edited by Debra J. Mashek, 81–102. London: Routledge, 2004.

Berthold, Fred. "Objectivity and Personal Encounter." *Journal of Religion* 45 (1965) 39–45.

Bertram, Robert W. "Brunner on Revelation." *Concordia Theological Monthly* 22 (1951) 625–43.

Bockmühl, Klaus. "Frank Buchmans Botschaft und ihre Bedeutung für die protestantischen Kirchen." In *Denken im Horizont der Wirklichkeit Gottes: Schriften zur Dogmatik und Theologiegeschichte*, edited by Klaus Bockmühl et al., 193–226. Giessen: Brunnen, 1999.

———. "Die Wende im Spätwerk Karl Barths." In *Denken im Horizont der Wirklichkeit Gottes: Schriften zur Dogmatik und Theologiegeschichte*, edited by Klaus Bockmühl et al., 280–90. Giessen: Brunnen, 1999.

Bockmühl, Klaus, et al., eds. *Denken im Horizont der Wirklichkeit Gottes: Schriften zur Dogmatik und Theologiegeschichte*. Giessen: Brunnen, 1999.

Boschki, Reinhold. *"Beziehung" als Leitbegriff der Religionspädagogik: Grundlegung einer dialogisch-kreativen Religionsdidaktik*. Ostfildern: Schwabenverlag, 2003.

Bowdle, Brian F., and Dedre Gentner. "The Career of Metaphor." *Psychological Review* 112 (2005) 193–216.

———. "Informativity and Asymmetry in Comparisons." *Cognitive Psychology* 34 (1997) 244–86.

———. "Metaphor Comprehension: From Comparison to Categorization." In *Proceedings of the Twenty First Annual Conference of the Cognitive Science Society: August 19–21, 1999, Simon Fraser University, Vancouver, British Columbia*, edited by Martin Hahn and Scott C. Stoness, 90–95. Mahwah, NJ: Erlbaum, 1999.

Bowlby, John. *Attachment and Loss*. London: Hogarth, 1969.

———. *Attachment and Loss: Anxiety and Anger*. London: Hogarth, 1973.

———. *Attachment and Loss: Sadness and Depression*. London: Hogarth, 1980.

Bowman, Clarice M. "Can Theologies Communicate?" *Journal of Bible and Religion* 25 (1957) 293–300.

Boyd, Gregory A. *Cross Vision: How the Crucifixion of Jesus Makes Sense of Old Testament Violence*. Minneapolis: Fortress, 2017.

———. *The Crucifixion of the Warrior God: Interpreting the Old Testament's Violent Portraits of God in Light of the Cross*. Minneapolis: Fortress, 2017.

———. *God of the Possible: A Biblical Introduction to the Open View of God*. Grand Rapids: Baker, 2001.

Boyd, Jay. "The Problem with 'A Personal Relationship with Jesus.'" *Homiletic & Pastoral Review*, July 10, 2014. http://www.hprweb.com/2014/07/the-problem-with-a-personal-relationship-with-jesus/.

Bracken, Joseph A. "Toward a New Philosophical Theology Based on Intersubjectivity." *Theological Studies* 59 (1998) 703–19.

Bradbury, Thomas N., and Benjamin R. Karney. *Intimate Relationships*. New York: Norton, 2010.

Bray, Gerald. *God Is Love: A Biblical and Systematic Theology*. Wheaton, IL: Crossway, 2012.

Brooks, David. *The Social Animal: The Hidden Sources of Love, Character, and Achievement*. New York: Random House, 2012.

Brown, Cynthia Bennett. *Believing Thinking, Bounded Theology: The Theological Methodology of Emil Brunner.* Eugene, OR: Pickwick, 2015.

———. "The Personal Imperative of Revelation: Emil Brunner, Dogmatics and Theological Existence." *Scottish Journal of Theology* 65 (2012) 421–34.

Brozio, Peter. *Vom pädagogischen Bezug zur pädagogischen Beziehung: Soziologische Grundlagen einer Erziehungstheorie.* Würzburg: Ergon, 1995.

Brümmer, Vincent. *The Model of Love: A Study in Philosophical Theology.* Cambridge: Cambridge University Press, 1993.

———. *Speaking of a Personal God: An Essay in Philosophical Theology.* Cambridge: Cambridge University Press, 1992.

Brunner, Emil. "Die andere Aufgabe der Theologie." In *Ein offenes Wort: Vorträge und Aufsätze, 1917–1962,* edited by Emil Brunner and Rudolf Wehrli, 171–93. Zürich: TVZ, 1981.

———. *Christianity and Civilisation: First Part: Foundations.* New York: Scribner's Sons, 1948.

———. *Dogmatics I: The Christian Doctrine of God.* Cambridge: Lutterworth, 2002.

———. *Dogmatics II: The Christian Doctrine of Creation and Redemption.* London: Lutterworth, 1952.

———. *Dogmatics III: The Christian Doctrine of the Church, Faith, and the Consummation.* London: Lutterworth, 1962.

———. *Dogmatik I: Die christliche Lehre von Gott.* Zürich: Zwingli-Verlag, 1953.

———. *Dogmatik II: Die christliche Lehre von Schöpfung und Erlösung.* Zürich: TVZ, 1972.

———. *Dogmatik III: Die christliche Lehre von der Kirche, vom Glauben und von der Vollendung.* Zürich: Zwingli-Verlag, 1964.

———. *Erlebnis, Erkenntnis und Glaube.* Tübingen: Mohr, 1933.

———. *Eternal Hope.* Philadelphia: Westminster, 1954.

———. *Das Ewige als Zukunft und Gegenwart.* Zürich: Zwingli-Verlag, 1953.

———. *Faith, Hope, and Love.* Philadelphia: Westminster, 1956.

———. "Die Frage nach dem 'Anknüpfungspunkt' als Problem der Theologie." In *Ein offenes Wort: Vorträge und Aufsätze 1917–1962,* edited by Emil Brunner and Rudolf Wehrli, 239–67. Zürich: TVZ, 1981.

———. *Für den Fall.* Personal letter before a surgical operation in case of his death. Staatsarchiv des Kantons Zürich, W I 55 122, 10.

———. "Für Ferdinand Ebner." In *Ein offenes Wort: Vorträge und Aufsätze, 1917–1962,* edited by Emil Brunner and Rudolf Wehrli, 7–9. Zürich: TVZ, 1981.

———. *Das Gebot und die Ordnungen: Entwurf einer protestantisch-theologischen Ethik.* Tübingen: Mohr, 1932.

———. *Gerechtigkeit: Eine Lehre von den Grundgesetzen der Gesellschaftsordnung.* Zürich: TVZ, 1981.

———. "Intellectual Autobiography of Emil Brunner." In *The Theology of Emil Brunner,* edited by Charles W. Kegley, 3–24. London: Macmillan, 1962.

———. *Justice and Social Order.* Cambridge: Lutterworth, 2002.

———. *Man in Revolt: A Christian Anthropology.* London: Lutterworth, 1939.

———. *The Mediator: A Study of the Central Doctrine of the Christian Faith.* Cambridge: Lutterworth, 2002.

———. "Meine Begegnung mit der Oxforder Gruppenbewegung." In *Ein offenes Wort: Vorträge und Aufsätze, 1917–1962*, edited by Emil Brunner and Rudolf Wehrli, 268–88. Zürich: TVZ, 1981.

———. *Der Mensch im Widerspruch: Die christliche Lehre vom wahren und vom wirklichen Menschen*. Berlin: Furche, 1937.

———. *Das Missverständnis der Kirche*. Zürich: TVZ, 1988.

———. *Der Mittler: Zur Besinnung über den Christusglauben*. Tübingen: Mohr, 1937.

———. *The Misunderstanding of the Church*. Cambridge: Lutterworth, 2002.

———. *Die Mystik und das Wort: Der Gegensatz zwischen moderner Religionsauffassung und christlichem Glauben dargestellt an der Theologie Schleiermachers*. Tübingen: Mohr, 1924.

———. "Natur und Gnade: Zum Gespräch mit Karl Barth." In *Ein offenes Wort: Vorträge und Aufsätze, 1917–1962*, edited by Emil Brunner and Rudolf Wehrli, 333–75. Zürich: TVZ, 1981.

———. *Natur und Gnade: Zum Gespräch mit Karl Barth*. Tübingen: Mohr, 1934.

———. "The New Barth: Observations on Karl Barth's Doctrine of Man." *Scottish Journal of Theology* 4 (1951) 123–35.

———. *Offenbarung und Vernunft: Die Lehre von der christlichen Glaubenserkenntnis*. Zürich: Zwingli-Verlag, 1961.

———. *Our Faith*. London: SCM, 1949.

———. *The Philosophy of Religion: From the Standpoint of Protestant Theology*. Westport, CT: Hyperion, 1979.

———. "Reply to Interpretation and Criticism." In *The Theology of Emil Brunner*, edited by Charles W. Kegley, 325–54. London: Macmillan, 1962.

———. *Revelation and Reason: The Christian Doctrine of Faith and Knowledge*. Philadelphia: Westminster, 1946.

———. *Das Symbolische in der Erkenntnis: Beiträge zu einer Theorie des religiösen Erkennens*. Tübingen: Laupp, 1914.

———. *The Theology of Crisis*. New York: Scribner's Sons, 1929.

———. "Toward a Missionary Theology." *The Christian Century* 66 (1949) 816–18.

———. *Truth as Encounter: A New Edition, Much Enlarged, of "The Divine-Human Encounter."* Philadelphia: Westminster, 1964.

———. *Unser Glaube: Eine christliche Unterweisung*. Zürich: Gotthelf, 1935.

———. *Vom Werk des heiligen Geistes*. Tübingen: Mohr, 1935.

———. *Wahrheit als Begegnung*. Zürich: Zwingli-Verlag, 1963.

———. *Weg zum Glauben*. Typoscript of an unpublished chapter of *Dogmatik III*. Staatsarchiv des Kantons Zürich, W I 55 97.

———. *The Word and the World*. London: SCM, 1932.

Brunner, Emil, and Rudolf Wehrli, eds. *Ein offenes Wort: Vorträge und Aufsätze, 1917–1962*. 2 vols. Zürich: TVZ, 1981.

Brunner, Hans Heinrich. *Mein Vater und sein Ältester: Emil Brunner in seiner und meiner Zeit*. Zürich: TVZ, 1986.

Buber, Martin. *I and Thou*. London: Continuum, 2004.

Burkhardt, Helmut. *Ein Gott in allen Religionen? Wiederkehr der Religiosität—Chance und Gefahr*. Giessen: Brunnen, 1993.

Cairns, David. "Brunner's Conception of Man as Responsive, Responsible Being." In *The Theology of Emil Brunner*, edited by Charles W. Kegley, 75–98. London: Macmillan, 1962.

———. "The Theology of Emil Brunner." *Scottish Journal of Theology* 1 (1948) 294–308.
Campbell, Lorne, and Timothy J. Loving, eds. *Interdisciplinary Research on Close Relationships: The Case for Integration*. Washington, DC: American Psychological Association, 2012.
Campbell, Lorne, and Jeffry A. Simpson. "The Blossoming of Relationship Science." In *The Oxford Handbook of Close Relationships*, edited by Jeffry A. Simpson and Lorne Campbell, 3–10. Oxford: Oxford University Press, 2013.
Campbell, Lorne, and Catherine Surra. "Research on Close Relationships: Call for an Interdisciplinary Integration." In *Interdisciplinary Research on Close Relationships: The Case for Integration*, edited by Lorne Campbell and Timothy J. Loving, 3–24. Washington, DC: American Psychological Association, 2012.
Caneday, Ardel. "Veiled Glory: God's Self-Revelation in Human Likeness—A Biblical Theology of God's Anthropomorphic Self-Disclosure." In *Beyond the Bounds: Open Theism and the Undermining of Biblical Christianity*, edited by John Piper and Justin Taylor, 149–99. Wheaton, IL: Crossway, 2003.
Caprez-Roffler, Greti. "Von Gebet und Introspektion." In *Emil Brunner in der Erinnerung seiner Schüler*, edited by Werner Kramer and Hugo Sonderegger, 86–89. Zürich: TVZ, 1989.
Cavallo, Justin V., et al. "Regulating Interpersonal Risk." In *The Oxford Handbook of Close Relationships*, edited by Jeffry A. Simpson and Lorne Campbell, 116–32. Oxford: Oxford University Press, 2013.
Cavey, Bruxy. *The End of Religion: Encountering the Subversive Spirituality of Jesus*. Colorado Springs, CO: NavPress, 2014.
Clark, Margaret S., and Oriana R. Aragón. "Communal (and Other) Relationships: History, Theory Development, Recent Findings, and Future Directions." In *The Oxford Handbook of Close Relationships*, edited by Jeffry A. Simpson and Lorne Campbell, 255–77. Oxford: Oxford University Press, 2013.
Collins, Nancy L., and Brooke C. Feeney. "An Attachment Theory Perspective on Closeness and Intimacy." In *Handbook of Closeness and Intimacy*, edited by Debra J. Mashek, 163–88. London: Routledge, 2004.
Comstock, Gary. "Truth or Meaning: Ricoeur versus Frei on Biblical Narrative." *Journal of Religion* 66 (1986) 741–66.
Cook, William L., and David A. Kenny. "The Actor–Partner Interdependence Model: A Model of Bidirectional Effects in Developmental Studies." *International Journal of Behavioral Development* 29 (2005) 101–9.
Covey, Stephen R. *The Seven Habits of Highly Effective People: Powerful Lessons in Personal Change*. New York: Simon & Schuster, 2004.
Cross, Susan E., and Jonathan S. Gore. "The Relational Self-Construal and Closeness." In *Handbook of Closeness and Intimacy*, edited by Debra J. Mashek, 229–46. London: Routledge, 2004.
Dalferth, Ingolf U. *Crucified and Resurrected: Restructuring the Grammar of Christology*. Grand Rapids: Baker Academic, 2015.
Dalferth, Ingolf U., and Eberhard Jüngel. "Person und Gottebenbildlichkeit." In *Anthropologie und Theologie*, edited by Albert Raffelt et al., 57–99. 2nd ed. Freiburg im Breisgau: Herder, 1981.
Deddo, Gary W. *Karl Barth's Theology of Relations: Trinitarian, Christological and Human: Towards an Ethic of the Family*. New York: Lang, 1999.

Dépelteau, François. "What Is the Direction of the 'Relational Turn'?" In *Conceptualizing Relational Sociology: Ontological and Theoretical Issues*, edited by Christopher Powell and François Dépelteau, 163–85. New York: Palgrave Macmillan, 2013.

DesCamp, Mary Therese, and Eve E. Sweetser. "Metaphors for God: Why and How Do Our Choices Matter for Humans? The Application of Contemporary Cognitive Linguistics Research to the Debate on God and Metaphor." *Pastoral Psychology* 53 (2005) 207–38.

Dietrich, Jan. "Responsive Anthropologie: Zum Bild des Menschen im Alten Testament am Beispiel der Tugend-Epistemologie." In *Relationale Erkenntnishorizonte in Exegese und Systematischer Theologie*, edited by Raphaela J. Meyer zu Hörste-Bührer and Walter Bührer, 145–60. Leipzig: Evangelische Verlagsanstalt, 2018.

Dix, Theodore, and Katharine Ann Buck. "The Emergence of Social Approach and Avoidance Motivation in Early Parent-Child Relationships." In *Interdisciplinary Research on Close Relationships: The Case for Integration*, edited by Lorne Campbell and Timothy J. Loving, 53–82. Washington, DC: American Psychological Association, 2012.

Dowey, Edward A. "Redeemer and Redeemed as Persons in History." In *The Theology of Emil Brunner*, edited by Charles W. Kegley, 189–206. London: Macmillan, 1962.

Duvall, J. Scott, and J. Daniel Hays. *God's Relational Presence: The Cohesive Center of Biblical Theology*. Grand Rapids: Baker Academic, 2019.

Earley, J. E. "By Parallel Reasoning: The Construction and Evaluation of Analogical Arguments." *Philosophical Review* 121 (2012) 451–57.

Ebeling, Gerhard. "Die Beunruhigung der Theologie durch die Frage nach den Früchten des Geistes: Arthur Rich zum 60. Geburtstag." *Zeitschrift für Theologie und Kirche* 66 (1969) 354–68.

Eckstein, Hans-Joachim. *Der aus Glauben Gerechte wird leben: Beiträge zur Theologie des Neuen Testaments*. Münster: LIT, 2003.

———. *Glaube als Beziehung: Von der menschlichen Wirklichkeit Gottes*. Holzgerlingen: Hänssler, 2006.

Edelstein, Robin S., and Phillip R. Shaver. "Avoidant Attachment: Exploration of an Oxymoron." In *Handbook of Closeness and Intimacy*, edited by Debra J. Mashek, 397–414. London: Routledge, 2004.

Ensminger, Sven. *Karl Barth's Theology as a Resource for a Christian Theology of Religions*. London: Bloomsbury, 2014.

Ernst, Hans. "Anekdoten und Sentenzen." In *Emil Brunner in der Erinnerung seiner Schüler*, edited by Werner Kramer and Hugo Sonderegger, 161–64. Zürich: TVZ, 1989.

Evangelisch-reformiertes Forum St. Gallen. "Emil Brunner – Leben und Werk, eine Einführung." *YouTube*, October 26, 2016. https://www.youtube.com/watch?v=m70-DezThiA.

Fehr, Beverly. "A Prototype Model of Intimacy Interactions in Same-Sex Friendship." In *Handbook of Closeness and Intimacy*, edited by Debra J. Mashek, 9–26. London: Routledge, 2004.

———. "The Social Psychology of Love." In *The Oxford Handbook of Close Relationships*, edited by Jeffry A. Simpson and Lorne Campbell, 201–28. Oxford: Oxford University Press, 2013.

Fernández, Eliseo. "Taking the Relational Turn: Biosemiotics and Some New Trends in Biology." *Biosemiotics* 3 (2010) 147–56.

Finkel, Eli J., et al. "The Psychology of Close Relationships: Fourteen Core Principles." *Annual Review of Psychology* 68 (2017) 383–411.

Finkenstaedt, Thomas. *You und Thou: Studien zur Anrede im Englischen, mit einem Exkurs über die Anrede im Deutschen*. Berlin: de Gruyter, 1963.

Firestone, Robert W., and Lisa Firestone. "Methods for Overcoming the Fear of Intimacy." In *Handbook of Closeness and Intimacy*, edited by Debra J. Mashek, 375–96. London: Routledge, 2004.

Fischer, Hermann. *Systematische Theologie: Konzeptionen und Probleme im 20. Jahrhundert*. Stuttgart: Kohlhammer, 1992.

Fiske, Susan T., and Jennifer Berdahl. "Social Power." In *Social Psychology: Handbook of Basic Principles*, edited by Arie W. Kruglanski and Edward T. Higgins, 678–94. 2nd ed. New York: Guilford, 2007.

Fletcher, Garth J. O., et al. *The Science of Intimate Relationships*. Chichester: Wiley-Blackwell, 2013.

Fretheim, Terence E. *God and World in the Old Testament: A Relational Theology of Creation*. Nashville: Abingdon, 2005.

———. *God So Enters into Relationships That . . . : A Biblical View*. Minneapolis: Augsburg Fortress, 2019.

Fuchs, Thomas. *Das Gehirn—ein Beziehungsorgan: Eine phänomenologisch-ökologische Konzeption*. Stuttgart: Kohlhammer, 2017.

Gaines, Stanley O., and Deletha P. Hardin. "Interdependence Revisited: Perspectives from Cultural Psychology." In *The Oxford Handbook of Close Relationships*, edited by Jeffry A. Simpson and Lorne Campbell, 553–69. Oxford: Oxford University Press, 2013.

Gentner, Dedre. "Structure-Mapping: A Theoretical Framework for Analogy." *Cognitive Science* 7 (1983) 155–70.

Gentner, Dedre, and Arthur B. Markman. "Structure Mapping in Analogy and Similarity." *American Psychologist* 52 (1997) 45–56.

Gentner, Dedre, et al., eds. *The Analogical Mind: Perspectives from Cognitive Science*. London: MIT Press, 2001.

Gentner, Dedre, et al. "Metaphor Is Like Analogy." In *The Analogical Mind: Perspectives from Cognitive Science*, edited by Dedre Gentner et al., 199–253. London: MIT Press, 2001.

Gergen, Kenneth J. *Relational Being: Beyond Self and Community*. Oxford: Oxford University Press, 2011.

Gill, Theodore A. "Emil Brunner as Teacher and Preacher." In *The Theology of Emil Brunner*, edited by Charles W. Kegley, 305–24. London: Macmillan, 1962.

Gillath, Omri, et al. "Introduction: Theoretical Integration and Interdisciplinarity in Relationship Science." In *Relationship Science: Integrating Evolutionary, Neuroscience, and Sociocultural Approaches*, edited by Omri Gillath et al., 3–10. Washington, DC: American Psychological Association, 2012.

———, eds. *Relationship Science: Integrating Evolutionary, Neuroscience, and Sociocultural Approaches*. Washington, DC: American Psychological Association, 2012.

Gillath, Omri, et al. "A Multilevel, Multimethod Interdisciplinary Approach to the Understanding of Attachment." In *Relationship Science: Integrating Evolutionary, Neuroscience, and Sociocultural Approaches*, edited by Omri Gillath et al., 219–40. Washington, DC: American Psychological Association, 2012.

Glaw, Annette M. *The Holy Spirit and Christian Ethics in the Theology of Klaus Bockmuehl*. Cambridge: Clarke & Co., 2013.
Gloege, Gerhard. "Gläubiges Denken." *Verkündigung und Forschung* 1/2 (1951) 57–78.
Göcke, Benedikt Paul. "Theologie als Regina Scientiae." Conference presentation at *Studientagung: Ist Theologie eine Wissenschaft?*, STH Basel, September 13, 2019.
Goodwin, Robin, and Urmila Pillay. "Relationships, Culture, and Social Change." In *The Cambridge Handbook of Personal Relationships*, edited by Anita L. Vangelisti and Daniel Perlman, 695–708. Cambridge: Cambridge University Press, 2006.
Granqvist, Pehr. *Attachment in Religion and Spirituality: A Wider View*. New York: Guilford, 2020.
Granqvist, Pehr, et al. "Religion as Attachment: Normative Processes and Individual Differences." *Personality and Social Psychology Review* 14 (2010) 49–59.
Grau, Ina, ed. *Sozialpsychologie der Partnerschaft*. Berlin: Springer, 2003.
Greene, Kathryn, et al. "Self-Disclosure in Personal Relationships." In *The Cambridge Handbook of Personal Relationships*, edited by Anita L. Vangelisti and Daniel Perlman, 409–27. Cambridge: Cambridge University Press, 2006.
Green, Melody, and David Hazard. *No Compromise: The Life Story of Keith Green*. Nashville: Thomas Nelson, 2008.
Grenz, Stanley J. *The Social God and the Relational Self: A Trinitarian Theology of the Imago Dei*. Louisville: Westminster John Knox, 2001.
Grenz, Stanley J., and Leighton Ford. *Created for Community: Connecting Christian Belief with Christian Living*. Grand Rapids: Baker, 2008.
Grenz, Stanley J., and Roger E. Olson. *20th-Century Theology: God and the World in a Transitional Age*. Grand Rapids: InterVarsity, 1993.
Greshake, Gisbert. *Der dreieine Gott: Eine trinitarische Theologie*. Freiburg im Breisgau: Herder, 2007.
Grudem, Wayne. *Systematic Theology: An Introduction to Biblical Doctrine*. Leicester: InterVarsity, 1994.
Guarini, Marcello, et al. "Resources for Research on Analogy: A Multidisciplinary Guide." *Informal Logic* 29 (2009) 84–197.
Gunton, Colin E. *The One, the Three, and the Many: God, Creation, and the Culture of Modernity*. Cambridge: Cambridge University Press, 1993.
———. *Promise of Trinitarian Theology*. London: Continuum, 2003.
Gushee, David P. *After Evangelicalism*. Louisville: Westminster John Knox, 2020.
Guthrie, Stewart E. "Anthropology and Anthropomorphism in Religion." In *Religion, Anthropology, and Cognitive Science*, edited by Harvey Whitehouse, 37–62. Durham, NC: Carolina Academic, 2007.
Härle, Wilfried. "Wie kam die Relationale Erkenntnistheorie und Ontologie in die Welt? Erinnerungen eines Zeitzeugen." In *Relationale Erkenntnishorizonte in Exegese und Systematischer Theologie*, edited by Raphaela J. Meyer zu Hörste-Bührer and Walter Bührer, 15–32. Leipzig: Evangelische Verlagsanstalt, 2018.
Härle, Wilfried, and Eilert Herms. *Rechtfertigung, das Wirklichkeitsverständnis des christlichen Glaubens: Ein Arbeitsbuch*. Göttingen: Vandenhoeck & Ruprecht, 1980.
Harris, Harriet A. "Should We Say That Personhood Is Relational?" *Scottish Journal of Theology* 51 (1998) 214.
Hart, John Woodward. *Karl Barth vs. Emil Brunner: The Formation and Dissolution of a Theological Alliance, 1916–1936*. New York: Lang, 2001.

Hartenstein, Friedhelm. "Relationalität als Schlüssel zum Verständnis JHWHs: Zur Beziehungslogik alttestamentlicher Gotteskonzepte." In *Relationale Erkenntnishorizonte in Exegese und Systematischer Theologie*, edited by Raphaela J. Meyer zu Hörste-Bührer and Walter Bührer, 161–80. Leipzig: Evangelische Verlagsanstalt, 2018.

Hartl, Johannes. "Abschied von einem Lehrer." *Johannes Hartl* (blog), April 21, 2020. https://web.archive.org/web/20200808164608/https://johanneshartl.org/abschied-von-einem-lehrer/

Harvey, John J., and Amy Wenzel. "Theoretical Perspectives in the Study of Close Relationships." In *The Cambridge Handbook of Personal Relationships*, edited by Anita L. Vangelisti and Daniel Perlman, 35–49. Cambridge: Cambridge University Press, 2006.

Hauge, Reidar. "Truth as Encounter." In *The Theology of Emil Brunner*, edited by Charles W. Kegley, 133–56. London: Macmillan, 1962.

Hazan, Cindy, and Phillip R. Shaver. "Attachment as an Organizational Framework for Research on Close Relationships." *Psychological Inquiry* 5 (1994) 1–22.

Heilig, Christoph. *Paulus als Erzähler? Eine narratologische Perspektive auf die Paulusbriefe*. Berlin: de Gruyter, 2020.

Heim, Erin M. *Adoption in Galatians and Romans: Contemporary Metaphor Theories and the Pauline Huiothesia Metaphors*. Leiden: Brill, 2017.

Hempelmann, Heinzpeter. "Editorial." *Theologische Beiträge* 51 (2020) 133–34.

———. "Wunder als Zeichen: Acht Thesen aus wissenschaftstheoretischer Perspektive." *Theologische Beiträge* 51 (2020) 200–216.

Henry, Carl F. H., and David S. Dockery. *Architect of Evangelicalism: Essential Essays of Carl F. H. Henry*. Bellingham, WA: Lexham, 2019.

Heschel, Abraham Joshua. *The Prophets*. New York: Perennial, 2001.

Hesselink, I. John. "Emil Brunner: A Reappraisal (Book Review)." *The Christian Century* 131 (2014) 39–41.

Hilberath, Bernd Jochen, et al., eds. *Communicative Theology: Reflections on the Culture of Our Practice of Theology*. Wien: LIT, 2007.

Hochman, Larry. *The Relationship Revolution: Closing the Customer Promise Gap*. Chichester: Wiley, 2010.

Holmes, Stephen R. *The Quest for the Trinity: The Doctrine of God in Scripture, History and Modernity*. Downers Grove, IL: InterVarsity, 2012.

Holtzen, William Curtis. "Dei Fide: A Relational Theology of the Faith of God." DTh diss., University of South Africa, 2009.

———. *The God Who Trusts: A Relational Theology of Divine Faith, Hope, and Love*. Westmont, IL: InterVarsity, 2019.

Horton, Michael. *Introducing Covenant Theology*. Grand Rapids: Baker, 2009.

Huddleston, Rodney D., et al. *The Cambridge Grammar of the English Language*. Cambridge: Cambridge University Press, 2010.

Ickes, William, et al. "Closeness as Intersubjectivity: Social Absorption and Social Individuation." In *Handbook of Closeness and Intimacy*, edited by Debra J. Mashek, 357–74. London: Routledge, 2004.

James, Lindsay. "Anthropomorphism." In *The International Standard Bible Encyclopaedia*, edited by James Orr et al., 152–54. Chicago: Howard-Severance, 1915.

Jehle, Frank. *Emil Brunner: Theologe im 20. Jahrhundert*. Zürich: TVZ, 2006.

Jenson, Robert W. *Systematic Theology, Volume 1: The Triune God*. New York: Oxford University Press, 2001.

Jewett, Paul King. *Emil Brunner's Concept of Revelation*. London: Clarke, 1954.

Johnson, Bill. *When Heaven Invades Earth: A Practical Guide to a Life of Miracles*. Shippensburg, PA: Destiny Image, 2003.

Johnson, David W., and Roger T. Johnson. "New Developments in Social Interdependence Theory." *Genetic, Social, and General Psychology Monographs* 131 (2005) 285–358.

Johnson, Wendell Gordon. "Soteriology as a Function of Epistemology in the Thought of Emil Brunner." PhD diss., Rice University, 1989.

Kanzian, Christian. "Der Begriff 'Koinzidenz' in der Mereologie." In *Analyomen/ Analyomen: Proceedings of the 1st Conference Perspectives in Analytical Philosophy*, edited by Georg Meggle and Ulla Wessels, 892–98. Berlin: de Gruyter, 1994.

Karremans, Johan C., and Paul A. M. van Lange. "The Role of Forgiveness in Shifting from 'Me' to 'We.'" *Self and Identity* 7 (2008) 75–88.

Keener, Craig S. *Miracles: The Credibility of the New Testament Accounts*. Grand Rapids: Baker Academic, 2011.

Kegley, Charles W., ed. *The Theology of Emil Brunner*. London: Macmillan, 1962.

Keil, Carl Friedrich, and Franz Delitzsch. *Biblischer Commentar über die Bücher Moses: Genesis und Exodus*. Leipzig: Dörffling und Franke, 1878.

Kelley, Harold H. *Personal Relationships: Their Structures and Processes*. Hillsdale, NJ: Erlbaum, 1979.

Kelley, Harold H., and John W. Thibaut. *Interpersonal Relations: A Theory of Interdependence*. New York: Wiley, 1978.

Kelley, Harold H., et al. *An Atlas of Interpersonal Situations*. Cambridge: Cambridge University Press, 2003.

Kelley, Harold H., et al. *Close Relationships*. New York: Freeman, 1983.

Kenrick, Douglas T., et al. "Relationships from an Evolutionary Life History Perspective." In *The Oxford Handbook of Close Relationships*, edited by Jeffry A. Simpson and Lorne Campbell, 13–35. Oxford: Oxford University Press, 2013.

Kirkpatrick, Lee A., and Phillip R. Shaver. "Attachment Theory and Religion: Childhood Attachments, Religious Beliefs, and Conversion." *Journal for the Scientific Study of Religion* 29 (1990) 315.

Kläden, Tobias. "Hartmut Rosa als Gesprächspartner für die Theologie." *Pastoraltheologie* 107 (2018) 394–400.

Klein, Albert. "Von der Tradition zum biblischen Zeugnis." In *Emil Brunner in der Erinnerung seiner Schüler*, edited by Werner Kramer and Hugo Sonderegger, 223–28. Zürich: TVZ, 1989.

Knauer, Peter. *Der Glaube kommt vom Hören: Ökumenische Fundamentaltheologie*. Freiburg: Herder, 1991.

———. "Ontología Relacional." In *Dios clemente y misericordioso: Enfoque antropológico; homenaje a Barbara Andrade*, edited by Javier Quezada del Río, 1–17. 1st ed. México, D.F: Universidad Iberoamericana, 2012.

———. *Verantwortung des Glaubens: Ein Gespräch mit Gerhard Ebeling aus katholischer Sicht*. Frankfurt am Main: Knecht, 1969.

Konstan, David. *Friendship in the Classical World*. Cambridge: Cambridge University Press, 1997.

Köstenberger, Andreas J. "Aesthetic Theology—Blessing or Curse? An Assessment of Narrative Theology." *Faith and Mission* 15 (1998) 27–37.

Kouneski, Edward F., and David H. Olson. "A Practical Look at Intimacy: ENRICH Couple Typology." In *Handbook of Closeness and Intimacy*, edited by Debra J. Mashek, 117–36. London: Routledge, 2004.

Kovacs, Kenneth E. *The Relational Theology of James E. Loder: Encounter and Conviction.* New York: Lang, 2011.

Kramer, Werner, and Hugo Sonderegger, eds. *Emil Brunner in der Erinnerung seiner Schüler.* Zürich: TVZ, 1989.

Krautz, Jochen, ed. *Beziehungsweisen und Bezogenheiten: Relationalität in Pädagogik, Kunst und Kunstpädagogik.* München: Kopead, 2017.

———. "Relationalität in Pädagogik, Kunst und Kunstpädagogik: Zur Einführung." In *Beziehungsweisen und Bezogenheiten: Relationalität in Pädagogik, Kunst und Kunstpädagogik*, edited by Jochen Krautz, 11–30. München: Kopead, 2017.

Kruglanski, Arie W., and Edward Tory Higgins, eds. *Social Psychology: Handbook of Basic Principles.* 2nd ed. New York: Guilford, 2007.

Künkler, Tobias. *Lernen in Beziehung: Zum Verhältnis von Subjektivität und Relationalität in Lernprozessen.* Bielefeld: Transcript, 2014.

———. "Die Relationalität menschlicher Existenz: Versuch einer (kategorialen) Systematisierung." In *Beziehungsweisen und Bezogenheiten: Relationalität in Pädagogik, Kunst und Kunstpädagogik*, edited by Jochen Krautz, 61–78. München: Kopead, 2017.

———. "Relationalität und relationale Subjektivität: Ein grundlagentheoretischer Beitrag zur Beziehungsforschung." In *Kinderrechte in pädagogischen Beziehungen*, edited by Annedore Prengel and Ursula Winklhofer, 25–43. Opladen: Verlag Barbara Budrich, 2014.

LaCugna, Catherine M. "The Relational God: Aquinas and Beyond." *Theological Studies* 46 (1985) 647–63.

Laube, Martin. "Eine bessere Welt ist möglich: Theologische Überlegungen zur Resonanztheorie Hartmut Rosas." *Pastoraltheologie* 107 (2018) 356–70.

Laurenceau, Jean-Philippe, and Brighid M. Kleinman. "Intimacy in Personal Relationships." In *The Cambridge Handbook of Personal Relationships*, edited by Anita L. Vangelisti and Daniel Perlman, 637–56. Cambridge: Cambridge University Press, 2006.

Laurenceau, Jean-Philippe, et al. "Intimacy as an Interpersonal Process: Current Status and Future Directions." In *Handbook of Closeness and Intimacy*, edited by Debra J. Mashek, 61–80. London: Routledge, 2004.

Laurenceau, Jean-Philippe, et al. "Intimacy as an Interpersonal Process: The Importance of Self-Disclosure, Partner Disclosure, and Perceived Partner Responsiveness in Interpersonal Exchanges." *Journal of Personality and Social Psychology* 74 (1998) 1238–51.

Laursen, Brett, et al. "Incorporating Interdependence into Developmental Research: Examples from the Study of Homophily and Homogeneity." In *Modeling Dyadic and Interdependent Data in the Developmental and Behavioral Sciences*, edited by James P. Selig et al., 11–37. London: Routledge, 2008.

Leiner, Martin. *Gottes Gegenwart: Martin Bubers Philosophie des Dialogs und der Ansatz ihrer theologischen Rezeption bei Friedrich Gogarten und Emil Brunner.* Gütersloh: Kaiser, 2000.

Leipold, Heinrich. *Missionarische Theologie: Emil Brunners Weg zur theologischen Anthropologie.* Göttingen: Vandenhoeck & Ruprecht, 1974.

Leithart, Peter J. "Common Spirit, Common Good." *First Things*, June 4, 2020. https://www.firstthings.com/web-exclusives/2020/06/common-spirit-common-good.
Leonhardt, Rochus. *Grundinformation Dogmatik: Ein Lehr- und Arbeitsbuch für das Studium der Theologie*. Göttingen: Vandenhoeck & Ruprecht, 2001.
Leuenberger, Robert. "Theologie als grosses Gespräch: Zur Wirkung Emil Brunners." In *Emil Brunner in der Erinnerung seiner Schüler*, edited by Werner Kramer and Hugo Sonderegger, 9–27. Zürich: TVZ, 1989.
Lewis, C. S. *The Complete Chronicles of Narnia*. London: Collins, 2000.
Lim, Timothy T. N. "Anthropomorphism and Anthropopathism." In *The Lexham Bible Dictionary*, edited by John D. Barry et al. Bellingham, WA: Lexham, 2016.
Loder, James E. *The Logic of the Spirit: Human Development in Theological Perspective*. San Francisco: Jossey-Bass, 1998.
Loos, Andreas. "Divine Action and the Trinity: A Brief Exploration of the Grounds of Trinitarian Speech about God in the Theology of Adolf Schlatter." *International Journal of Systematic Theology* 4 (2002) 255–77.
———. "Die Krise der Trinitätslehre in der protestantischen Theologie." In *Das Geheimnis der Dreieinigkeit im Zeugnis der Kirche: Trinitarisch anbeten—lehren—leben; ein bekenntnis-ökumenisches Handbuch*, edited by Peter Beyerhaus, 221–32. Nuremberg: VTR, 2009.
Lösel, Friedrich, and Doris Bender. "Theorien und Modelle der Paarbeziehung." In *Sozialpsychologie der Partnerschaft*, edited by Ina Grau, 43–76. Berlin: Springer, 2003.
Loving, Timothy J., and Ted L. Huston. "Back to the Future: Resurrecting and Vitalizing the Unrealized Call for Interdisciplinary Research on Close Relationships." In *Interdisciplinary Research on Close Relationships: The Case for Integration*, edited by Lorne Campbell and Timothy J. Loving, 273–82. Washington, DC: American Psychological Association, 2012.
Lüdemann, Uwe. *Denken—Glauben—Predigen: Eine kritische Auseinandersetzung mit Emil Brunners Lehre vom Mensch im Widerspruch*. Frankfurt am Main: Lang, 1998.
Luhrmann, T. M. *When God Talks Back: Understanding the American Evangelical Relationship with God*. New York: Knopf, 2012.
Lütz, Dietmar. *Der Weg zum Glauben: Emil Brunner und das unerledigte Kapitel protestantischer Dogmatik*. Berlin: WDL, 2000.
Lynch, Chloe. *Ecclesial Leadership as Friendship*. Milton Park: Routledge, 2019.
Lyotard, Jean-François. *La condition postmoderne: Rapport sur le savoir*. Paris: Les Éditions de Minuit, 2002.
Majerus, Brian D., and Steven J. Sandage. "Differentiation of Self and Christian Spiritual Maturity: Social Science and Theological Integration." *Journal of Psychology and Theology* 38 (2010) 41–51.
Mashek, Debra J., ed. *Handbook of Closeness and Intimacy*. London: Routledge, 2004.
Mashek, Debra J., and Michelle D. Sherman. "Desiring Less Closeness with Intimate Others." In *Handbook of Closeness and Intimacy*, edited by Debra J. Mashek, 343–56. London: Routledge, 2004.
Maurer, Ernstpeter. "Die Metapher als eigentliche Rede: Zur Verwicklung von Sprache und Wirklichkeit." In *Relationale Erkenntnishorizonte in Exegese und Systematischer Theologie*, edited by Raphaela J. Meyer zu Hörste-Bührer and Walter Bührer, 33–54. Leipzig: Evangelische Verlagsanstalt, 2018.

Maurer, Hans. "Keine neue Orthodoxie." In *Emil Brunner in der Erinnerung seiner Schüler*, edited by Werner Kramer and Hugo Sonderegger, 94–99. Zürich: TVZ, 1989.

Mauz, Andreas. "Theology and Narration: Reflections on the 'Narrative Theology'-Debate and Beyond." In *Narratology in the Age of Cross-Disciplinary Narrative Research*, edited by Sandra Heinen and Roy Sommer, 261–85. Berlin: de Gruyter, 2009.

McDowell, John C. "Karl Barth, Emil Brunner, and the Subjectivity of the Object of Christian Hope." *International Journal of Systematic Theology* 8 (2006) 25–41.

McEnhill, Peter, and G. M. Newlands. *Fifty Key Christian Thinkers*. London: Routledge, 2004.

McFague, Sallie. *Metaphorical Theology: Models of God in Religious Language*. Philadelphia: Fortress, 2010.

McFarlane, Graham. *A Model for Evangelical Theology: Integrating Scripture, Tradition, Reason, Experience, and Community*. Grand Rapids: Baker Academic, 2020.

McGrath, Alister E. *The Christian Theology Reader*. Newark: Wiley-Blackwell, 2016.

———. *Emil Brunner: A Reappraisal*. Chichester: Wiley-Blackwell, 2016.

———. *Mere Apologetics: How to Help Seekers and Skeptics Find Faith*. Grand Rapids: Baker, 2011.

McIlroy, David H. "Towards a Relational and Trinitarian Theology of Atonement." *Evangelical Quarterly* 80 (2008) 13–32.

McInroy, Mark J. "Karl Barth and Personalist Philosophy: A Critical Appropriation." *Scottish Journal of Theology* 64 (2011) 45–63.

McKim, Mark G. "Brunner the Ecumenist: Emil Brunner as a Vox Media of Protestant Theology." *Calvin Theological Journal* 32 (1997) 91–104.

Meland, Bernard E. "The Thought of Emil Brunner: An Evaluation." *Journal of the American Academy of Religion* 16 (1948) 165–68.

Merkle, Benjamin L. *Discontinuity to Continuity: A Survey of Dispensational and Covenantal Theologies*. Bellingham, WA: Lexham, 2020.

Merton, Thomas. *New Seeds of Contemplation*. New York: New Directions, 2007.

Meyer zu Hörste-Bührer, Raphaela J. *Gott und Menschen in Beziehungen*. Neukirchen-Vluyn: Neukirchener, 2016.

Meyer zu Hörste-Bührer, Raphaela J., and Walter Bührer. "Relationale Erkenntnishoizonte als Bindeglied zwischen Exegese und systematischer Theologie?" In *Relationale Erkenntnishorizonte in Exegese und Systematischer Theologie*, edited by Raphaela J. Meyer zu Hörste-Bührer and Walter Bührer, 1–13. Leipzig: Evangelische Verlagsanstalt, 2018.

———. "Relationale Erkenntnishorizonte als hermeneutischer Schlüssel zu Pluralität und Einheit des Alten Testaments." In *Relationale Erkenntnishorizonte in Exegese und Systematischer Theologie*, edited by Raphaela J. Meyer zu Hörste-Bührer and Walter Bührer, 181–219. Leipzig: Evangelische Verlagsanstalt, 2018.

———, eds. *Relationale Erkenntnishorizonte in Exegese und Systematischer Theologie*. Leipzig: Evangelische Verlagsanstalt, 2018.

Mielke, Robert H. E. "The Doctrine of Imago Dei in the Theology of Emil Brunner." PhD diss., Drew University, 1951.

Mikulincer, Mario, and Phillip R. Shaver. "The Role of Attachment Security in Adolescent and Adult Close Relationships." In *The Oxford Handbook of Close Relationships*, edited by Jeffry A. Simpson and Lorne Campbell, 66–83. Oxford: Oxford University Press, 2013.

Miller, Rowland S. *Intimate Relationships*. New York: McGraw Hill, 2012.

Bibliography

Miner, Maureen H. "Applying Relational and Contextual Reasoning (RCR) to Understand Human–Divine Relationships." *Theology and Science* 7 (2009) 245–59.

Moltmann, Jürgen. "God's Kenosis in the Creation and Consummation of the World." In *The Work of Love: Creation as Kenosis*, edited by John Polkinghorne, 137–51. Grand Rapids: Eerdmans, 2001.

Moriarty, Glendon L., et al. "Understanding the God Image through Attachment Theory." *Journal of Spirituality in Mental Health* 9 (2006) 43–56.

Mühling, Markus. *Post-Systematische Theologie I: Denkwege—eine theologische Philosophie*. Paderborn: Fink, 2020.

———. "Relationalität, Narrativität und Werte: Grundzüge einer wahrhaft relationalen theologischen Ethik—7 Thesen." In *Relationale Erkenntnishorizonte in Exegese und Systematischer Theologie*, edited by Raphaela J. Meyer zu Hörste-Bührer and Walter Bührer, 55–68. Leipzig: Evangelische Verlagsanstalt, 2018.

Müller, Eberhard. "The Church in Action." In *The Theology of Emil Brunner*, edited by Charles W. Kegley, 41–54. London: Macmillan, 1962.

Muller, Richard A. "Christ—the Revelation or the Revealer? Brunner and Reformed Orthodoxy on the Doctrine of the Word of God." *Journal of Evangelical Theological Society* 26 (1983) 307–19.

Noll, Mark A., et al., eds. *Evangelicals: Who They Have Been, Are Now, and Could Be*. Grand Rapids: Eerdmans, 2019.

Noller, Patricia. "Bringing It All Together: A Theoretical Approach." In *The Cambridge Handbook of Personal Relationships*, edited by Anita L. Vangelisti and Daniel Perlman, 769–90. Cambridge: Cambridge University Press, 2006.

Nygren, Anders. *Agape and Eros*. Chicago: University of Chicago Press, 1982.

———. "Emil Brunner's Doctrine of God." In *The Theology of Emil Brunner*, edited by Charles W. Kegley, 177–88. London: Macmillan, 1962.

O'Donovan, Joan E. "Man in the Image of God: The Disagreement between Barth and Brunner Reconsidered." *Scottish Journal of Theology* 39 (1986) 433–59.

Oei, Amos Winarto. "The Impassible God Who 'Cried.'" *Themelios* 41 (2016) 238–47.

Olson, Roger E. "A Favorite Theologian Revisited: Emil Brunner (Review of Alister McGrath's Book: Part One)." *Patheos* (blog), April 15, 2014. https://www.patheos.com/blogs/rogereolson/2014/04/favorite-theologian-revisited-emil-brunner-review-of-alister-mcgraths-book-part-one/.

———. "A Favorite Theologian Revisited: Emil Brunner (Review of Alister McGrath's Book: Part Two)." *Patheos* (blog), April 19, 2014. https://www.patheos.com/blogs/rogereolson/2014/04/a-favorite-theologian-revisted-emil-brunner-review-of-alister-mcgraths-book-part-two/

———. "Gems of Wisdom from Emil Brunner: Transcendence and Free Decision." *Patheos* (blog), December 21, 2015. https://www.patheos.com/blogs/rogereolson/2015/12/gems-of-wisdom-from-emil-brunner-transcendence-and-free-decision/.

———. "Narrative Theology Explained." *Patheos* (blog), January 15, 2016. https://www.patheos.com/blogs/rogereolson/2016/01/narrative-theology-explained/.

Oman, Doug. "Defining Religion and Spirituality." In *Handbook of the Psychology of Religion and Spirituality*, edited by Raymond F. Paloutzian and Crystal L. Park, 23–47. 2nd ed. New York: Guilford, 2015.

Oord, Thomas Jay. "Relational Love." In *Relational Theology: A Contemporary Introduction*, edited by Thomas J. Oord et al., 24–27. Eugene, OR: Wipf & Stock, 2012.

———. *The Uncontrolling Love of God: An Open and Relational Account of Providence.* Downers Grove, IL: IVP Academic, 2015.

Oord, Thomas Jay, et al., eds. *Relational Theology: A Contemporary Introduction.* Eugene, OR: Wipf & Stock, 2012.

Oster, Stefan. *Person-Sein vor Gott: Theologische Erkundungen mit dem Bischof von Passau.* Freiburg im Breisgau: Herder, 2015.

Palma, Robert J. "Thomas F. Torrance's Reformed Theology." *Reformed Review* 38 (1984) 2–46.

Paloutzian, Raymond F., and Crystal L. Park, eds. *Handbook of the Psychology of Religion and Spirituality.* 2nd ed. New York: Guilford, 2015.

———. "Recent Progress and Core Issues in the Science of the Psychology of Religion and Spirituality." In *Handbook of the Psychology of Religion and Spirituality*, edited by Raymond F. Paloutzian and Crystal L. Park, 3–22. 2nd ed. New York: Guilford, 2015.

Peckham, John C. *The Love of God: A Canonical Model.* Downers Grove, IL: InterVarsity, 2015.

Perlman, Daniel, and Steve Duck. "The Seven Seas of the Study of Personal Relationships: From 'The Thousand Islands' to Interconnected Waterways." In *The Cambridge Handbook of Personal Relationships*, edited by Anita L. Vangelisti and Daniel Perlman, 11–34. Cambridge: Cambridge University Press, 2006.

Peterson, Jordan B. *12 Rules for Life: An Antidote to Chaos.* London: Penguin, 2018.

Petzoldt, Matthias. "Wahrheit als Begegnung: Dialogisches Wahrheitsverständnis im Licht der Analyse performativer Sprache." In *Veritas et Communicatio: Ökumenische Theologie auf der Suche nach einem verbindlichen Zeugnis*, edited by Heiko Franke and Thomas Krobath, 79–93. Göttingen: Vandenhoeck & Ruprecht, 1992.

Pinnock, Clark H. *The Openness of God: A Biblical Challenge to the Traditional Understanding of God.* Downers Grove, IL: InterVarsity, 1994.

Polkinghorne, John. "Kenotic Creation and Divine Action." In *The Work of Love: Creation as Kenosis*, edited by John Polkinghorne, 90–106. Grand Rapids: Eerdmans, 2001.

———. *The Trinity and an Entangled World: Relationality in Physical Science and Theology.* Grand Rapids: Eerdmans, 2010.

———, ed. *The Work of Love: Creation as Kenosis.* Grand Rapids: Eerdmans, 2001.

Poythress, Vern S. *Redeeming Sociology: A God-Centered Approach.* Wheaton, IL: Crossway, 2011.

Prager, Karen J., and Linda J. Roberts. "Deep Intimate Connection: Self and Intimacy in Couple Relationships." In *Handbook of Closeness and Intimacy*, edited by Debra J. Mashek, 43–60. London: Routledge, 2004.

Preston Sprinkle. "Is Having a Personal Relationship with Jesus a Biblical Concept?" *Patheos* (blog), October 8, 2014. https://www.patheos.com/blogs/theologyintheraw/2014/10/is-having-a-personal-relationship-with-jesus-a-biblical-concept/.

Putthoff, Tyson L. *Ontological Aspects of Early Jewish Anthropology: The Malleable Self and the Presence of God.* Leiden: Brill, 2016.

Quick, Kathryn S. "Taking a Relational Turn in Leadership Studies." *Public Administration Review* 74 (2014) 542–44.

Rabens, Volker. *The Holy Spirit and Ethics in Paul: Transformation and Empowering for Religious-Ethical Life.* Minneapolis: Fortress, 2014.

Bibliography

———. "Sein und Werden in Beziehungen: Grundzüge relationaler Theologie bei Paulus und Johannes." In *Relationale Erkenntnishorizonte in Exegese und Systematischer Theologie*, edited by Raphaela J. Meyer zu Hörste-Bührer and Walter Bührer, 91–143. Leipzig: Evangelische Verlagsanstalt, 2018.

Rahner, Karl. *Grundkurs des Glaubens: Einführung in den Begriff des Christentums.* Freiburg: Herder, 1977.

Regan, Pamela C. *Close Relationships.* London: Routledge, 2011.

Rehfeld, Emmanuel L. *Relationale Ontologie bei Paulus: Die ontische Wirksamkeit der Christusbezogenheit im Denken des Heidenapostels.* Tübingen: Mohr Siebeck, 2012.

———. "Seinskonstitutive Christusbezogenheit: Relational-ontologische Denkstrukturen und 'In-Christus-Sein' bei Paulus." In *Relationale Erkenntnishorizonte in Exegese und Systematischer Theologie*, edited by Raphaela J. Meyer zu Hörste-Bührer and Walter Bührer, 69–90. Leipzig: Evangelische Verlagsanstalt, 2018.

Reis, Harry T. "Perceived Partner Responsiveness as an Organizing Theme for the Study of Relationships and Well-Being." In *Interdisciplinary Research on Close Relationships: The Case for Integration*, edited by Lorne Campbell and Timothy J. Loving, 27–52. Washington, DC: American Psychological Association, 2012.

Reis, Harry T., and Margaret S. Clark. "Responsiveness." In *The Oxford Handbook of Close Relationships*, edited by Jeffry A. Simpson and Lorne Campbell, 400–418. Oxford: Oxford University Press, 2013.

Reis, Harry T., et al. "Ellen Berscheid, Elaine Hatfield, and the Emergence of Relationship Science." *Perspectives on Psychological Science* 8 (2013) 558–72.

Reis, Harry T., et al. "Perceived Partner Responsiveness as an Organizing Construct in the Study of Intimacy and Closeness." In *Handbook of Closeness and Intimacy*, edited by Debra J. Mashek, 201–28. London: Routledge, 2004.

Rich, Arthur. "Denken, das weh tut." In *Emil Brunner in der Erinnerung seiner Schüler*, edited by Werner Kramer and Hugo Sonderegger, 78–82. Zürich: TVZ, 1989.

Richards, E. Randolph, and Richard James. *Misreading Scripture with Individualist Eyes: Patronage, Honor, and Shame in the Biblical World.* Downers Grove, IL: InterVarsity, 2020.

Robinson, William E. W. *Metaphor, Morality, and the Spirit in Romans 8:1–17.* Atlanta: SBL, 2016.

Rollefson, Richard Griffith, and David Jay Gouwens. *Thinking with Kierkegaard and Wittgenstein: The Philosophical Theology of Paul L. Holmer.* Eugene, OR: Pickwick, 2014.

Rosa, Hartmut. *Resonance: A Sociology of the Relationship to the World.* Cambridge: Polity, 2019.

———. *Resonanz: Eine Soziologie der Weltbeziehung.* Berlin: Suhrkamp, 2018.

Rosenstock, Roland. "Etwas, was nicht ist und doch nicht nur nicht ist: Konturen einer resonanzsensiblen Theologie im Gespräch mit Hartmut Rosa." *Pastoraltheologie* 107 (2018) 401–7.

Ross, James F. "Analogy in Theology." In *Encyclopedia of Philosophy*, edited by Donald M. Borchert, 138–43. 2nd ed. Detroit: Macmillan Reference, 2006.

Rössler, Roman. *Person und Glaube: Der Personalismus der Gottesbeziehung bei Emil Brunner.* München: Kaiser, 1965.

Rusbult, Caryl E., and Paul A. M. van Lange. "Interdependence, Interaction, and Relationships." *Annual Review of Psychology* 54 (2003) 351–75.

———. "Why We Need Interdependence Theory." *Social and Personality Psychology Compass* 2 (2008) 2049–70.

Rusbult, Caryl E., et al. "Commitment." In *The Cambridge Handbook of Personal Relationships*, edited by Anita L. Vangelisti and Daniel Perlman, 615–36. Cambridge: Cambridge University Press, 2006.

Rusbult, Caryl E., et al. "Interdependence, Closeness, and Relationships." In *Handbook of Closeness and Intimacy*, edited by Debra J. Mashek, 137–62. London: Routledge, 2004.

Rusbult, Caryl E., et al. "Self Processes in Interdependent Relationships: Partner Affirmation and the Michelangelo Phenomenon." *Interaction Studies* 6 (2005) 375–91.

Salakka, Yrjö. *Person und Offenbarung in der Theologie Emil Brunners während der Jahre, 1914–1937*. Helsinki: Luther-Agricola-Gesellschaft, 1960.

Sandage, Steven J., and Jeannine K. Brown. "Relational Integration, Part I: Differentiated Relationality between Psychology and Theology." *Journal of Psychology and Theology* 43 (2015) 165–78.

———. "Relational Integration, Part II: Relational Integration as Developmental and Intercultural." *Journal of Psychology and Theology* 43 (2015) 179–91.

Sandage, Steven J., et al. "Relational Spirituality and Transformation: Risking Intimacy and Alterity." *Journal of Spiritual Formation and Soul Care* 1 (2008) 182–206.

Sanders, John. *The God Who Risks: A Theology of Divine Providence*. Downers Grove, IL: InterVarsity, 2007.

———. *Theology in the Flesh: How Embodiment and Culture Shape the Way We Think about Truth, Morality, and God*. Minneapolis: Fortress, 2016.

Sanderson, Catherine A. "The Link between the Pursuit of Intimacy Goals and Satisfaction in Close Relationships: An Examination of the Underlying Processes." In *Handbook of Closeness and Intimacy*, edited by Debra J. Mashek, 247–66. London: Routledge, 2004.

Sattler, Dorothea. *Beziehungsdenken in der Erlösungslehre: Bedeutung und Grenzen*. Freiburg im Breisgau: Herder, 1997.

Scheld, Stefan. *Die Christologie Emil Brunners: Beitrag zur Überwindung liberaler Jesulogie und dialektisch-doketischer Christologie im Zuge geschichtlich-dialogischen Denkens*. Wiesbaden: Steiner, 1981.

Schirrmacher, Thomas. "Emil Brunner: Die Väter der Situationsethik." *Bibel und Gemeinde* 3 (2004) 11–22.

———."Das Missverständnis der Kirche und das Missverständnis des Emil Brunner: Emil Brunners Bibliologie als Ursache für das Scheitern seiner Ekklesiologie." *Bibel und Gemeinde* 3 (1989) 279–305.

Schlippe, Arist von, and Jochen Schweitzer. *Lehrbuch der systemischen Therapie und Beratung I: Das Grundlagenwissen*. Göttingen: Vandenhoeck & Ruprecht, 2016.

Schmid, Johannes Heinrich. *Die Lehre von Gott: Martin Buber, Heinrich Ott, Wolfhart Pannenberg, Eberhard Jüngel, Sören Kierkegaard, Emil Brunner*. Riehen: ArteMedia, 2013.

Schmid, Manuel. *Gott ist ein Abenteurer: Der Offene Theismus und die Herausforderungen biblischer Gottesrede*. Göttingen: Vandenhoeck & Ruprecht, 2019.

Schneewind, Klaus, and Eva Wunderer. "Prozessmodelle der Partnerschaftsentwicklung." In *Sozialpsychologie der Partnerschaft*, edited by Ina Grau, 221–56. Berlin: Springer, 2003.

Schnelle, Udo. *Das Evangelium nach Johannes*. Leipzig: Evangelische Verlagsanstalt, 2009.

Schrotenboer, Paul G. *A New Apologetics: An Analysis and Appraisal of the Eristic Theology of Emil Brunner*. Kampen: Kok, 1955.
Schulte, Joachim. *Wittgenstein: Eine Einführung*. Stuttgart: Reclam, 2016.
Schulz, Claudia, and David Plüss. "Evangelikalismus und die Vielfalt der Frömmigkeitsprofile unter Studierenden." *Praktische Theologie* 54 (2019) 113–18.
Schuurman, Douglas James. *Creation, Eschaton, and Ethics: The Ethical Significance of the Creation-Eschaton Relation in the Thought of Emil Brunner and Jürgen Moltmann*. New York: Lang, 1991.
Schweitzer, Beat. "Nur eine Illusion? Gott als Produkt des Gehirns." *Forum für Kommunikative Theologie* 22/23 (2019) 1–12. https://tsc.education/uploads/pdf/communicatio/communicatio-magazin1901-beat-schweitzer-gott-als-produkt-des-gehirns-skript.pdf.
Schwöbel, Christoph. *Gott in Beziehung: Studien zur Dogmatik*. Tübingen: Mohr Siebeck, 2002.
Selg, Peeter. "Two Faces of the 'Relational Turn.'" *Political Science & Politics* 49 (2016) 27–31.
Seubert, Harald. "Kommunizieren in unserer Zeit: Philosophische Perspektiven." *Communicatio* 1 (2020) 4–9.
Shults, F. LeRon. *Reforming the Doctrine of God*. Grand Rapids: Eerdmans, 2005.
———. *Reforming Theological Anthropology: After the Philosophical Turn to Relationality*. Grand Rapids: Eerdmans, 2003.
Shults, F. LeRon, and Steven J. Sandage. *Transforming Spirituality: Integrating Theology and Psychology*. Grand Rapids: Baker Academic, 2006.
Simpson, Jeffry A. "Foundations of Interpersonal Trust." In *Social Psychology: Handbook of Basic Principles*, edited by Arie W. Kruglanski and Edward T. Higgins, 587–607. 2nd ed. New York: Guilford, 2007.
Simpson, Jeffry A., and Lorne Campbell, eds. *The Oxford Handbook of Close Relationships*. Oxford: Oxford University Press, 2013.
Smail, Thomas Allan. *Like Father, Like Son: The Trinity Imaged in Our Humanity*. Grand Rapids: Eerdmans, 2006.
Smedes, Taede A. "Emil Brunner Revisited: On the Cognitive Science of Religion, the Imago Dei, and Revelation." *Zygon* 49 (2014) 190–207.
Smith, James K. A. *Speech and Theology: Language and the Logic of Incarnation*. London: Routledge, 2002.
Sonderegger, Hugo. "Pfarramt und Gegenwartsleben." In *Emil Brunner in der Erinnerung seiner Schüler*, edited by Werner Kramer and Hugo Sonderegger, 128–34. Zürich: TVZ, 1989.
Spaemann, Robert. "Wirklichkeit als Anthropomorphismus." In *Beziehungsweisen und Bezogenheiten: Relationalität in Pädagogik, Kunst und Kunstpädagogik*, edited by Jochen Krautz, 39–50. München: Kopead, 2017.
Spalink, Benjamin. "Personal Relationship with God? Let's Use Better Language." *City Grace Church*, April 13, 2016. http://www.citygraceny.com/Personal-Relationship-With-God.
Sprecher, Susan, and Susan S. Hendrick. "Self-Disclosure in Intimate Relationships: Associations with Individual and Relationship Characteristics over Time." *Journal of Social and Clinical Psychology* 23 (2004) 857–77.
Sproul, R. C. *What Can We Know about God?* Orlando: Reformation Trust, 2017.

Spycher, Hans Ulrich. "Miniaturen der Erinnerung." In *Emil Brunner in der Erinnerung seiner Schüler*, edited by Werner Kramer and Hugo Sonderegger, 135–42. Zürich: TVZ, 1989.

Stanley, Brian. *The Global Diffusion of Evangelicalism: The Age of Billy Graham and John Stott*. Downers Grove, IL: InterVarsity, 2013.

Stienstra, Nelly. *YHWH Is the Husband of His People: Analysis of a Biblical Metaphor with Special Reference to Translation*. Kampen: Kok, 1993.

Stosch, Klaus von. *Einführung in die Systematische Theologie*. Stuttgart: UTB, 2009.

Suk, John D. *Not Sure: A Pastor's Journey from Faith to Doubt*. Grand Rapids: Eerdmans, 2011.

———. "A Personal Relationship with Jesus?" *Reformed Journal*, November 16, 2005. https://reformedjournal.com/a-personal-relationship-with-jesus/.

Swarat, Uwe. "Gesetz und Evangelium bei Emil Brunner." In *Verbindlich werden: Reformierte Existenz in ökumenischer Begegnung / Festschrift für Michael Weinrich zum 65. Geburtstag*, edited by Marco Hofheinz et al., 185–204. Neukirchen-Vluyn: Neukirchener, 2015.

Tanner, Kathryn. *Christ the Key*. Cambridge: Cambridge University Press, 2010.

Thibaut, John W., and Harold H. Kelley. *The Social Psychology of Groups*. Oxford: Wiley, 1959.

Thompson, Curtis L. "Emil Brunner: Polemically Promoting Kierkegaard's Christian Philosophy of Encounter." In *Kierkegaard's Influence on Theology*, edited by Jon Stewart, 65–104. Farnham, UK: Ashgate, 2012.

Tillich, Paul. "Some Questions on Brunner's Epistemology." In *The Theology of Emil Brunner*, edited by Charles W. Kegley, 99–110. London: Macmillan, 1962.

Torrance, Andrew B. *The Freedom to Become a Christian: A Kierkegaardian Account of Human Transformation in Relationship with God*. London: Bloomsbury, 2016.

Torrance, Thomas F. *The Trinitarian Faith: The Evangelical Theology of the Ancient Catholic Church*. London: Bloomsbury, 2016.

Twelftree, Graham H., ed. *The Cambridge Companion to Miracles*. Cambridge: Cambridge University Press, 2011.

———. *Jesus the Miracle Worker: A Historical and Theological Study*. Downers Grove, IL: InterVarsity, 1999.

———. *Paul and the Miraculous: A Historical Reconstruction*. Grand Rapids: Baker Academic, 2013.

Urban, Christina. *Das Menschenbild nach dem Johannesevangelium: Grundlagen johanneischer Anthropologie*. Tübingen: Mohr Siebeck, 2001.

Vacek, Edward C. *Love, Human and Divine: The Heart of Christian Ethics*. Washington, DC: Georgetown University Press, 1996.

van Lange, Paul A. M., and Daniel Balliet. "Interdependence Theory." In *APA Handbook of Personality and Social Psychology*, edited by Mario Mikulincer and Phillip R. Shaver, 65–92. Washington, DC: American Psychological Association, 2015.

Vangelisti, Anita L., and Daniel Perlman, eds. *The Cambridge Handbook of Personal Relationships*. Cambridge: Cambridge University Press, 2006.

Vanhoozer, Kevin J., ed. *The Cambridge Companion to Postmodern Theology*. Cambridge: Cambridge University Press, 2003.

———. *The Drama of Doctrine: A Canonical-Linguistic Approach to Christian Theology*. Louisville: Westminster John Knox, 2005.

———. *Remythologizing Theology: Divine Action, Passion, and Authorship*. Cambridge: Cambridge University Press, 2010.
VanLear, Arthur C., et al. "Relationship Typologies." In *The Cambridge Handbook of Personal Relationships*, edited by Anita L. Vangelisti and Daniel Perlman, 91–110. Cambridge: Cambridge University Press, 2006.
Viola, Frank. "Origin of 'Personal Savior' & The Idea of Having a 'Personal Relationship' with Christ." *Patheos* (blog), January 11, 2021. https://www.patheos.com/blogs/frankviola/personalsavior/.
Vogelsanger, Peter. "Brunner as Apologist." In *The Theology of Emil Brunner*, edited by Charles W. Kegley, 289–304. London: Macmillan, 1962.
Volf, Miroslav, and Matthew Croasmun. *For the Life of the World: Theology That Makes a Difference*. Grand Rapids: Brazos, 2019.
Volk, Hermann. *Emil Brunners Lehre von dem Sünder*. Münster: Regensberg, 1950.
———. *Emil Brunners Lehre von der ursprünglichen Gottebenbildlichkeit des Menschen*. Emsdetten: Lechte, 1939.
Volken, Laurenz. *Der Glaube bei Emil Brunner*. Fribourg: Paulusverlag, 1947.
Wales, Kathleen M. "Thou and You in Early Modern English: Brown and Gilman Re-Appraised." *Studia Linguistica* 37 (1983) 107–25.
Wan, Enoch. "The Paradigm of 'Relational Realism.'" *Occasional Bulletin (EMS)* 19 (2006) 1–4.
———. "Relational Theology and Relational Missiology." *Occasional Bulletin (EMS)* 21 (2007) 1–7.
Ward, Keith. "Cosmos and Kenosis." In *The Work of Love: Creation as Kenosis*, edited by John Polkinghorne, 152–66. Grand Rapids: Eerdmans, 2001.
Waters, Guy Prentiss, ed. *Covenant Theology: Biblical, Theological, and Historical Perspectives*. Wheaton, IL: Crossway, 2020.
Welker, Michael. "Beziehung—menschlich und göttlich." In *Was ist der Mensch, dass du seiner gedenkst? (Psalm 8,5) Aspekte einer theologischen Anthropologie / Festschrift für Bernd Janowski zum 65. Geburtstag*, edited by Michaela Bauks et al., 541–51. Neukirchen-Vluyn: Neukirchener, 2008.
———. "Romantic Love, Covenantal Love, Kenotic Love." In *The Work of Love: Creation as Kenosis*, edited by John Polkinghorne, 127–36. Grand Rapids: Eerdmans, 2001.
Wheeless, Lawrence R., and Janis Grotz. "The Measurement of Trust and Its Relationship to Self-Disclosure." *Human Communication Research* 3 (1977) 250–57.
White, Charles Jason. "The Literal vs. the Metaphorical God: A Description, Critique, and Clarification of Classical and Open Theist Methodologies within Conservative Evangelicalism." PhD diss., McMaster Divinity College, 2016.
White, Hugh Vernon. "Brunner's Missionary Theology." In *The Theology of Emil Brunner*, edited by Charles W. Kegley, 55–74. London: Macmillan, 1962.
Wieselquist, Jennifer, et al. "Commitment, Pro-Relationship Behavior, and Trust in Close Relationships." *Journal of Personality and Social Psychology* 77 (1999) 942–66.
Williams, Daniel D. "Brunner and Barth on Philosophy." *Journal of Religion* 27 (1947) 241–54.
Williams, Michael. "Systematic Theology as a Biblical Discipline." In *All for Jesus: A Celebration of the 50th Anniversary of Covenant Theological Seminary*, edited by Robert A. Peterson and Sean M. Lucas, 167–96. Fearn, UK: Christian Focus, 2006.

Wisse, Maarten. "Towards a Truly Relational Theology: A Conversation with F. LeRon Shults." *Ars Disputandi* 4 (2004) 148–60.

Witten, Marsha Grace. *All Is Forgiven: The Secular Message in American Protestantism*. Princeton: Princeton University Press, 1993.

Wittgenstein, Ludwig. *Philosophical Investigations: The German Text, with an English Translation*. Oxford: Wiley-Blackwell, 2009.

Wolf, Herbert C. "An Introduction to the Idea of God as Person." *Journal of the American Academy of Religion* 32 (1964) 26–32.

Wolff, Phillip, and Dedre Gentner. "Structure-Mapping in Metaphor Comprehension." *Cognitive Science* 35 (2011) 1456–88.

Wright, N. T. *The Day the Revolution Began: Reconsidering the Meaning of Jesus's Crucifixion*. San Francisco: HarperOne, 2016.

Yong, Amos. *Beyond the Impasse: Toward a Pneumatological Theology of Religions*. Grand Rapids: Baker Academic, 2003.

Young, William P. *The Shack*. London: Hodder & Stoughton, 2008.

Zahl, Bonnie Poon, and Nicholas J. S. Gibson. "God Representations, Attachment to God, and Satisfaction with Life: A Comparison of Doctrinal and Experiential Representations of God in Christian Young Adults." *International Journal for the Psychology of Religion* 22 (2012) 216–30.

Zeindler, Matthias. "Emil Brunner (1889–1966)." In *Schweizer Ethiker im 20. Jahrhundert: Der Beitrag theologischer Denker*, edited by Wolfgang Lienemann, 85–104. Zürich: TVZ, 2005.

Zizioulas, John D. *Being as Communion: Studies in Personhood and the Church*. London: Darton, Longman & Todd, 2004.

www.ingramcontent.com/pod-product-compliance
Lightning Source LLC
Chambersburg PA
CBHW050347230426
43663CB00010B/2021